D0585143

From Siberia, with Love

Also by Geoffrey Elliott

I Spy, Little, Brown, 1997

(with Harold Shukman)
Secret Classrooms: An Untold Story of the Cold War,
St Ermin's Press, 2002

From Siberia, with Love

A story of exile, revolution and cigarettes

Geoffrey Elliott

Methuen

Published by Methuen 2004

1 3 5 7 9 10 8 6 4 2

Copyright © 2004 by Geoffrey Elliott

The right of Geoffrey Elliott to be identified as the author of this
work has been asserted by him in accordance with the
Copyright, Designs and Patents Act 1988.

Published in 2004 by
Methuen Publishing Ltd
215 Vauxhall Bridge Road
London SW1V 1EJ
www.methuen.co.uk

Methuen Publishing Limited Reg. No. 3543167

ISBN 0 413 77459 7

A CIP catalogue for this title is available from the British Library.

Typeset by SX Composing DTP, Rayleigh, Essex

Printed and bound in Great Britain
by Mackays of Chatham plc, Chatham, Kent

For Thomas and James again, and for NMN

'I am fully alive to the defects and incomplete character of the sketches which I now venture to present to the public; and I now ask therefore for indulgence if I have not contributed as much as I might have done to the instruction or amusement of my readers.'

H. D. Seymour MP, *Russia on the Black Sea and Sea of Azof*, 1855

Contents

Acknowledgements

Family thanks first. To Edgar and Nina Nathan, and Natasha Nightingale, all much missed and fondly remembered, for their personal memories of David and Manya. It is sad that Nina and Edgar's daughter Daphne Mendes is no longer here to cast a wry eye on a story which belongs to her too. Daphne's brother John Nathan, who followed our grandfather's trail along the Trans-Siberian Railway, gave me many valuable pointers. I also thank Dr Isidore Redstone (for his insights into family and Sobranie history, the Chaliapin drawing and the singer's endorsement letters), Mrs Edith Redstone (for valuable papers kept by her late husband, Charles, and for many direct memories), and Manon Nightingale for her Whitechapel discoveries.

From the lawyer-encircled wagon train, which is all that remains of the UK tobacco trade, David Lewis of the premier cigar importers Hunter & Frankau Ltd introduced me to Robert Emory of Sobranie's very first retail outlet James J. Fox and Robert Lewis Ltd, who generously gave me one of the rare porcelain cigarette boxes which were one of the firm's hallmarks.

For their research contributions, gratitude goes to Helen Belopolsky of St Antony's College, Oxford, and Mark Gamsa of Queen's College. Also at St Antony's, Robert Service helped me understand the Mensheviks, and the indefatigable librarian of its Russian Centre, Jackie Wilcox, magically produced the key Rozental book. In Russia I thank Sergei Vasilyev of the Kuznetsov Museum in Chita and Lyudmilla Boiko in Odessa. In Yakutsk I am indebted to

Zoya Grigoryevna, curator of the Romanovka, Masha Alekseyevna, architect for many of the city's 'new' timber buildings in the historic style, the staff of TourService Centre, and Yuri Solovyev, who was interested enough in the story to interview me at length for the main local newspaper and courteous enough to do so without correcting my clumsy Russian as we talked.

Chris Wheal was as always diligent and professional in researching the story of Sobranie, shipping records and other more arcane subjects. At the Scott Polar Research Institute, Piers Vitebsky and Keith Hill generously provided access to their archives. Richard Davies MBE, Keeper of Special Collections at the Brotherton Library of the University of Leeds, was always on call for help, and identified the source of my Babel quotation to which Professor Gregory Freidin of Stanford also gave me helpful compass bearings. Chris Thomas of the British Library kindly gave me time, space and books. Michael Petchey of CSI was painstaking in conjuring up obscure Redstone family data from the Public Records Office and Greg Hamlen of Goodman, Derrick & Co. also helped greatly in this area.

For tracking down many of the books I have tapped, I am obliged to Anthony C. Hall, G. Heywood Hill and Maggs Brothers. I also read in the London Library, the Marx Memorial Library and, for the background on Queen Charlotte's, in the Library of the Royal College of Obstetricians and Gynaecologists. Nicholas Zvegintzov briefed me on what to expect in Yakutsk and with Brigitte Pakendorff whetted my appetite by providing me with several good photographs of the Romanovka.

As the manuscript took final shape Harry Shukman of St. Antony's did me the great kindness of reading it with the care of a scholar and the sympathy of one whose family story has some parallels with my own. Angela Burgess was as always an unflappable centre of gravity.

Finally, for her help in processing much of the material, for her patience with what must have seemed an interminable project, and for venturing with me to Siberia, my special thanks to Fay Elliott.

With all this support and two pairs of editorial eyes in Linda Osband and then Methuen's Joanna Taylor, there should be no errors. But there always are; not, I hope, too many.

The author, editor and publisher acknowledge with thanks the permissions granted to use the text extracts and illustrations included within this publication. Every effort has been made to trace copyright owners for the use of text extracts and illustrations. If any errors or omissions have accidentally occurred they will be corrected in subsequent editions if notification is sent to the publisher.

Extract from *Summoned by Bells* by John Betjeman (John Murray, London, 2001) reprinted by permission of Hodder Headline, London.

Illustrations

1. David and Manya after their wedding in Irkutsk, Christmas Day 1905. **Author's collection**
2. A sketch of an Irkutsk Prison cell by George Frost. **Author's collection**
3. Irkutsk Prison, where David and Manya met, August 1905. **Kennan Archive/Library of Congress**
4. Odess'a Cathedral Square, c. 1900. **Maria Karavina**
5. The faces of Manya's Siberian childhood, as drawn by George Frost. **Author's collection**
6. A one-way ticket, the train to Siberia. **Postcard reproduced on www.transib.ru**
7. Exiles and a guard on the train to Siberia. **De Baye**
8. Political and criminal prisoners being herded on to a steamer to travel down the Lena. **Kennan Archive**
9. Some of the protestors crammed inside the Romanovka.. **Author's collection**
10. The Cossacks must have seemed terrifying to the Romanovka group. **Martin, 1887**
11. The siege as dramatised by a contemporary artist. **Yakutsk Museum**
12. Romanovka 'Marksman' and veteran Bolshevik fighter, Victor Kurnatovsky. **Yakutsk Museum**
13. Weapons destroyed by the defenders before surrender. **Yakutsk Museum**

Barents Sea

RUS

St Petersburg

Trans-Siberian Railway

Moscow

London

EUROPE

BESSARABIA

Odessa

Belgorod-
Dnestrovsky

Black Sea

Sofia

Constantinople
(Istanbul)

Port Said

| 0 | 500 | 1000 | 1500 miles |

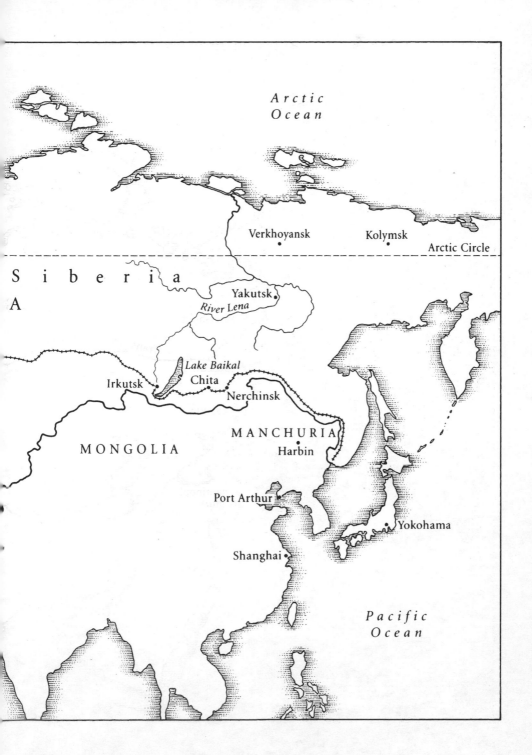

Foreword

It is folklore rather than logic which dictates the special resonance surrounding a centenary. It is no more than coincidence that I am writing this one hundred years after the siege and shoot-out in a small sub-zero Siberian town which almost cost my grandfather his life. It was a happier coincidence that the bloodstains on the snow led directly to my grandfather's jailhouse meeting with my Siberian-born grandmother. David and Manya Redstone were my mother's parents, two ordinary people in a turn-of-the-century Russian population of 130 million; ordinary people forced by the drama of Russian history into extraordinary lives.

By the mind-numbing norms of twenty-first century political mayhem, the stand-off in February 1904 between the Tsar's Cossacks and more than fifty desperate political exiles who had barricaded themselves inside a little wooden house would hardly be headline material. Three dead, a few wounded. Yet this almost suicidal protest against a harsh exile regime reverberated around Europe. It was applauded as a major explosion in the rolling barrage of revolution which had been rocking Russia to the roots for over fifty years, and which in 1917 would finally blow away the last members of the dynasty which had ruled Russia as autocrats for hundreds of years.

I had known some of my grandparents' story from family chatter, and a few years ago I included what I then knew in an account of my father's adventures on different battlefields. But with the self-centred myopia of childhood and adolescence I never took the trouble to ask them much about it while they were alive. It was only in recent years, peering back nostalgically through the bottle-glass lenses of my own old age, that I came to see their story not only as the dangerous romance that it was, but also as a study in contrasts, and I wanted to find out more.

The first contrast was between David and Manya themselves, on the surface as ill-matched a pair as one could imagine, but in fact two personalities which meshed perfectly in love and support. Second, their life together was played out in two sharply contrasting acts. In Act One we see them against a background of jail, guns, exile, hard labour in the silver mines, or even the threat of a firing squad. Then there is a move to London, homesickness, and a return to Siberia to raise a family to the accompaniment of the hoofbeats of revolution, counter-revolution, Red and White terror, and raids by mad Manchurian mercenaries. Completing Act One is a spell in what must have been the utterly mysterious ambience of an un-Westernised Japan.

Act Two, some of which I witnessed myself, could not have been more different. It was a quiet life in a quiet North London house, whose front door was varnished by a craftsman when they moved in and which, rather like my grandparents, remained bright and free from cracks until they died there forty years later. It was a life centred on family rather than on changing the world; and on the family business, Balkan Sobranie, which made fine pipe tobacco and exotic cigarettes – Black Russian, Turkish, Egyptian, the multi-hued Cocktail – for connoisseurs, rather than bombs for revolutionaries. David, now transformed into a genial salesman, was its public face.

When I made up my mind to do better justice to their story, I was amazed by the wealth of material I found. It all happened so long ago, so far away, and its centrepiece was an incident which, however loudly it was acclaimed at the time, was no Battleship Potemkin, but several of those involved wrote their memories down while they were still fresh. These I read with astonishment, admiration and, when I came across a couple of lines which set the scene of my grandparents' meeting in the Irkutsk jail, with a jolt of surprise and a lump in my throat. I found obscure Russian newspapers, tobacco trade memorabilia, fading revolutionary journals. And the biggest surprise of all was that the little house owned by the merchant Romanov in faraway Yakutsk was still standing, despite all that has happened in Russia over the last hundred years, and the ravages of the world's harshest climate. It is a lasting monument to my grandparents' story, as I hope this book will be.

Geoffrey Elliott
July 2004

Love Lane

'Love Laughs at Locksmiths'

My grandparents met on 16 August 1905 in the stone-flagged corridor outside cell No. 9 of the main block of the prison in Irkutsk in Siberia – an unlikely setting for what my grandmother always claimed happily was love at first sight.

The clanging doors, the 'murderous stench' (in a visitor's words) from the *parashi* – the wooden toilet buckets – in each cell, the gruff warders and the claustrophobic cube of the cell must have added to Manya Flegontova's sense of shock. Just a few hours earlier, she and one of her sisters, Elizaveta, both nurses, had been arrested for handing out 'seditious' leaflets when the police waded vigorously into a street demonstration in Siberia's second largest city on a balmy day just a few weeks before the weather's abrupt switch – predictable almost to the hour – to the brief glories of autumn and the ever shorter and colder days that all of a sudden became the endless winter.

One moment they were in the midst of the excited crowds in the main square, bracketed between God and Mammon by the almost-Roman bell towers of the Cathedral of the Epiphany, the Catholic cathedral, conventionally Gothic with Russian flourishes, and the confidence-inspiring granite bulk of the State Bank. The next they and half-a-dozen others were grabbed, manhandled into a horse-drawn *chyornyi voron* (Russians called them 'Black Ravens' rather than 'Black Marias'), searched, and their personal details laboriously written into the big leather-bound police ledger. Excitement shrivelled into fright as they bounced down the wide unpaved and rutted road and into the jail courtyard. Now they were standing in the narrow corridor, ten cells on each side, opening out into a 'common room' at the end, clutching each other's hands while the warders grumbled at my grandfather to hurry up and shift his little bundle of belongings to the cell next door. David Redstone* would have taken it all in his stride. Already serving a ten-year term in exile, after nearly eighteen months in jail, for involvement with the anti-Tsarist underground, he was now facing twelve years' hard labour for his part in a shoot-out in an even more remote Siberian town.

This is the story of what led to that strange encounter, and of their long wanderings together afterwards. Appropriately for so Russian a tale, it is like a nest of enamel-painted *matryoshka* dolls. Layer by layer, new images emerge. Though they are images of times long gone, of parts of the world even today unfamiliar and hostile, of a family that never made the headlines, the underlying issues and values are much on our minds today: the ineradicable curse of terrorism, the systemic cruelty and criminality of authoritarian regimes and their legions of servants and officials, massive social upheaval and suffering, and quiet courage in the face of adversity.

In my childhood during the Second World War and right through the 1950s, David and Manya were surrogate parents. They supported their younger daughter – my mother – and housed her and her three children when my father was away in wartime Yugoslavia, operating as a British agent in Cold War Hungary, and later, after the slow-motion train-wreck of the marriage, as an alimony-dodging expatriate in Jamaica. They had to tidy up the debris and take care of the shaken young passengers. If I could add up all the time I spent in their little house when I was growing up, it would be measured in

*He was born Davyd Roitenshtern – a Russian genealogist tells me that 'Davyd' comes from the Hebrew 'Beloved' – and later became Rothenstern, but to keep things simple we will stick to the Anglicised name he subsequently adopted and by which he was far more widely known. For the same reason I have not altered Russian dates to adjust for the thirteen-day difference from the pre-1917 Julian calendar. My grandmother was christened Mariya, the name which appears in the Russian accounts of the story, but I have stayed with 'Manya', the affectionate diminutive by which David and her family knew her.

years, not months. So I meet Dr Johnson's criterion that 'nobody can write the life of a man but those who have eat[en] and drunk and lived in social intercourse with him'. Stretching a point, I too have lived an exile's life for many years, by choice, not compulsion, in comfort rather than in struggle. My choice of the 'soft option' in the sun was out of weakness, rather than courage. There is really no comparison between my grandparents' iron-spiked experiences and my marsh-mallow life. They could never go back to where they were born. I can; though when I do, I feel ever more disconnected, *déraciné*, what Stalin called a 'rootless cosmopolitan', while at the same time till the day I die I shall be seen as a foreigner in the place I now regard as home. So it reinforces my interest in trying to understand how others, my father included, come to terms with this feeling that you don't quite belong.

The lives of my grandparents and my mother and her sister were slivers of stone in the confused mosaic of the history of the Russian Revolution. This book makes no claim to be a study of that history. It is just the story of two ordinary people, neither aristocrats, nor intellectuals, nor revolutionary leaders, who had extraordinary lives.

They made an odd couple. When they met, David Redstone was a bearded, 26-year-old Jewish revolutionary from the Black Sea coast of Bessarabia, with a chequered past and an uncertain future, one of five children of a prosperous grain merchant. Manya Flegontova, half a head taller than her firebrand lover, was born and raised in Siberia, a trained nurse and midwife, the devoutly Russian Orthodox daughter of a fur trader with eleven other children. Despite the mismatch, or maybe because of it, they were to stay together for over fifty years, many full of fear and confusion, when they were no more than tiny figures scrambling across a battlefield clutching their little family and a couple of suitcases. Some, thankfully quite a few, of their years were also serene.

To us they were '*Dyedushka*' and '*Babushka*' – other English families had 'Grandpa' and 'Granny' – and using their first names in these pages strikes me even after all those years as a little impertinent. I, as well as their other grandchildren and great-grandchildren, saw a lot of them. We all loved them dearly. We loved them in the here and now, as younger people do. What we picked up from them and my mother of their past sounded infinitely remote, a 'quarrel in a far-away country between people of whom we knew nothing', as prime minister Neville Chamberlain remarked in the last moments before the Second World War. For me to brag at school about a father who had parachuted behind enemy lines was just about acceptable, though pushy, but the fact that he had gone AWOL domestically was in those days a matter best skirted. A Russian revolutionary grandfather with a beard and a heavy accent who had been in jail was harder to put across at Sports Day to a bunch of blazered, very British boys, and thus also best left as a story untold. Even if I had asked more, the story had long since been condensed and airbrushed into David's political exile to Siberia, followed by a few disagreeable years in London, a voluntary return to Siberia to make a new life, a hard time scrambling between Reds, Whites and bandits to get out of Russia, and spells in Manchuria and Japan before finally making it back to London and new beginnings. The shootings, deaths and dangers were largely left out. David was neither Baron Münchausen nor Walter Mitty and was without a drop of self-pity in his veins, but he enjoyed telling a good story. That meant a story that amused his audience without alarming them. It would have been hard, for instance, to tell the story of 'The Great Escape' without explaining why he was in jail in the first place, and dead soldiers in the snow and a forest suicide were not the stuff of after-dinner chatter.

Though they were naturalised and long settled in England, David and Manya wore the Brand of Cain as exiles in a country whose people did not take kindly to foreigners anyway, and whose middle classes would make an effort to pass by on the other side of the road rather than meet anyone who had been in jail, even for a good cause. Even though Britain had a long tradition of providing refuge for foreign dissidents and revolutionaries, the Home Office might well have looked askance had they known they had granted citizenship to someone who had been as close to the front line as David. On balance, 'Don't ask, don't tell' suited everyone.

As I pulled off doll after doll and saw what lay beneath, I found it harder and harder to square the grandfather I remembered with the portrait that emerged of an underground agitator imprisoned and exiled for his beliefs, an armed resister, a comrade of one of Stalin and Lenin's toughest early henchmen, his photograph taken with a leading woman terrorist. Was this the man portrayed by the *Financial Times* as ' "Uncle David" . . . one of the best-loved personalities in the tobacco industry'? Was the genial man, who in one of my earliest memories rowed me around a sunny lake in summertime, the same David Redstone who saw men shot in the Siberian snow? Was the David Redstone who yelled 'Down with autocracy' from a court-room dock the embarrassed man who was deputed by my mother to explain the facts of life to me while we walked around the slopes of Golders Hill Park, behind the Finchley Road, while I tried to look suitably awed at the retelling of weighty matters long since explained with less circumlocution in my school playground? When I was musing about the many who praised David's capacity for making friends, something brought to my mind a childhood supper at my grandparents' house when their guest was a nice man in a heavily badged blazer who was due to referee the England–Scotland football game at Wembley the next day. Being even as a child totally useless at, and thus uninterested in, any sport, I was probably not as impressed as I should have been; I don't think I even bothered to ask if he had a spare ticket. But as I think back, what on earth was the man with one of sport's golden whistles doing having an informal meal with a man in the tobacco trade who long ago and far away had waved a less than golden gun? And in a contrast of a different kind, how to reconcile my image of a thoughtful man, but not one given to expressing strong opinions, with the polymath polemicist who wrote busily for Siberian journals in the First World War and who as an exile a couple of years later was commended by the British for his work as a 'propaganda agent for the Harbin War Publicity Committee' around 1919?

David was small – a little over five feet tall – eyes twinkling behind his spectacles, and always formally dressed. His shirts were the kind that required bone and brass collar studs back and front, and cufflinks, and his three-piece suits were impregnated with the fragrance of the rich Yenidje tobacco that was the lifeblood of his business, much as an elderly priest's soutane might carry the faint breath of incense.

My grandmother's aura was that of 4711 Eau de Cologne. Her white hair always tightly rolled in a neat bun, she cooked, washed, pushed her wheeled wickerwork basket to the shops, and worried about us, hands twisted by arthritis, a very Russian blend of religious conviction and deep-seated superstitions. What on earth had she been doing in a street demonstration? How did she possibly cope with three children, one of them terminally ill with tuberculosis, in escape scenes straight out of *Dr Zhivago*, living for months in a railway carriage in a Manchurian siding, in cheap lodgings in Shanghai, a city where opium dens, brothels and nightclubs far outnumbered the churches, or in a house in Yokohama, whose paper walls fascinated the children but for David and Manya were an ever present reminder of the risk of earthquakes?

Also puzzling was the short period that they spent in another Siberian troublespot when David came out of jail. Then their faltering steps in Edwardian London and another puzzle: why did they return to Russia? Then a lull, but again a strange one, since they and my mother and her sister lived for several placid years back in Siberia while the First World War raged in Europe. The Revolution destroyed their lives, forcing them into dangerous flight through Manchuria to Shanghai and Yokohama, not because they were among the thousands of noble families escaping vengeance, but because David, though a Socialist, was on the wrong end of the political spectrum when the Bolshevik hit men came round to settle scores. As the final and, yet again, sharply contrasting act of the drama, we find him partnering his brother in building a well-respected London family business, whose Sobranie brands are still widely known today. How did the pieces of the doll all fit together as a story?

2

A Shelf of Clues

Over the years I spent in my grandparents' home, I read just about everything crammed into David Redstone's bookcase in that wartime alcove of shelter under the stairs, and a smaller set of shelves in the stipple-plastered, smoke-pickled (it was what the French would call a *tabagie*) sitting room. Like all good collections, his books, stacked two and three deep, were a mixed bag reflecting the eclectic interests of a voracious reader: André Maurois, Aldous Huxley, a life of Byron, a collected Shakespeare, and a long run of King Penguin and Pelican. A Webster's dictionary printed around 1904 and yellow-jacketed volumes from Victor Gollancz's Left Book Club stick in my mind. So does Tom Wintringham's *New Ways of War*, which appealed to my boyhood imagination with its advice about how to string steel wire across country lanes to decapitate German motorcycle dispatch riders. *I Chose Freedom*, the memoirs of an early post-war Soviet defector, rubbed covers with what I recall as a rather triumphalist survey, published shortly after the Second World War by the US Strategic Air Command to illustrate the devastation it had wrought on Nazi Germany, replete with grainy photos of liberators droning through the clouds – pin-up girls painted on their fuselages and messages of the 'A Present for Adolf' variety chalked on their bombs – and cities and their inhabitants mashed together into piles of rubble. There were perhaps a dozen folio-sized scrapbooks in which year after year David had neatly pasted cuttings from British newspapers, notably the *Manchester Guardian* and *News Chronicle*, both liberal-leaning, on the course of the Second World War campaigns and on the shape of the post-war world, mixed in with David Low's political cartoons. There were now-forgotten monthly and weekly magazines such as *Argosy*, *Strand*, *Punch*, *Lilliput* (good for a furtive glimpse of pin-up girls with prudishly neutered pudenda) and, as if my grand-parents had not travelled enough, glimpses of faraway places in the *National Geographic* and *World Wide*. There was even for some reason the *New Yorker*, whose advertisements suggested to an impression-able teenager that there was another, technicolor world out there. There was a paperback, I think in two volumes, of Hašek's satirical masterpiece of the 1920s, *The Good Soldier Svejk*. Discreetly keeping all this company was a turn-of-the-century Russian midwifery textbook belonging to my grandmother, in which the detailed anatomical engravings were more perturbing than prurient.

When I began to finger my way along those shelves in my memory, I realised that some of my grandfather's books were not just classics or evening reading. They were, rather, 'paper milestones', which must have sparked for David as many memories and associations of life's potholed highway as an old photograph album, among them Pushkin's collected works and the first edition, published in Milan in Russian, of Pasternak's *Doctor Zhivago*. Also, in a way far more bound up with the story than I realised, were Isaac Deutscher's life of Trotsky, *The Prophet Armed* – David's copy of which for some reason I still have after all these years – and Arthur Koestler's *Darkness at Noon*, which must have resonated more with David than many other of its readers. A one-off edition of *Murder off Miami*, a detective story by Dennis Wheatley in unique 'police file' format, also had its special place in the tale we are telling. Even *Svejk* turns out to have a little-known Siberian connection.

The most important book of all was one I never read in David's lifetime. I am not sure I ever even took much notice of it, since it was in Russian, a language I acquired only when I was older and my visits to my grandparents' house were less regular, and any lingering curiosity about my grandparents had been overtaken by my own marriage and family. If, as I now look back, some of his other books were linked to his past in ways I did not appreciate, this would loom over the 'milestones' much like the twelve-foot-high stone obelisk at Perm, which for earlier generations of exiles who trudged into banishment on foot marked the boundary between the Russia they knew and the grim unknown of Siberia. Published in St Petersburg, its 450 pages were the first account of what happened in the Romanovka and the aftermath. Until I read it a long time later, I had no idea of the part David Redstone had played in the affair or that he had taken many of the shorthand notes of events on which the book was based. I came across it in the bookcase only after his death. For years I meant to sit down and read it. I did not and, to compound my failure, in a misplaced fit of generosity I lent it, still mainly unread, to an understandably manic-depressive and unreliable Gulag survivor in the Bronx who was revising a dictionary of Siberian prison slang. As poor Sasha became more incoherently maudlin with each telephone call, I gave up trying to get it back from him and found another copy in the Bodleian Library in Oxford.

It was written by one of David's co-conspirators, Pavel Teplov, a 35-year-old surveyor and, according to the pedantic phrasing of the police, a 'man of letters' from a peasant family. *Istoryia Yakutskogo Protesta – Delo Romanovtsev (The Story of the Yakutsk Protest – the Men and Women of the Romanovka)* combines narrative with the text of almost every relevant official document, including all the *démarches* to the authorities, the indictments, the courtroom speeches and judgments, summaries of the police dossiers on all those involved, and even supporting resolutions from exiles elsewhere in Siberia and abroad. When the book was published – with surprising speed, less than a year after the events it described – the cycle of reform and repression in Russia was taking another downward lurch for the worse. It would have been risky to give the Tsar's secret police ammunition for another round of retribution, so Teplov carefully blurred questions of the group's organisation and leadership, or of who had fired the fatal shots, and gave few descriptions of the colourful and courageous personalities.

Though Teplov was the key starting point, I then found many other untapped Russian-language sources on the Romanovka and other pieces of the Redstone puzzle. One important addition was published in 1924. Written by another central character in the drama, Dr Pavel Rozental, and partly based on a diary he wrote and somehow managed to hang on to through everything that happened, it is much shorter but much richer in its human detail. It is likely that as Soviet revisionism began to repaint history red, Rozental's 'subtext' was to get on record that what happened had not been an exclusively Bolshevik affair; many other shades of political opinion had raised their colours in those wooden walls. It is to Rozental that I owe the brief account of my grandparents' jailhouse meeting. He can have had no idea who would read his book and I doubt he ever dreamed it would even be seen outside Russia. That a grandson of the Redstones would yell with pleasure when he spotted the reference while leafing through the book in a Bermuda garden over seventy-five years later would have astonished and, I hope, gratified him. Russian dictionaries, at least those I have, do not contain a word for 'serendipity'. An evocative first-hand account of the grandeur of the scenery, and the atmosphere of Yakutsk as my grandfather knew it, but from the very different standpoint of a free man, has come down to us from Vladimir Berenshtam, one of the protestors' defence lawyers.

There was a surprising number of other books and papers in later years, continuing into the 1990s. Among them were the memoirs of the distinguished Menshevik – a term we shall come to later – Eva Broido, whose husband was one of the group. Notably there was a mine of reminiscence in the greying pages of a Russian journal with the uncompromising title *Katorga i Ssylka (Hard Labour and Exile)*. It was published between 1921 and 1930, at which point the Kremlin probably realised that, given its ambitions for the Gulag, a periodical devoted to the heroism of Siberian exile resistance in the fight against a brutal, authoritarian regime might be open to misinterpretation. The most valuable issue for our purpose was in 1929, when a number of surviving participants wrote about their memories and their friends to mark the twenty-fifth anniversary of their shared experience behind the wooden barricades.

There were Russian newspapers going back to my grandfather's childhood, and Manya's early life in Siberia, found in the US Library of Congress, and, a discovery of which I am rather proud, the 'Frost drawings'. George Kennan was an American writer (distantly related to the eponymous twentieth-century diplomat) who came to Russia first to plan out a cross-Empire telephone line, and then turned to journalism and produced the first exposé of the tsarist exile system. His companion on a trip so arduous that most modern travel writers would never dream of undertaking it was an accomplished Massachusetts artist named George Frost. Kennan's two-volume work is much improved by engravings from Frost's drawings, and I thus recognised them with a start when I was snuffling like a truffle hunter through the underbrush of a London dealer's stock. I was shown a crammed grey cardboard box just sent over by an antiquarian bookseller dealer in New England, who had no idea what they were and was in search of a London buyer. Many of them were very fine and detailed, some little more than doodles on scraps of paper or card, some on frail tracing paper, some marked up for the engraver, drawn from jolting sledges, with numbed fingers on freezing hillsides, inside smoky post-houses and several prisons and labour camps, including Irkutsk prison where David and Manya met. The thrill of the discovery got the better of my commercial instincts and I ended up paying more than I might have done had I maintained a professional buyer's studied disinterest.

Then there were the three museums. Two are tiny, narrowly focused places but museums nonetheless, each with mementoes of my grandfather's singular life. Half a world away from London, the *Dom-Muzeiya Istoriya Politicheskoi Ssylki* (The Museum of the History of Political Exile) in Yakutsk is in the original wooden Romanovka building and still proudly displays the guns David and his group left behind, their photographs and the makeshift 'armour plate' hurriedly hammered together out of balks of timber to take the impact of the hail of Cossack bullets.

The second is more substantial but even so, after all that has happened in Russia, Siberia and the world, was a remarkable source. Armies have rampaged and looted there. Secret policemen have rifled the records to remove traces of their crimes. Contradictory, sometimes deadly cycles of political correctness have led to furtive late-night weeding and 'deaccessioning' into the dumpster. Files have been recycled as typing paper, or bundled onto stoves to keep their archivists warm. It was thus astonishing to find behind the almost Georgian front door and impressively pillared front of the Kuznetsov Museum in Chita traces of David's later political involvement and even a photograph of him and Manya's brother grouped with, among others, one of the Revolution's most remarkable woman terrorists.

The Siberian museums are not far from the Arctic Circle. Museum No. 3 is close to London's Circle Line and Whites, Boodles and Brooks's clubs in St James's Street, an altogether more hospitable environment. Like the Romanovka, 'Freddy Fox's Room' also has a wooden theme: in this case, old panelling impregnated with the aroma of three centuries of the finest Havana and Turkish and Egyptian tobaccos. It is the treasure house of memory of the patrician cigar and of tobacco merchants now known as James J. Fox & Robert Lewis. It preserves as part of its history of the Lewis side of the firm several fine examples (some of which would not be out of place in the Victoria and Albert Museum) of the luxurious porcelain boxes and stylish packages that were the hallmarks of the House of Sobranie, the Redstone family business to whose early success Lewis made an important contribution.

I also had the help of family memories. Those of the Redstones' elder daughter Nina were in the form of staccato notes for a lecture and her taped comments for a BBC TV programme about the Revolution. Towards the end of his long life, her husband Edgar Nathan, a meticulous and sympathetic observer, wrote down what he remembered of David's recollection of events. My late sister Natalie also put down what she remembered of her chats with Manya, an especially poignant record since she was reaching back to her beginnings while facing her own far too early end.

3

Russian Roulette

Our matryoshka dolls come from a Russia that is the stuff of history books, a Russia first heading blindly into, and then being torn up by, the jaws of revolution.

Other than loving each other, about the only thing my grandparents had in common was that they were subjects 'Out of Fear and Out of Conscience', as Russian law declared, of the Emperor and Autocrat of All the Russias. The features that separated them – religion; education; warm south versus frozen north; one growing up in a cosmopolitan city, the other on the borders of Mongolia; even, as I discovered later when I learned their language, the idiom and the accents of their spoken Russian – epitomised an empire which combined hundreds of nations large and small, and almost as many languages and dialects, beliefs, climates and time zones.

Nearly 90 per cent of the Empire's population were classed as peasants. Less than half were actually Russian. The rest was a patchwork of national and ethnic groups, many 'Russified' only by force of arms. (When my grandparents were born, Russia had already been fighting the Chechens unsuccessfully for seventy years; the first Russian outpost in Grozny was built in 1818. The name means 'Terrible', as rightly applied to Tsar Ivan. As one historian wrote prophetically half a century ago, General Yermolov's ferocious but unsuccessful attempts to pacify the Caucasus may have 'won Russia more bitter enemies than reliable subjects'.)

In their day, David and Manya would both have been proud to be

Russians, feeling quite entitled to criticise the Empire and, in David's case, to try hard to change it, but ready to defend it and its traditions and values against all outsiders. Their country was still clinging on to its role as one of the Great Powers of Europe. It was industrialising. It pulsed with cultural vitality. Pushkin, Lermontov, Dostoevsky, Gogol, Tolstoy and later Chekhov and Gorky wrote with magic, often tragic, pens. Borodin, Balakirev, Glinka, Rimsky-Korsakov and Tchaikovsky set the Russian soul to music. Scriabin too; although one of his cousins took a different life path, adopted the revolutionary name of 'Molotov' ('The Hammer Man') and survived to become Stalin's dour Foreign Minister.

Though they were far from the centre, Odessa and the major Siberian cities had theatres, opera houses, concerts, museums, libraries, hospitals, universities, schools at every level offering a broad range of classical or modern courses and technical institutes. Those who could read were remarkably well informed. The Odessa and Irkutsk newspapers of the period carried many up-to-date, even though brief, reports from around the world and across Russia and kept their readers informed about political developments in the capital, even though censorship meant that it is hard to find any overt attacks or criticism, and the prominence and deference given to the doings and anniversaries of the royal family are evident. That was not an exclusively Russian trait; the court reports read not too differently from those in the London *Times*. Literacy was limited since the authorities fought shy of educating peasant masses, frightened of the forces it might unleash, and like the professions many higher educational institutions offered only limited access to Jews.

For David to seek change, to feel anger and dismay that despite all this Russia had 90 per cent of its people mired in squalor and indignity, was not disloyalty. Nor was the special sense of grievance that he must have had as part of a maligned minority. Manya had different genes. She was an educated woman, a trained nurse and intellectually aware, but the thought patterns of childhood are deeply ingrained. She was religious, but raised in a remote land where the shadows of spirits hung over the hills, and folk fables had as much resonance as gospel truth. So I suspect that she would have been inclined to think that the structure of Russian society was pre-ordained and largely immutable. As a young girl she would have had no reason to question the beliefs and superstitions that were part of her life fabric, among them the conviction that Russia 'rested on the backs of three whales' with the Tsar at the head of a monolithic structure, of which her church and its priests were an integral part.

The majority of thinking Russians was aware that for all its repressive powers, its strutting on the world stage, its pomp and circumstance, the system was unsustainable. As Thomas Carlyle wrote of the French Revolution less than a century before my grandfather was born: 'The relentlessly selfish aristocrats and royal family could expect nothing more than a destructive apocalypse.' Looking back at the land he left, Vladimir Nabokov put it even more succinctly: 'Fatal poverty and fatalistic wealth'.

Like so many phrases we bandy about today, 'Russian Revolution' has taken on a slightly different freight and has come to be seen as an explosion of popular support for the Bolsheviks in 1917, a one-off event. For the Redstones and their fellow countrymen who lived through it, it was less an explosion than a rolling barrage which started in 1905 (others might say even in 1825 with the abortive attempt by the Decembrist nobles to depose the Tsar) and ended around 1922 only after Russia had been ravaged by years of civil war, foreign intervention, human displacement, savagery and starvation. It was not so much a revolution won by the Bolsheviks to popular acclaim as a coup d'état in a country of chaos by a ruthless and determined minority. It was a revolution, moreover, which replaced the despised tsarist autocracy with a despotism which proclaimed itself as a 'dictatorship of the proletariat', but in truth was just an industrialised, far crueller version of the old tyranny.

Part of this is the fault of our age, which has distilled the 'Revolution' into stereotype film images of heroic men and women storming the Winter Palace, the pram tumbling down the Odessa Steps, Trotsky orating, Lenin mummified into a yellow-skinned Barbie doll, or *Doctor Zhivago*, its message now reduced to little more than the ripping of silk bodices, by guttering candlelight to the music of gypsy violins, while peasants look simultaneously downtrodden and revolting as they trudge through the machine-blown snow outside.

Another stereotype is the image of the revolutionaries themselves. They took the moral high ground throughout their struggles, the dashing bravado of young idealists risking their lives in a battle with a pitiless police force, puppets of whiskered old fogies in St Petersburg, maintaining by force of arms a regime that was out of date, despotic and inept. It goes without saying that, like David himself, they were brave, deeply committed young people for the most part, prepared to die for what they believed in, but some were quite prepared to kill too, lobbing nail-filled bombs at their opponents or gunning down their families. Somehow this has come down through the ages as a red badge of courage rather than a mark of shame; one generation's terrorist is another's freedom fighter.

Even 'Bolshevik' is a misnomer. It means 'member of the majority', which Lenin and his supporters were not. It would be too diverting to go into all the parties, factions and trains of thought in the Russian cataclysm, but the Bolsheviks are most often contrasted with the 'Mensheviks', a label that David took on in later years and which means 'member of the minority', again for a long time the opposite of the truth. It is a tribute to Lenin's brilliant opportunism that he took advantage of a relatively minor party squabble to capture and cling to the 'majority' label even though he conceded that at the time his supporters were 'the weaker several times over – the Mensheviks have more money, more literature, more transport, more "names", more collaborators. It would be unforgivable childishness not to see this.'

Because of David, the term 'Mensheviks' comes up several times in our story. It is therefore worth saying a few words on what they were about since in a way it helps define the man himself, though as a practical matter it is of little consequence. They lost, and went into history's 'Deleted Items'. Who now remembers what the opposition parties in the Reichstag stood for after Hitler came to power? Yet another stereotype presents the Mensheviks as akin to the present-day British Liberal Democrats; far from it. By today's standards they were dangerously left-wing, and their differences with the Bolsheviks lay in the Mensheviks' belief in constitutional process, that the people should decide their form of government, and, in what now seems an arcane point of Marxist dogma, that before there could be a revolution Russia must first pass through a phase of 'capitalist transition'. I suspect that for David an even better set of labels than strict party affiliation would have been some combination of 'liberal', 'democrat', 'romantic', 'impulsive' and 'idealist'. As we are about to see, he was clearly also a 'doer', though not an extremist and, though he later became a well-informed columnist, seems never to have had the slightest urge to become one of the shabby theoreticians hunched in steamy Zurich cafés or the Reading Room of the British Museum wrapped in heavy scarves and a penumbra of theories about the inevitability of the downfall of capitalism.

Canute-like, the Tsar and his ministers and officials fought back the tide of revolution with a mixture of 'velvet glove' reforms and attempts at liberalisation, always too little and too late and often arbitrarily reversed, and 'iron fist'. The reforms had little effect. The emancipation of the serfs and an attempt at land distribution were 'hard on the wretched and the weak', the historian Edward Crankshaw observed. 'The strong, the able, the energetic, the greedy, forged swiftly ahead buying up the land of the feeble, the feckless and the gentle, who were reduced to near starvation, bankrupted or driven to the factories or to work for their powerful neighbours.' (History always repeats itself; the same words could equally have been the epitaph for the Yeltsin-era 'privatisations' in the 1990s, which allowed the so-called 'oligarchs' to steal billions of dollars of state assets.)

When concession failed to produce the right results, the authorities' 'iron fist', with which they were always more comfortable, brought brutality and violence backed by the power of the state, wreaking even more havoc and unrest, and leading inexorably to still more terrorism. Since there was no ballot box, the bullet and the bomb seemed to many to be the only effective tools and the paving stones of nineteenth-century Russia carried the bloodstains of assassinations and of the victims of police and Cossack responses; a familiar pattern.

Still the Tsar and his ministers believed passionately that it was his divine right to rule, and that God was in their corner with the holy water bottle sponging them down between rounds and urging them to fight on. They were as blind as the Bourbons or the Hapsburgs to the world outside their windows, as unable to learn from history, and they paid the price. It was only years later, when the world could see what the Bolsheviks had wrought to their long-suffering country, that perspectives began to change and the Tsar began to be seen as more inept and detached than evil.

Reuters, the worldwide news agency, had long since prepared its St Petersburg bureau. Its system relied on masking correspondents' messages in commercial codes, partly to save money (because cables were paid for by the word) but mainly to prevent cable clerks along the international routes filching their scoops and selling them to rivals. Its 1889 codebook, which for unknown reasons used French, covered most permutations of what experienced men thought likely to happen to the Tsar: he might be stabbed, slightly or seriously wounded, or shot. *'Banquiers opposent difficulté'* ('Bankers are raising objections') meant that the autocrat was dead, while the more circumstantial *'Télégraphez à mon associé retourner sans attendre réception ma lettre'* ('Cable my colleague to return without waiting for my letter') was to be read in Reuters' Old Jewry newsroom as 'An assassin shot and killed the Tsar.'

David would have been more aware than Manya of Russia as an anti-Semitic 'police state', in which, though freedom of speech and thought were severely curtailed for all, the Jews were special targets. Laws governed where they could live, what and where they could study, and the professions and trades they could follow. The urban and rural lower classes were left with shopkeeping, running taverns and small-scale trading, activities that were bound to create resentments with the Russian peasantry, who were their clientele and debtors. This, combined with their alien worship and un-Russian ways, made the Jews into even handier scapegoats to be thrashed, and their shops and homes destroyed, in the frequent pogroms, which if not inspired, were often tacitly connived at by the Tsarist authorities.

This is David's story and this will be how he saw it. That at higher levels of society there were wealthy Jews who owned land, gold and coal mines, swathes of timber-producing forests, railways, distilleries, breweries, major trading houses and banks, is ammunition for Marxist or anti-Semitic polemic but for us irrelevant. We can assume they never cowered in their mansions while mobs of peasants milled in the streets outside yelling, *'Bei Zhidov'* ('Beat up the Yids'). In Bessarabia and across Russia, the hate-twisted faces, backlit by flaring tar-dipped torches in the night and heavy sticks crashing down, were imprinted on the folk memory.

The Tsar, a bred-in-the-bone anti-Semite, like his Court, his Church (unwavering proponents of the 'Killers of Christ' thesis), his ministers and indeed most Russians and Poles had excluded the Jewish community from any participation in his coronation. He once wrote petulantly to his mother that, 'Ninety per cent of our revolutionaries are Yids'. Konstantin Pobedonostsev was a close advisor to the Tsar who brought to his role as Procurator of the Russian Orthodox Holy Synod more of the flint-hard reactionary essence of the regime than the images of mercy and compassion on his Church's gilded icons. He told an American visitor in words that could as readily have been screamed to a Nuremberg rally: 'A Jew is a parasite; separate him from the living organism in which – and at the expense of which – he thrives and transfer him to a rock and he will perish.' His chilling view of where the anti-Jewish measures would lead was that 'one third will die, one third will leave the country and the last third will be completely assimilated into the Russian people'. A more measured if hardly more positive view had been expressed some years earlier by the US Consul in Russia, Eugene Schuyler, who told Washington: 'The disabilities and exceptional position of the Israelites in Russia are based not on grounds of religious intolerance but on the idea that the Hebrew race has a natural tendency to exploit the population in the midst of which it is settled and the Hebrews are therefore harmful to the state . . . The Hebrews are an alien race living in Russia and owing allegiance to the Imperial Government subject to all the burdens and endowed with few of the benefits of Russian subjects. On the assumed theory of their being harmful to the population at large, they are under the special supervision of the government and are restricted in their place of abode, their occupations, acquisition of property, mode of life, dress, education and manner of worship.'

It was hardly surprising that the revolutionary movement as a whole included a disproportionate number of Jewish men and women, excluded from the country's mainstream intellectual and professional life. 'The Jews were the artisans of the revolution,' as one commentator said. However, in marked contrast to the Court and Church attitude, Lenin, who took a rather dim view of the character and mental capacity of the mass of his fellow countrymen, once remarked approvingly that 'an intelligent Russian is almost always a Jew or someone with Jewish blood in his veins'.

Fifty years before David was born, an earlier Tsar had re-established the *Oprichnina* of Ivan the Terrible as the Third Department of the Imperial Chancery for 'the collection of all information relating to higher police [matters], political security, religious sects and schismatics, counterfeiting and forgery'. It had responsibility for the 'surveillance and banishment to remote provinces of "politically unreliable persons and the supervision of foreigners in Russia"'. It ran the jails where 'state criminals' were confined, collected statistics and 'reported on all events without exception'. It also took over theatre censorship, a line of mind control that by 1850 had burgeoned into a dozen different censorship bureaus sniffing for heresy and dissent, not only in the press but also in everything from church publications to all written material imported from abroad. By the end of the century, the Third Department became the core of the Ministry of the Interior. Much as MI5 in Britain has always used the police Special Branch to turn its secret investigations into arrests, the Third Department was a small, mainly civilian unit that worked hand in glove with the Corps of Gendarmes. It ran a network of case officers, informants and spies at home and abroad and, like exile and many other elements of the Tsarist system of social control and espionage, did not require much adaptation to meet the needs of the Bolsheviks and Communists in the years to come. Its staff was wholly Russian; Poles and Jews were excluded from its ranks 'on principle', though many were recruited or coerced into acting as *agents provocateurs* or undercover informants.

'Pogrom' is another word whose jagged edges have become blunted over time. To those inured to the terrible images of Nazi brutality against the Jews of Eastern Europe, its Russian variant has come to suggest anti-Jewish mobs yelling in the streets, smashing shop windows and spewing hatred, like Mosley's Fascists in London's East End; nasty, deplorable but not widely lethal. In fact Russian pogroms were far closer to the German 'model', lacking only the mechanical advances and organisational efficiency of the Nazis. Tacitly allowed and all too often instigated by the authorities as a diversionary tactic in the face of some military or political defeat, or economic hardship for which someone had to suffer, they sent waves of Cossack horsemen smashing into a defenceless crowd, backed up by yelling, drink-inflamed locals and quite often blessed by the local priest as they lurched into action. There was no corner of Russia where even the rumour, let alone the menacing presence, of Cossacks did not trigger shivers of fear. They looked, and were, merciless. Their horses were trained to move through crowds in unwavering formation, trampling down anyone in their way, while their riders glared down, whips in hand and sabres always ready to be drawn with a menacing metallic flourish from polished scabbards. They wore dark blue jackets crossed with glossy leather cartridge belts, red striped breeches, fur cloaks and high black sheepskin caps. Most had moustaches and beards that were grown and trimmed to add an intimidating frame for even an ordinary face. There was murder, rape, mutilation of young and old, pregnant women with their bellies slashed open and live cats crudely stitched inside, fathers impaled on bayonet-sharp tree stumps, graveyards and synagogues defiled, villages put to the torch, shops and livelihoods ruined. Thus this was a deeply troubled Russia, but not one in which every young man or woman took to the barricades, or ended in jail. What was David's path to the front line?

4

The Warm South

A 1950s film version of David's background would have set the stage with a fake-antique parchment map unrolling slowly down the screen while a deep off-screen voice announced, 'Bessarabia . . . fertile land of antiquity, land of mystery . . .'

Bessarabia misleads the Western ear. It has nothing to do with the Middle East. It is the legacy of Besarab, a medieval Transylvanian tribal chieftain in the Vlad the Impaler mould. It is also hard to find as an entity on a modern map. Squabbled and fought over for centuries by the Ottoman Empire, Russia and Romania, and occupied by the Germans in the Second World War, much of it is now Moldova and the rest, including Odessa, is part of the Ukraine. It is best located by looking north and east of Odessa for its water boundaries – the Rivers Prut and Dniester and the Chilia arm of the Danube.

David was born on 22 February 1878, the son of Aron, a grain merchant, and Tsivia, no doubt a formidable matriarch. He was the eldest of three brothers and two sisters. At the time, his home town, across the Dniester River estuary from Odessa, was called Akkerman, the Turkish for 'White Fort'. It had begun as the Greek settlement of Tiras, part of Scythia, in an age when Herodotus could enthuse over the crystal waters of the Dniester as 'most productive not only of all the Scythian rivers but of all others except the Egyptian Nile'. It must be a long while since the whales Herodotus saw spouting in the Black Sea (which he knew as Pontus Euxinus and the Turks as Kara Deniz) around 450 BC last surprised local fishermen. Less than 200 miles from

Akkerman, the Roman Emperor Trajan built his towering wall to defend the Empire against the tribes of South Russia; chunks of it still stand today. Even though Akkerman was a sleepy, fly-blown and dusty place, of far less importance and grandeur than Odessa, there must have been a strong sense of civilisations far older than that of Russia recorded in the mosaics, foundation stones and inscriptions, memorials to the successive waves of polyglot occupants. Locals had long claimed that the city had sheltered the poet Ovid when he was banished by Emperor Augustus in the first century AD. That his actual destination turns out to have been what is now the Romanian port of Constanta has not prevented one of the fort's towers still carrying the name 'The Ovidius'; and a small town on the Odessa side of the estuary is proud to be called Ovidiopol.

When David was growing up, Akkerman was part of Russia though it still had its Turkish name, borrowed in part from the Romans', 'Alba Julia'; the 'Fort', some of it still standing, is based on a structure built by the Genoese in the fourteenth century which they named 'Moncastro'. It stands at the tip of the little promontory around which the town clustered in David's time. From its central square, with its tree-shaded open-air cafés, there radiated about a dozen streets. Most of them ended at the line of trees marking the boundaries of 'The Bishop's Park'. The term conjures up images of dappled cows placidly grazing on the riverside meadows of a cathedral in Hampshire, or Gothic towers looming over Esztergom on the Danube. In fact, this and similar 'parks' (as so often, the Russian word has several shades of meaning – 'court', 'courtyard', 'home' or 'farmstead') were often little more than a cluster of inns, schools, hostels and thatched farm buildings, where the region's bishop would stay and preach as he made his stately rounds, icons and banners held aloft by his acolytes, and where hundreds of people would gather for his blessing. In the case of especially venerated clerics like John of Kronstadt, just the association was enough, and fashionable ladies paid high prices to lodge and pray in his 'courtyard' even though he might never arrive, hoping for some Lourdes-like miracle cure to emanate from the aura of his sanctity.

Akkerman's little harbour was an exciting sight for David and his friends. The cobbled quayside bustled with carts creaking under loads of oak and fir, grain, hides, grapes and tobacco, but as the indispensable 'Black Sea Pilot' cautioned, it had to be approached through the tricky shores with circumspection through two narrow breaches in the sandbank, which closed off almost the entire estuary mouth. A litany of navigation instructions told mariners how to line up signal masts, buoys and church spires to find the right course. The water was so shallow that larger freighters had to moor offshore and offload some of their cargo by barge, until they were riding high enough in the water to approach the harbour. The shipping added to the sense of history a press of movement and the pull of distant horizons.

In the sleepy heat of summer, boats brought Russian tourists to Akkerman on their way to the little villages further up the Dniester to take the mineral waters, mud baths or simply to swim. There they rented rooms or little dachas for the season. Fathers in crumpled linen suits and panama hats frowned over week-old newspapers on the porch, mothers gossiped over tea with their neighbours, children yelled, splashing and digging in the sand as their kerchiefed, white-aproned *babushki* and fussy nursemaids beamed and clucked warnings, the whole scene a mix of Chekhov and *Monsieur Hulot's Holiday*. However, it was no holiday staying in Akkerman itself. Of its three tiny hotels, only one had bathrooms and a communal steam bath.

The rutted road out of Akkerman to the south-west meandered through farms and peasant huts into the countryside between the 50,000 acres of vineyards – the town's crest was a grapevine on a red background – orchards and tobacco fields on the hillsides along the estuary. Within a long day it would have taken an early-rising traveller on horseback through Kulechka across the lake lands to the Danube and the port of Izmail, where, after handing over a few coins to sweeten the surly guards at the wooden frontier post, he would find himself, tired, dusty and probably slightly apprehensive, in Romania. Across the broad river and the marshlands with their reed-thatched fishermen's shacks lay the fortified hill town of Tulcea. Some of the stones in its walls dated back to the seventh century BC, and seen from a distance by an early French traveller it was 'a most pleasant sight; it is a host of mills hurrying, each of them, as if vying to be the first to finish the job'.

When the Romanians got their manicured hands on Akkerman after the Great War (they are the only army known to have gone into the conflict bolstered by regulations restricting the use of cosmetics to officers above a certain rank) and again briefly in the Second World War, they translated the Turkish directly to Cetatea Alba; hopefully the current form, Belgorod-Dnestrovsky, 'White City on the Dniester', will prove more lasting.

There had been a Jewish community in the town since the sixteenth century and by 1897 it was some 5,600 strong – 20 per cent of the population. Many of them had come as 'colonists' to farm (like Trotsky's family, the Bronsteins, on the other side of Odessa), or ran agricultural merchants' businesses. Most other occupations and professions were closed to them. Even so, as Isaac Deutscher, Trotsky's biographer, pointed out, farming was so foreign to the Jewish way of life that very few of those able to eke out a precarious living in the towns would choose it. Those who did were tough, had nothing to lose, and had few or no ties with the synagogue. According to Deutscher, the Jewish idiom for 'a man of the land', 'Am Haaretz', also meant a vulgarian who did not have even a smattering of the Scriptures and being outside the mainstream of Jewish life was less scrupulous about its dogmas and disciplines. They were not free of the scourge of the pogrom, but one has the impression of a community in and around Odessa that was more confident, less fearful and less harried than in the cities, in part perhaps because of the region's multi-ethnic nature and history; in part, too, because even before the Bund (the trade union movement which also organised squads of young men to combat pogrom attacks), some of the Jewish settlements had well-organised and well-armed 'self defence units' ready to rough up or even shoot Russian trouble-makers in search of mayhem. Looked at from a distance, the Jewish settlements were islands surrounded by an anti-Semitic sea, whose waves varied in intensity from suspicious indifference through resentment to overt hostility.

Where the two communities coexisted, the tensions were sharper. Many villages had both a synagogue and an Orthodox church, and some ultra-Orthodox Jews had been known to turn away and mutter *sotto voce* prayers when they saw Russian church processions with their white beards, gold and red banners, and icons and portraits of the Tsar held high. But some things were shared: disease, natural disaster and famine. Sometimes both houses of worship found themselves offering the same prayers, for instance when news came that the *Rotnik*, or district police superintendent, was about to descend on one of his periodic inspections. Each congregation beseeched the heavens in its own way that he would find nothing to upset him, as he was known to explode in a frenzy of kicks and curses and order his men to beat up anyone who crossed his path.

Memoirs of life in the villages around Akkerman, such as Harry Burroughs', across the estuary highlight the rural beauty of the setting and cite the communities' 'abundant *Parnossah*', which then meant a sense of shared financial well-being. 'And where there is *Parnossah* one does not begrudge the other and jealousy gains no power.' (The word is related to the Hittite symbol *par-na-sa* expressing the sense of 'home' and even Greece's sacred Mount Parnassus. In more modern literature, the word seems to have taken on the meaning of the elders of a community responsible among other things for distributing its wealth.) Others remember the storks returning to nest at the same house year after year. Before they left again in winter, they would line up in flight formation in one of the fields, the older birds strutting up and down as if giving orders to the young.

Though grain was the area's main source of income, vine-growing, wine-making and wine-selling were not only profitable but enjoyable as the endless tasting rituals were spun out in the twilight. The writer Isaac Babel, who grew up in Odessa and etched indelible word portraits of its traders, publicans and sinners, and who had drunk many bottles of it, observed in his Odessa story 'Lyubka the Cossack' that Bessarabian wine 'has a bouquet of sunshine and bedbugs'. That struck me as a flight of literary fantasy until I was told by a pretty girl from modern Odessa that her mother still has a vine on her terrace within the city itself, whose grapes do indeed, when peeled, give off the unmistakable musty smell of bedbugs, themselves as much a part of Russian life over the centuries as cabbage pie, prayer and vodka. Money came from tobacco-growing and processing, and even (which would have struck a chord with Manya's father) the curing and processing of sheepskins, which were shipped upriver to the Great Fair at Balta, some 150 miles north of Odessa.

As the income trickled down, so it kept comfortably alive the local artisans and craftsmen, the coopers, saddlers, vegetable-sellers and menders of pots and pans, whose tiny shops and barrows filled the market squares, which, depending on the season, were either shrouded in choking dust or knee-deep in mud. Even peasant communities had a pecking order, with shoemakers at the bottom of the craft ladder and tailors just a cut above, so to speak. Memories of the period also underscore Deutscher's point that while the communities were Jewish, most families saw no contradiction between Judaism and giving their children a worldly education. Several later émigrés have stressed the 'general humanistic values' instilled in them as children and David was no exception; his family were among what were called the *maskilim* or 'people of modern impulse', maybe because, unlike those confined to city ghettoes, reality for the merchants was the wider world, the effects of wars, storms, poor harvests, fluctuations in currency exchange rates, dealing with sharp foreigners in foreign languages, and competition from deep-pocketed international firms such as Dreyfus and Bunge, who had the lion's share of the Odessa export market. It was a business on a major scale; in the 1890s grain represented 47 per cent of Russia's total exports. Bessarabia also had a large German community, farmers for the most part, which had put down its first roots in 1804; of some 280 villages listed at the end of the nineteenth century, at least half had unequivocally German names from Alte Elft through Furstenfeld to Teplitz and Wagner Gut (the latter needing only a closing exclamation mark to qualify as literate graffiti for a Bayreuth wall).

We know so little of David's schooling. We do know that Akkerman had a mix of liberal and religious education, slanted more towards the former than the recital of prayers and sacred texts. We also know that the boys there wandered the countryside, the sandbanks and the mudflats with their friends, maybe on one of those heavy early bicycles with solid tyres and 'sit up and beg' handlebars. The Coventry-made Triumph and Raleigh were widely advertised locally. David would also have seen the first moving picture shows, short – 60 feet – sets of flickering images, three 'stories' to a reel, hand-cranked onto whitewashed walls or tightly stretched bed-sheets by itinerant projectionists; the writer Maxim Gorky first saw the new phenomenon in 1890, describing it as 'the Kingdom of the Shadows'.

Even the background noise of Akkerman must have been unique: the bells of the Russian churches; the different peals, on a different timetable, of the German Lutheran churches; Jewish music; Russian music; but probably most of all the plangent keening of Balkan melodies, a heady mix of fiddles, lutes, accordions, goatskin bagpipes and the clarinet-like taragot. Gypsy brass-players wandered from village to village, delighting children with their adapted and regur-gitated Ottoman oompah-pah rhythms of the military bands of the Turkish janissaries. They can even be heard today, as if by some quirk of fate John Philip Sousa and the quintet of the Hot Club of France had found themselves in an impromptu jam session over the trestle tables of a smoky, sweaty bar in a muddy Moldovan market square.

So Akkerman was exotic in its own way, and a comfortable place in which to grow up, but it was still provincial. The magnet was Odessa, to which the passenger steamers *Turgenev* and *Vasilyev* shuttled across the estuary twice a day; the third-class fare 'without deck access' was a few coins. Odessa, where David, like so many others from the outlying areas, went on to the trade school, was a bustle of polyglot prosperity, designed by the émigré Duc de Richelieu (role model for Byron's Don Juan) for Catherine the Great on the site of what had once been a sleepy settlement named Hadji-Bey. It was a city with magnificent architecture, where the sun shone for six months of the year, the sea sparkling beyond the 1200-metre breakwater that shielded the broad, crammed harbour and splashing on the nearby beaches – one of them named Arkadia – lined like the little villages along the Dniester by rather grander summer villages with spas offering curative waters and pungent mud and sulphur baths. Though frost could bite in the winter, the summers were long and languorous. This – and the foreigners who lived and traded there, or brought their ships into its port, Russia's largest by shipping volume – gave it a uniquely foreign flavour, far more Marseilles than Minsk. By the 1900s it was one of Russia's largest and most economically vibrant cities (its population of 425,000 compared to St Petersburg's 1.4 million), ranking only behind the latter, Moscow and Warsaw in the quality of its universities and educational institutions. Foreign banks and trading houses were prominent and one account put the mercantile community alone at over 500,000. Only half its population were native Russian-speakers and street names in the city centre were posted in Russian, French and Greek. It had six daily newspapers, two for the German community and one which to judge from its masthead, 'The Defence of the Interests of the Russian People', was of a strongly nationalistic and probably anti-Semitic cast. The city even had its own branch of the Court jeweller Fabergé and a bottling plant of the French Champagne house Roederer. The perceptive writer Anna Reid tells us that its waterworks were British-built, its trees grown from saplings brought from Vienna, its gas lighting installed by Germans, and its tramways built by Belgians. Its turn-of-the-century guidebook chose to give its latitude and longitude in relation to Paris rather than Greenwich; back then, time zones were measured with a precision inherited from Sir Isaac Newton and the guidebook noted that noontime in Odessa was precisely 10.06 and 24 seconds in Paris. Even the Steps owed some of their design to a British engineer, who, in keeping with the city's louche traditions, had jumped bail in London while facing fraud charges. Despite all the city's modernity, the 'Black Sea Pilot', counselled with a nice homely touch that if weather forced an incoming navigator to moor outside the harbour, the best way to find a berth was to take a bearing 'from the tip of the Quarantine Port Mole to the third house from the left-hand corner of the Place Richelieu'. Another approach was 'to line up the semaphore mast on the cliff with the cathedral bell tower'.

The city was actually and temperamentally closer to the Balkans, Turkey and the city my grandfather knew as Constantinople (a day away by steamer), and the Crimea than to Moscow, which probably explains why the British Consul, Colonel Stewart, spent far more time in his offices at 21 Troitskaya Street briefing and debriefing agents slipping in and out of Central Asia across the Black Sea in the heady days of the 'Great Game' of Russian and British rivalries in India than he did stamping passports or dealing with what the Foreign Office regulations even today classify as 'Distressed British Subjects'. A forty or fifty-mile carriage ride would have taken a traveller to towns with distinctly un-Slavonic names such as Izmail and Mahmudia.

In the earlier part of the century Odessa had left its mark on Russia's own Byron. The poet Pushkin had spent an intellectually fruitful if personally complicated twelve months of his shooting-star life there in 1823, when he was 24, falling foul of the Viceroy Count Vorontsov by falling in love with the Countess. He had even crossed to Akkerman with his friend Liprandi, an army officer, to visit the White Fort's Governor, marking the visit with a poem in Ovid's honour: 'Ovid, I am living near the quiet shores to which you once brought the exiled gods of your fathers and where you left your ashes,' he wrote, yet another visitor who had the facts wrong, though dry facts should never get in the way of good poetry. Pushkin, who had been ordered out of Moscow by the Tsar, clearly felt in tune with his exiled forerunner. (In 1825 the Polish national poet Adam Mickieiwicz also found himself in Odessan exile and made the same side trip to Akkerman.) The manuscript of the first chapter of *Evgeny Onegin* is annotated by Pushkin as 'written in Bessarabia', as were *The Gypsies* and *The Fountain of Bachisarai*. Pushkin dropped his stanzas on Odessa from the first published version of *Onegin*, but they capture the city's flavour in terms that fifty or so years later the young student David Redstone would have recognised, even though by his time the roads had been paved and he would not have had to 'ford the streets on stilts' when rains turned the city into a mud bath.

The long, light summer days – in mid June the sun rises at 4 a.m. and does not dip below the waves until 8 p.m. – the seascape of sails, white rigging, multi-coloured flags and gently swaying masts of ships from every port under the sun, the mix of people, all echo Pushkin's impression that 'Europe and the South are in the air'. There were, Pushkin wrote,

> '. . . A bouillabaisse of races,
> Foreign accents, swarthy faces,
> Greeks and Dagoes, French, Armenians,
> Pushy Slavs, thickset Ruthenians,
> That Corsair there: he made his pile
> Marauding out from the mouth of the Nile.'

Odessa's first school, set up in 1803, reflects the nature of the place even then. The forty boys could be taught in Russian, Greek or Italian. Wealth and growth brought culture and education. The city's history claims that in the mid-nineteenth century, only St Petersburg had more students per head of population and that families from all over Russia vied to send their children to Odessa schools.

Odessa offered country boys a high life of the mind diluted with the temptations of a low life. Whether David joined in the writers' drinking evenings in one of the city's 250 wine shops in the courtyard of the Bruns bar on Yekaterinovskaya Street or on the open verandas of the Robin and Fakoni cafés, we will never know. According to the *Odessa Almanakh*, it was bad form among the intellectuals to drink yourself senseless, and even worse for some now totally obscure reason to be seen drinking with the lay-brothers of the Mutual Burial Society, 'who feed from the tables of other men's grief' (probably a reflection of their habit of freeloading and pilfering when they went to collect a member's linen-wrapped corpse).

Nor do I know – though out of a fastidious sense of respect I choose to doubt it – whether David and his friends caroused in the bordellos on Zaporozhskaya Street, to which Babel's petty hoods travelled in varnished carriages carrying bunches of flowers for the whores. Madame Joska's was renowned as the house where 'a father might encounter his son, the shopkeeper one of his counter clerks and the high school teacher one of his pupils'. (The common Russian term for 'brothel' at that time was *publichny dom*, literally 'a public house'. Were Russian émigrés to London confused to learn that there were 'public houses' on almost every corner and did they wonder about possible hidden meanings in the painted signs proclaiming: 'I Am The Only Running Footman' or 'The Sun and Thirteen Cantons'?) David would certainly have known the legend of the large cannon mounted on a plinth at the end of Primorskaya Boulevard, which had been captured during the Crimean War from the British frigate HMS *Tiger*. According to Odessa folklore, if a young man wanted to be sure that his fiancée was the virgin she claimed to be, he should sit her astride the cannon. If it fired spontaneously, she was telling the truth.

David would have strolled past the Italianate façade of the 'English Club' – membership of which was as hard to achieve as in any of the London clubs surrounding Freddy Fox's Museum – and the Londonskaya Hotel (one of the fifteen officially listed as 'first class'), and would have remembered taking short cuts between the Parisian-scale boulevards through the old Odessa courtyards where so much of life was lived. Most of the buildings were peeling two or three-storey rabbit warrens. Some were no more than wooden shacks on stilts, called 'huts on chickens legs'. As an anonymous writer recorded in the *Almanakh*, 'The women washed their kids, bottled fruit, dried their linen, filleted their fish . . . and in the stuffy summer nights everyone slept out under the old acacia tree, bringing with them their aches and pains, their joys, their troubles and their hopes; there they arranged marriages and there they mourned their dead.' When night fog blanketed the bay, the steady tolling of the warning bell from the lightship in the harbour could be heard across the city.

Even after all this time, the city's pulse can be felt by flicking through the microfilms of one of the local newspapers. It put out both a morning and an afternoon edition, offering world news, many loyal column inches about the Tsar's doings, medal awards and pronouncements, grain and currency prices from the major European markets, and reports of major grain deals in the city. There were advertisements for operas (The Vienna Opera with *Die Fledermaus* was appropriate for an opera house which looked as though it had been transported brick by brick from the Ringstrasse) and concerts, with as much Saint-Saëns, Berlioz and Massenet as Tchaikovsky and

Rimsky-Korsakov. The newspaper also saved the gendarmes a lot of trouble by naming the new arrivals at the principal hotels, offering in the process a nice glimpse of the social habits of the time. Taking one day at random, the business travellers stayed at the Odesskaya, a troupe of visiting actors filled the Versailles, and army officers and civil servants flocked en masse to the Dvoryanskaya. The Maybach was the preserve of German settlers in transit to their new homes. Odessa's role as a major military centre and the political climate of the 1890s are reflected in the law reports: whereas the London *Times*, for example, would have recorded proceedings in the high courts, the Odessa accounts are all of hearings before the military district tribunal, which dealt with civil crimes as well as the whole range of military offences.

It was a city where the rich lived very well, but even the less well-to-do could find fresh food in abundance. In the summer, vendors hawked local honeydew melons and watermelons, blackberries, raspberries, gooseberries, cherries, peaches, pears and apricots. As autumn approached, cornucopias of the succulent Akkerman *Izabella* grapes overflowed the edges of the market stalls. Even in winter, aubergines, cucumbers, squash and tomatoes were shipped in daily from Constantinople along with mussels, crabs, langoustine and lobster. From the waters of the Dniester, Danube and Dnepr Rivers, silver, red and white fish were brought by the wicker-basketful to the quaysides, to be offloaded alongside the still flapping plaice, mullet, mackerel, bullheads and perch trawled from the sea.

Writing in the United States many years later, Harry Burroughs (we do not know his Russian name) remembers arriving from the countryside, his first trip to a big city and his first journey by train. To the wide-eyed Jewish teenager the broad streets of Odessa were 'swept as clean as the floor of an Orthodox home at Passover'. Proud horses drew fine carriages through the broad boulevards laid out in a tidy grid pattern, while in the acacia-shaded squares moustache-twirling men of evident distinction and parasol-twirling women of evident charm bowed and exchanged formal greetings. Sailors in tufted caps, ribboned collars and starched uniforms ogled the girls, while red-bereted 'commissionaires', who carried parcels and messages for a few coins, scurried between the traffic. But Burroughs found it 'grotesque' that this display of bourgeois tranquillity continued undisturbed when just a few moments later, having walked no further than two or three streets away, he saw Jewish shopkeepers frantically rattling down their shutters as butchers in bloody white coats, who were also on call as the area's Defence League, swarmed out of the local kosher slaughterhouse to fight off a marauding band of hooligans before their jeering and stone-throwing boiled over into something more primeval.

It was in Odessa that David caught the revolutionary bug. But before we follow him down that long, winding path which ended in Siberia, let us bring Manya up on the screen.

5

Furs, Frost and Happy Families

Though they later shared the indelible Siberian experience, David and Manya came to it from very different beginnings. He was a prisoner. For her, it was her childhood home, a place of delight and wonder, not punishment. It was a world that revolved on a different axis, looking east not west. Mongolia was a reality at the end of Manya's garden and she grew up far nearer Beijing or Tokyo than the gilded palaces of St Petersburg. In an ordinary day at the market, she would see as many ruddy-cheeked, bearded, narrow-eyed Buryats as Russians, mingling with Chinese in long quilted coats and clusters of chattering Mongols in embroidered jackets, fur hats and patterned leather riding boots, the toes curved upwards at an impossible angle like the six-inch fingernails of some wizened mandarin. As a child she also met some of the exiled intellectuals, many of them in those days Poles, who had been shipped out wholesale after the Polish uprising against Russian rule in 1863. They were allowed to give private lessons, and some of them gave her and her siblings their grounding in reading, writing and arithmetic.

The extremes of climate, the remoteness, the natural beauty, the tribesmen, the mountains and the 'frontier spirit' were in Manya's blood. She trotted through the meadows on shaggy Siberian ponies many years before she ever saw the inside of a car. To David and the other exiles from European Russia, all of these aspects were negatives, regarded with a fear and loathing much intensified by their fragile status as outcasts even more at the mercy of arbitrary authority than 'regular' convicts whose lives, harsh and terrible as they were, were governed by the judicial and penal system.

Manya's Siberia lagged behind European Russia in worldliness much as the Chicago of that era felt inferior to New York. But like the American Midwest, it had factories and mines, the first telephones and some electric light in the major cities. The railway was arriving to strike terror into the stone-age tribesmen and bring new waves of settlers. Its mountains, forests and boggy tundra were rich in game birds, fish and wildlife, including bears, snow leopards and the occasional tiger. Buried beneath them were diamonds and a King Solomon's Mine of other precious stones: gold, silver, antimony, wolfram, lead, copper, coal and iron ore. There were also the bones of mammoths, who, in the local belief, lived eternally in the frozen darkness but died and shrivelled the instant their hiding places were opened to the light. Though the trade was soon to be threatened by the manufacture of artificial ivory, mammoth tusks were still highly prized and Yakutsk, where much of our story takes place, had a centuries-old annual market where around 20,000 kilos changed hands every year, many collected by the natives from the shores of the Arctic and the banks of the northern rivers. Most were sent to the Bogomolov factory in Moscow, sawn, lathed and polished into billiard balls and combs. Even into the early twentieth century, travellers spotted sledges whose runners were made from mammoth ribs. Siberia also had Arctic shores, stony windswept plains, forests, marshlands, deserts, mountain ranges, hidden gorges that must have concealed many a Shangri-La and endless rushing rivers, down which in the brief summers splashed large paddle steamers (some of them built in British shipyards) and which in the long winter froze almost solid – not the smooth ice of skating rinks and lakes, but cruelly jagged ice piled into crags and cliffs, ice that could sometimes come alive, groaning in pain as it buckled and reformed. In Lake Baikal was the world's largest mass of fresh water, the size of Switzerland. To Manya's generation, it was an expanse of magic and danger, usually referred to as 'The Sea', 'The Old Man', or simply 'He'. The local villagers had at least a dozen dialect terms to distinguish the different winds that suddenly sprang up from every point of the compass out of a clear blue sky and whipped the placid surface into a boat-swallowing froth. Siberia also had Cossacks and caviar, scientists and village witchdoctors, exiled poets and pitiful peasants, as well as the grim prisons and mines which have become its stereotype, where convicts and lost souls toiled.

Manya's world was built on the liturgies and certainties of the Orthodox Church, but though there were Jewish communities and synagogues in Siberia, and the Buryats around her were Buddhists, she would also have tuned in to the transcendental currents of the nomadic tribesmen's shamanism, folk ways as old as mammoth bones. The nomads lived by a simple calendar in which winter months were simply known by their numbers, while those of the spring and summer had names which evoked the season, such as 'the harvest', 'the dropping of foals', 'the melting of the snows'.

Though their tribes were ruled at an earthly level by the *tojon* (chief), on a spiritual plane there were underworlds, a pantheon of animistic gods and evil spirits to be petitioned or placated. Bears, ravens and eagles were revered and everything in nature – rocks, rivers, lakes, trees, thunder – had its own spirits, whose effigies – a goose, beaver, elk, eagle or swan – were hidden in sanctuaries in the forest used for ritual ceremonies to ward off epidemic diseases or prepare for war. The tribal priests or shamans, who also doubled as healers, exorcists and arbiters in community squabbles, presided over the rites, sacrificing horses, reindeer or other animals under a tree, smearing the mouths of the spirit effigies with blood to 'feed' them, and offering libations of fermented mares' milk and melted butter. Mystic 'rivers', along which only shamans could travel, ran between what in a Christian structure would be heaven, the Earth, and hell. Though a nineteenth-century English traveller fulminated that shamanism was 'a most rascally system of knavery' propagated by 'evil spirits who terrify their followers from a threat of haunting them in this world and the next', the ethos, cult, belief, or whatever is the right word to apply, lives on strongly today.

Manya would also have been aware of other strict (and to today's eyes downright weird) sects and mystic movements such as the Milk Drinkers, the Runaways, the Wanderers, the Non-Prayers, the White

Robed Ones and the Khlysty, who had much in common with the Whirling Dervishes of North Africa. None, however, could match the radical demands imposed on their adherents by the *Skoptsy*, or Castrati, who believed in enlightenment by 'excision of the instrument of sin'. Though denounced as heretic as far back as 1807, by the 1850s the police were reporting that the sect had a lot of money at its disposal and was continuing to flourish, despite the deep breaths candidates for membership (or, rather, deprivation of membership), must have taken before signing up. Step one, the Small Seal, was castration. Step two, the Grand Seal, called for even more radical surgery. One prominent adherent, a merchant in Morchansk, was said to have 'a secret iron-barred cellar under his house where the shocking mutilations . . . were perpetrated'. Many *Skoptsy* communities were exiled to Siberia for their considerable pains, and were respected for their neatness and industry, though Trotsky shook his head after a visit to one of their villages: 'Somehow it is boring here. Life is lacking. Children are lacking. Mothers are lacking. Faces are bloated and, despite honest looks, unpleasant . . .'

Over the centuries, many travellers, from Venice, Rome, Paris, New York and London, have tried to comprehend the incomprehensibility of Siberia. As George Kennan told his American readers, this was a landmass of 5,493,629 square miles, compared to 3,501,414 for 'The United States and Alaska'. The province of Yakutsk alone was more than twelve times the size of Great Britain and the city itself was a major outpost of the Russian American Trading Company, which was founded in the eighteenth century and which dominated trade with the North-western United States. Until what seems now a curiously short-sighted sale in 1867, the company had owned much of present-day Alaska.

Contemporary visitors to Siberia are struck by the contrast between the majesty and the misery, the crumbling infrastructure, polluted rivers and isolated settlements ravaged by disease and hopelessness. But they all share with earlier voyagers the shock of the weather. In 1591 the English poet Giles Fletcher on a diplomatic mission to Siberia recorded anecdotes that mirror to the letter the stories David Redstone told us about putting an ungloved hand on a metal window handle and leaving strips of flesh behind, or water freezing before it hit the ground; knowing his audience, my grandfather would annoy my mother by telling her giggling children that was the least that would happen if a man was stupid enough to urinate outside.

Venetians, Jesuits, explorers from Bering, merchants, writers, missionaries, diplomats, railway engineers, teachers and salesmen promoting British-made icebreakers and fire engines, all made the long trek over the centuries. They were all of enquiring minds. In the eighteenth century a party of well-heeled and skilled French cartographers produced four calf-bound volumes of detailed maps, panoramas and a survey of mineral resources. A German naturalist wrote about the area in detail in 1768 and a British gazetteer of 1823 contains a description of Siberia's terrain, people and climate, which would be broadly valid even today. In 1829, Londoners could go to the Theatre Royal in Covent Garden to gaze in wonder at a 'moving diorama' of the British Navy's perilous search among the ice floes for the North-West Passage between Siberia and America.

In the early nineteenth century Captain Cochrane of the Royal Navy wrote 'A Pedestrian Tour' of Siberia, apparently referring to his means of locomotion rather than the drabness of his journeying, but perhaps pride of place in earlier writings about the region, at least for its *chutzpah* should go to a book written by the 'blind traveller Holman'. A later author sniffed that while both books 'increased public interest in . . . the narrators, they somewhat diminished their confidence in the accuracy of the information'. The comment is unfair on James Holman, whose account of his Siberian travels proved very popular when it appeared in 1825. Clearly a man with what American writer Tom Wolfe nearly two hundred years later characterised as 'the right stuff', he joined the navy at thirteen, rose through the ranks and gained his commission only to be blinded by scurvy in his twenties. After several years of frustrated idleness, he set off sightless on his personal version of The Grand Tour, a journey that included a solo swim two miles off Marseilles, a climb to the basilica of St Peter's in Rome and a foolhardy stroll around the ring of Mount Vesuvius. After a brief spell in England to write up his account of these bravura exploits, he set off eastwards, managing to get as far as Irkutsk, a major feat even today for a traveller with all his faculties and modern transport. 'Blindman's Bluff', the incredulous gendarmerie must have thought, since they arrested him as a spy and carted him back in chains to Moscow, where like so many of the characters in our story he spent a nasty spell in jail before being deported. Later a Fellow of the Royal Society, Holman thought his handicap actually gave him 'a stronger zest to curiosity'.

An intrepid Victorian, with unshakeable English certainty about the background of his potential readers, wrote that the dormitories in the military cadet barracks at Omsk 'were most comfortable, far more so than the Long Chamber at Eton'. His predecessor Giles Fletcher – whose fortitude given the medieval times is even more to be admired – was himself an Old Etonian and Fellow of King's, Cambridge, and it may be that public school hardships were indeed the right sort of background for an appreciation of Siberia.

In the 1850s another mildly eccentric Englishman went out of his way to give apparently unsolicited praise to the watercolour-makers Winsor and Newton, whose 'moist colours' had proved useable at one extreme in the burning plains of central Asia and also, though frozen 'as solid as a mass of iron', in Siberian winter lows of -43 degrees C. Yakutsk itself claims rather proudly to have the biggest temperature swing of 'any other region in the world', from -64 C to a summer peak of $+38$ C, with an average winter temperature of almost -43 C.

The weather played strange tricks. As the temperature fell, the air and sky became steadily cloudier until the world was blanketed by an eerie yellow fog. Like some apocalyptic vision, even the hardiest of birds on the wing would tumble out of the sky as ice-covered lumps, frozen solid in mid-air by some ferocious downdraft.

Kate Marsden, a pugnacious and some might say obsessive New Zealander of Boadicean build, came halfway round the world in the 1890s to draw attention to the plight of Siberia's leper colonies, whose inmates were left to fester and die in the wilderness. The summer and its mosquitoes almost crushed even her indomitable spirit: 'There are three charming varieties and each is made in a special way for torturing you. The very large ones are known to bleed horses and men to death, and can bite through even your thickest leather gloves, pushing their long probes through the stitches, and biting through all your clothes to the skin. The second kind can only tackle thinner clothing and of course any scrap of skin you are foolish enough to leave uncovered. The last are so small as to be almost invisible and get into your nose, ears and eyes, down your neck, up your gloves and down your boots. We burned manure in the hut, we covered ourselves with netting, we tried everything, but nothing stopped them.'

Though only half English, 'Crawley The Albino' put down very British roots when he came to rest in Tomsk in the late nineteenth century. Son of an 'Abyssinian' father and an English mother, he and his siblings had been exhibited in freak shows in London and across Europe as far as Turkey. When the troupe disbanded after displays in St Petersburg and Moscow, Crawley, who was said by then to have mastered five languages, hoped to start again as a solo act in China. Finding that his unusual features attracted less and less curiosity as he waded through the ever thickening genetic stew towards Asia, he settled in Tomsk and opened the first 'pub' there to boast a billiards room, making enough money in the process to buy a house and live out his life in comfort.

Spreading a different kind of British gospel were two early-nineteenth-century missionaries, Swan and Stallybrass, who spent twenty-three years in Selenginsk just south of Lake Baikal trying valiantly to convert the Buryats to Christianity, with a stunning lack of success that would have driven less devoted men home long before, even though they did succeed in producing the first printed translation of the Bible into Buryat. When out of frustration they turned their attentions to members of the Russian Orthodox Church, they were promptly deported.

Then there were the descendants of Scots, who had signed up as mercenaries in the sixteenth century to help the Tsars beat back Chinese incursions into Siberia; one of them is said to have become a member of the nobility and Lermontov himself was proud of his descent from the family of the Scottish immigrant Learmonth. There were also three British engineers from Newcastle, who had arrived in Siberia to supervise the building of the ice-breaking ferry which, before the last leg of the Trans-Siberian Railway was laid, was the only means of crossing Lake Baikal. In a remarkable feat of transportation and engineering the ice breaker had been sent out from England as a caravan of crates filled with iron plates, engine pipes, fittings, even nuts and bolts, and put together like a giant Meccano set in a lakeside shipyard. The British lived in lonely dread in a village that was notorious as 'a nest of crime and robbery', venturing out only to go to the shipyard and scurrying back behind locked doors at day's end.

Though firmly planted in the East, Manya's family had its own European history. Her father claimed that he was the son of a French drummer boy, who had tramped all the way to Russia with Napoleon's army and never gone home. While this may be romanticised and the surname Flegontov is Russian enough (though derived from the Greek for 'ardent' or 'excitable'), her father's first name, Kandit, is the Russian version of the undeniably French 'Candide' (by Russian tradition she and her sisters took the feminine version of their father's name, Kanditovna 'daughter of Kandit', as their middle name or patronymic and their brothers similarly the male form, Kandityevich). We know that some 400,000 of the Grande Armée never made it home. Many were killed; some were captured and some just wandered off.

How the most banal of words can migrate from one language is a science in itself. The French who found themselves adrift and penniless in Russia had to beg for every scrap of food. '*Cher ami . . .*', they entreated any peasant who would listen. Some 150 years later, corrupted into '*sharamyga*', the word was still used in Gulag prisoners' slang for someone who conned and wheedled their way to better treatment. In turn the French borrowed from Russian that quintessentially French word: '*bistro*'. In Russian it means 'hurry up', 'quickly', and it imprinted itself in France when the Tsar's troops, plundering and bullying Cossacks in the van, stamped into Paris with the triumphant Allied armies after Napoleon's defeat at Waterloo, shouting at the cowering French to 'get a move on'. Given the heavy influence of French culture and the Age of Enlightenment on the court and intellectuals in Peter the Great's Russia, it is hardly surprising that a recently published 855-page dictionary of foreign words imported into Russian is replete with Gallic borrowings, though it raises some intriguing questions. How did the French *'cauchemar'* – 'nightmare' – became the Russian *'koshmar'*? Did Russian bad dreams only begin after their first encounters with the French? Why did the Russians adopt the venerable Caran d'Ache trademark as their generic word *'karandash'* for 'pencil' and how did the French 'fileur', ('spinner') become *'filyor'*, meaning 'plain-clothes policeman'? Happily these are questions best left to others to pursue.

Manya was born in Nerchinsk, in the Transbaikal region, 150 miles east of Chita. I have no clear idea when; it was not the sort of question you asked. I have always assumed that she was probably a year or two younger than David. Using a standard of comparison more readily understood in his day, a turn-of-the-century geographer pointed out that the region – a land of high mountains, countless forests, rushing rivers and immense deposits of silver – was 'the size of Austro-Hungary'. It had a population of over 700,000, the majority Buryat rather than Russian. Nerchinsk was itself tiny – some 6,700 inhabitants and 727 houses (suggesting either poor statistics or serious overcrowding) – but quite remarkably prosperous. It had a girls' high school, a parish school, a seminary, three stone churches, two synagogues, a museum, a public garden 'with a fountain', its civic handbook noted proudly, and a town library which had 25,000 books. Much of it was paid for by the generosity of Mikhail Butin, an early 'oligarch' who owned two of the local silver mines and who dwelt in splendour in a Moorish palace at which Manya and her brothers and sisters must have goggled open-mouthed. To come across such wealth in the midst of so much bleakness and poverty clearly flabbergasted George Kennan: 'As I entered the splendid ballroom I caught the reflection of myself in the largest mirror in the world' (bought by Butin from Brussels). 'There were hardwood marquetry floors, silken curtains, hangings of delicate tapestry, stained-glass windows, splendid chandeliers, soft oriental rugs, white and gold furniture upholstered with satin . . . an extensive conservatory filled with palms, lemon trees and rare orchids . . .'

Although Kennan was told that Butin was going through a cash flow crisis at the time, he seems to have snapped back well. When he died in 1907, he left the bulk of his still impressive fortune for the building and upkeep of ten village schools in the region, a secondary school and a children's shelter. The silver mines and smelters of Nerchinsk had been opened in the 1700s. They were spread over a wide area along the Mongolian border, up to 180 miles from Nerchinsk itself, and were known collectively as Nerchinsky Zavod. (In contemporary Russian, *Zavod* means 'factory'; back then it was applied to the sites of silver, gold and lead mines and smelters.) In the middle of the eighteenth century, the Zavod mines began to use exiles to supplement their colonist workforce, under conditions which remained savage up to Kennan's time and beyond. There were many more criminal exiles than 'politicals'.

At some point the Flegontov family moved out to the Zavod area since one of Manya's earliest memories was of a house on the banks of the Argun River, so close to the frontier that, as she joked in later life, 'If you rolled out of the house and down the river bank, you were in Mongolia.' In summer the river sparkled. By October it was swirling with floating grey patches of snow and ice known locally as '*shuga*' and in Russian as '*salo*' (edible lard), reminding one visitor of 'cold fat on mutton gravy'. In two weeks it would be frozen solid, though another nearby river ran so fast that it could not freeze, and it could be followed along the valley for miles because of the clouds of steam pluming upwards as the relative warmth of the rushing water hit the frigid cold air above.

The sense of Asia predominating over any vestige of Europe must have been reinforced by the fact that, travelling south, the nearest towns large enough to be included on the map were called Chi La Lin and Tang Ping Chua. Manya's father made a comfortable living as a trader, mainly in furs but also handling anything else from timber to grain where a profit could be turned. (The *Guide to the Great Siberian Railway*, those steel lines of life and death stretching from one side of Russia to the other, which are central to the country's turn-of-the-century story and ours as well, notes matter-of-factly that even in 1900 opium was among the products traded in Manchuria. There was also a lively traffic in ginseng root, which along with the antlers of the young *maral* deer, known rather nicely in the circumstances as '*panty*', were much prized by Chinese men past their prime 'for restoring lost vigour'.)

Manya used to tell her grandchildren that her family had twelve servants, 'one for each child', suggesting that theirs was a comfortable life even though the 'servants' were unlikely to have been a house-keeper in grey gabardine, a bowing butler or white-aproned maids, but more probably peasant girls with goitres and gnarled old handymen.

Nerchinsk itself had become a major centre of Russian fur exports in 1697, when a customs post was set up to tax sales to China. Like grain in Bessarabia, fur trading was not a gentleman's business. Furs had been one of the first of Siberia's resources to be exploited, first by way of 'tribute' to feed the Tsar's treasury – in the middle of the seventeenth century they accounted for 20 per cent of budget revenues – and then as a staple of trade. Around the time of our story, Russia still provided some 40 per cent of the world's furs. The trade was based on barter rather than money and the merchants needed not just capital but at least three essential skills. The first was a bluff insensitivity to exploiting the natives who brought in the pelts. Even more important was a very sharp mind in dealing with the buyers higher up the trading 'hierarchy'. In an interesting ranking that reversed the usual Russian suspicion, one shrewd observer of the Siberian trading scene put Armenians first on the list of those given to cheating, followed by Greeks, Chinese (who displayed 'extreme dexterity . . . in every sort of chicanery'), Russians and only lastly Jews. One of George Frost's sketches of a local marketplace carries the scribbled note that some of the most tumbled-down shacks were run by 'Chinese Shylocks'.

As in any other trade, the third and perhaps key skill was to know what you were looking at. Sables were the most highly prized, and to survive as a trader Flegontov had to have the 'nose' to know, for instance, that the best skins came from north of Lake Baikal, that pale lips were the sign of an animal freshly killed and that the uncured pelts faded unless kept in the dark. Another arcane distinction was that sables trapped by Yakuts were inferior since they gutted the animals via the mouth rather than the recommended route which started at the opposite end. Next came ermine, whose tail showed a highly prized black tip in winter, and then lynx, blue, black, red and white foxes, marten, wolf, polecat, muskrat, squirrel and, on the Arctic shores, the sea otter. Flegontov also dealt as a sideline in the violet plumage of the duck known as '*gogarki*', used for making ladies' caps and dress trimmings.

It was a long way from a haphazard stack of bloodstained pelts on Flegontov's wooden counter top to wholesale houses in Vienna and the hushed, mirrored furriers' salons of Europe or New York, and by the time some elegant matron or mistress had the final product draped over her alabaster shoulders, the price per skin had multiplied several thousand-fold. The system the traders used sounds, and was, harsh, but it was of its time and no different from that operated by gold dealers in the Klondike, early diamond prospectors, or merchants of ivory in the Congo. Though some hunters were Russian, most were tribesmen for whom the hunt, usually starting around October, was a family affair, sometimes groups of families together. The trader supplied the food, fodder, traps, bait, guns and warm clothing, sometimes even the reindeer, horses and sledges, and agreed the prices to be paid for the pelts they brought back. Russian hunters usually came back with the whole carcass. The nomads, hungrier and less fastidious, would bring back bloody pelts after hacking off and eating the meat. 'Paid' did not usually mean in cash. The trader would first set against the notional value of the take the amount he had laid out in supplies, subtracting and adding margins of profit as he went, the deftness of his arithmetic baffling the unsophisticated eye of the native. Any balance still due would be handed over as tobacco, cloth, rifles (the longer the barrel, the higher the stack of pelts in exchange), tools, ornaments and rot-gut alcohol. When desperate hunters still begged for cash, unscrupulous merchants had been known to send them on their way with finely engraved coloured labels from champagne bottles and chocolate boxes. The tribesmen were locked in a cycle of cashless dependency, and out of season were often to be seen slumped in the streets drunk and begging. 'Tighten your belt' ('tighten your belly' in Russian) was literal: the tribesmen thought hunger could be warded off by pulling in their belts across their stomachs as hard as they could. Or they could blank out the world by smoking Yukagir-style: the strongest tobacco, mixed with sawdust, would be inhaled and the smoke simply swallowed into the stomach, producing 'some of the delicious effects which the opium eater enjoys'.

Manya remembered merchants from China calling at their home – it must have been more of a compound – to gossip, '. . . they say caravan teas are up . . .', buy and sell. Two or three times a year, Flegontov would make the trek to one of the huge trading fairs, in the summer at Arginskaya near Chita, or Spaso Preobrazhenskoe, and in the winter at Verkhneudinsk. Neatly blending ancient and modern, the *Guide to the Great Siberian Railway* listed the stations where travellers could link up with the caravan routes into Turkestan. As Manya remembered half a century later, the first oranges she ever saw had been brought back proudly by her father from one of the fairs. Even in 1906 a Chita shopkeeper felt it worth taking out a newspaper advertisement to announce the arrival of a consignment of oranges and lemons. It might be less obvious why another did the same when he received a fresh supply of mustard; in fact, the yellow spice was used not just for flavouring but as a meat preservative and often a simple household cleaning powder. For the rest of her life, Manya would spurn yellow butter in favour of white on the grounds that all those years ago peddlers had fobbed off on her father rancid butter from the milk of ailing cows, or even other unknown animals, heavily laced with dye to make it look appetising.

Her mother Anna ran a disciplined household, where the children had to wash themselves and brush their hair before coming to breakfast and say a polite 'good morning' to their parents. Manya painted for us the sort of childhood pictured in Russian novels: meadows, fishing, picking berries and mushrooms (when I once asked for help with a translation, she rattled off to me the names of at least a dozen different varieties, very few of which I can now recall), riding ponies, trapping fish in the icy fast-flowing streams with nets made out of horsehair, learning to sew and embroider, and making their own dresses. It was a household whose folk remedies for coughs, colds and stomach-ache, and whose superstitions, she was to carry across the world.

At the fairs Flegontov visited, camel trains and convoys of bullock carts swayed in from the Gobi desert with tea, spices, carpets, shawls, tallow and exotic silks. Though camels are equated with deserts, Frost has two intriguing sketches of them in unlikely contexts. One shows three camels swimming across the Irtysh River, driven by nomads on horseback; one of the beasts has a cart lashed precariously across its humps. Another even more unexpected image is of a camel-drawn sledge, turn-of-the-century statistics recording that Chita alone had nearly 10,000 camels, most owned by the nomads.

Kiakhta, on the Chinese border south of Irkutsk, was the main channel for tea. The Kiakhta Tea Merchants' Company (which also dealt in sugar, coffee and cocoa, as well as a product enigmatically advertised as 'Chinese black of different sorts . . . per lb. or one stick') had its headquarters in St Petersburg, where it had eleven stores in the city alone, a large warehouse there and two more in Odessa and Kiakhta itself, as well as offices and branches all across Russia and in Europe as far away as Genoa and Nice. Its top 'Tsin Iui' brand came wrapped in paper, or in glass jars and tins. At the bottom of the quality list came 'bricks', solid slabs of tea about an inch thick, nine inches high and six inches wide, compressed under heavy weights and stamped with the maker's Chinese ideograms. Those that proved consistently reliable in weight and quality became a currency in themselves – at one time twenty would buy a horse and twelve a sheep. Monetary theorists would scratch their heads at the findings of a researcher that, even into the 1930s, Siberian native nomads still preferred 'tea money' to cash, all the more since they had more than once seen paper money become worthless overnight. They were prone to lung disease, and tea was an efficient remedy against coughs and colds that might develop into something worse; they could thus put their money to practical use, scraping the bricks with a knife into boiling water to produce a pungent black liquor, which was usually mixed with butter rather than milk. At their cheapest, these bricks were the sweepings of the tea factory floor mixed with twigs, straw, soot and the occasional nugget of yak dung.

In the early 1900s, the *Guide* felt constrained to point out that the two hotels in Verkhneudinsk 'are under the management of Jews'. (The *Guide* was not alone in this sort of barbed warning. *Baedeker*, the international travellers' Bible, was at pains to call its readers' attention in its 1900 edition to various Russian cities with what it felt was a high quotient of Jews or Israelites; by its inspectors' calculations, Odessa was one-third Jewish, Minsk 50 per cent, and Grodno and Bialystok three-quarters – an ethnic variant of the Michelin star.)

The hotels were a far cry in every sense from the sophistication of Odessa. The British traveller John Foster Fraser spent some disturbed nights in an Irkutsk hotel around 1900. It could have been in Dodge City. Around 10 p.m. it exploded 'into rollicking uproar', as officers and petty officials barged in to drink, eat, play cards, all to the background of a jangling piano whose brass keys plucked fragments of melodies from a perforated paper roll. 'And this in a shed of a hotel with no handles on the doors, where your clothes' hook was a nail and the gaps in the woodwork so open you could see your neighbour going to bed. It was always four in the morning before quiet came.' Siberian nightlife had clearly not changed since intrepid Captain Cochrane made his tour. His main memory of one small town was 'the incivility of its inhabitants who with the commissars and the doctor were all noisily intoxicated'. (Other travellers also note the Russian passion for uniforms. The Court had uniforms for every time of day, every ceremony and every gradation of rank, as of course did the military. Ministers and civil servants had their distinctive gear, as did postmen, stationmasters, porters, tram drivers, university students and even, by one account, window cleaners.) Verkhneudinsk is now Ulan-Ude, Siberia's third largest city, with twenty Buddhist temples serving its Buryat people. But though Armani suits have replaced uniforms, Georgian champagne is now the drink of choice, and peroxide-blonde singers with bee-stung lips pout their sad lyrics where the player piano once ruled supreme, the nocturnal habits of its hotel guests are said not to have changed too much. And John Foster Fraser would find the nightlife in Yakutsk's Hotel Lena rather familiar.

Nerchinsk was Manya's happy exotic world, bounded by mountains, threaded by rushing rivers, and studded with lakes and meadows, but it was a world on which darkness could and did descend in an instant, like the blizzards of winter. Her mother died giving birth to her last child. Kandit Flegontov 'fell apart' ('*Papa srazu upal*', as she told my sister) and his business and the family income collapsed too. The children went their separate ways – though, as we shall see, years later Manya and one of her brothers, Pavel, a doctor, found each other again. Manya and her sister Elizaveta scraped together just enough money to train as nurses, and she later claimed that they were so poor they had only one pair of fine stockings between them, so could never go out to tea parties together. They found a good niche nursing rich ladies who needed more cosseting than medical attention. That brought the two sisters to Irkutsk, to their random arrest in the demonstration and to Manya's romantic meeting with David outside the unromantic cell No. 9.

To understand what brought David there, via the Romanovka, we have to lift another layer or two off the matryoshka doll.

6

Rebel with a Cause

Like so many Russian revolutionaries, David came from a comfortable middle-class background. And like so many of the others, no one will ever know when and why his heart tuned in to dreams of change. He told his son-in-law Edgar Nathan years later that as a teenager he took to hanging around Odessa Central Station on Kulikovo Field Square and got into 'friendly discussions with some of the railway officials and then the crews'. One of them invited him to help out on the footplate when another man fell sick. He became a part-time 'driver's mate', travelling across Russia and even as far as Hamburg, and 'spending time in all the cities he visited with local railwaymen and their families, and sleeping in workers' hostels'.

At first I found the recycled tale too good to be true – it sounded more like adolescent wish-fulfilment – but at the risk of using the arid language of a Marxist historian, I realised the story might just make sense if we put it into a political context and saw it as one of the lingering traces of what was known as the 'Populist Movement'. Its followers, mainly middle-class young men and some women who believed in 'going to the workers' with their message of change, fanned out with the bright-eyed zeal of Mormon missionaries to bring socialism to the peasants in the Bessarabian countryside and the artisans – plasterers, carpenters, plumbers – who had been drawn to Odessa from across Russia as its mercantile magnificence multiplied. Two of the standard tracts they handed out were *Skullduggery* and *A Tale of Four Brothers* (to be found by the police with either meant a one-way ticket to Siberia), and they preached the theories of Marx, John Stuart Mill and the lessons to be drawn from the 1871 Paris Commune. Learning a trade – one took up shoemaking – was an essential part of reaching the hearts and minds of the proletariat, and one group even set up its own workshop to mend pots and pans. Seen in this light, shovelling coal in the cab of a locomotive could well have been another way of reaching out. Since it was a busy line, some of David's proselytising trips on the footplate would have taken him up and down the track north into the Ukraine to the sprawling ironworks and coal-mining complex now called Donetsk. Back then it was known as Yuzovka, from the Russian pronunciation of the name of its developer John Hughes, a brilliant engineer, son of a Merthyr Tydfil blacksmith, who had first come to Russia to build the huge fort at Kronstadt in 1868. In an extraordinary demonstration of Victorian-era British capitalism and industrial ingenuity, he and a group of Welsh and English specialists, supported by a Russian and Polish workforce of about 12,000, built what soon became one the world's largest coal-mining and steel-making complexes. One of its less visible claims to fame was that it was the most remote dependency of the diocese of the Anglican Bishop of Gibraltar. Another was that the Soviet leader, Nikita Khrushchev, as a young miner, had played for the local football team. Yuzovka's Welsh engineers first introduced football to Russia, and are credited with forming its first brass band.

Another Oddessite who had followed the same path to the people in his early years was Aleksandr Helfand, better known in history as 'Parvus' and one of the Revolution's most fascinating figures. Praised by his friend Trotsky as 'a person of extensive knowledge and outstanding political and literary talent', Parvus was a Marxist theoretician and writer, a consummate underground organiser and a successful financial speculator, who accumulated millions serving his own ends alongside those of the cause. He went on to play a vital role in securing German moral and financial backing for Lenin and the Bolsheviks, a story vividly etched by Solzhenitsyn in his novel *Lenin in Zurich*, though overlaid with the author's barely concealed anti-Semitism. He portrays Parvus as a man for whom making money 'was almost a biological function' and as a stateless 'Wandering Jew'. Parvus, whose extraordinary life cries out for a fuller biography than has so far been produced, was eleven years older than David. He went to an Odessa city grammar school, which stressed the Classics, but at eighteen he and a friend decided to learn a trade as their way of 'going to the workers'. They apprenticed themselves to a metal-worker and 'tramped from one workshop to another'.

By the time David went to Odessa, populism had atrophied, foundering on what one realistic member termed the workers' 'granite, unheeding wall of impenetrable indifference and stolid fatalism' as well as the 'Central Asian savagery of the gendarmes', who eventually rounded up most of the group. But it is easy to see that among romantic idealists such as David and his friends, the idea of 'going to the people' lingered on, and the further one could travel in the process the more stimulating it must have become. He told Edgar Nathan that his experiences in the railway period, his sense of the world's inequalities, awakened his interest in 'human socialism'.

The long-suffering parents of revolutionaries deserve a special and sympathetic study of their own. In David's case, it is clear that no amount of fatherly finger-wagging, or bowls of chicken soup served to a background of apron wringing and heavy sobs, could keep the headstrong boy safely at home. It is not fanciful to hear distinct echoes of Trotsky's own troubled adolescence. For a while the teenager who was fated to become Stalin's Public Enemy No. 1 joined what was almost a commune outside Odessa, where the 'big-whiskered' Trotsky senior appeared more than once in search of his errant son, angrily yelling at his comrades, 'So you're another runaway, are you?'

It was not just the populists who were at risk. Any form of political activity was high risk in Russia, and all the more in Odessa which Trotsky claimed was 'the most police-ridden city in the whole of police-ridden Russia' ('ridden' is relative; Russia had fewer policemen than France). From 1874 to 1878 alone there were fifteen trials involving thirty-seven defendants mostly by military tribunal for various forms of subversive activity, excluding the much longer but untallied roster of police 'administrative actions'.

And it is David's police record, an unusual source for a grandson to be able to tap, which in the terse language of the bureaucratic machine the world over provides the key insights into this period of his life: 'A Gunner in the 2nd Mobile Artillery Depot. Graduated from the Trade School. Metalworker. In jail for 15 months before being sentenced. By Command of the All Highest dishonourably discharged from the ranks on 3rd April 1903 and exiled to eastern Siberia for ten years. Designated for settlement in the remotest part of the Yakutsk region. Before joining the army [Redstone] had got to know agitators then living in Odessa, maintained contact with them after joining up and obtained underground publications from them. Assigned to the Kolyma region.' Even though at that time Kolyma had yet to become a killing factory, those last few words were condemnation to the world's outer darkness.

I wonder why David went to the trade school rather than the university. Perhaps it was out of some lingering populist spirit; perhaps the university was not an option because it limited Jewish admission. Most likely it was because while the university was in the cold grip of the Ministry of Education, the trade schools were supervised by the Ministry of Trade and Industry, and many students were prepared to put up with the compulsory technical courses as the price of access to 'a much better, more varied and interesting course of study'.

A bigger puzzle is the trade he allegedly learned. The Russian word 'slesar' for the trade given in his police file is borrowed from the German 'Schlosser', and is nowadays translated for simplicity as 'metalworker' or 'locksmith'. In the late nineteenth century it had a far wider meaning, ranging from a craftsman in metal to anyone who could turn his hand to mending or making anything metal, from saucepans to scythes. But none of this fits the grandfather I knew. Not only was David not a craftsman, but it is also hard to remember him as any sort of handyman. I may be doing him an injustice but in all the years I knew him, I cannot recall him ever changing a light bulb, and I saw him using his hands only when he was fiddling with that essential tool of the pipe smoker, an instrument combining scrapers, tampers and spikes, the sort of thing Boy Scouts might use on especially recalcitrant stones in horses' hooves. He would certainly not have come to mind as the man to call if there was a problem with the front-door Yale lock. It seems most likely that 'slesar' was simply what the trade school clerks routinely wrote on students' certificates, for want of anything more precise.

But whatever his trade, it makes better sense if one sees it as essentially part of his political education. It also brings us back to the hero of another of those milestone books, Isaac Deutscher's *Trotsky*, whose subject's many talents included a way with words that makes it irritatingly hard to avoid quoting him. He once declared that, 'Anyone who does not know . . . that revolution is attractive like a young, passionate woman with arms flung wide, showering kisses on you with hot, feverish lips, has never been young.' A later bomb-thrower was eulogised for having 'loved revolution profoundly, tenderly as only those who have committed their lives to it can love'. A more measured assessment had been made earlier in the period by an official of the Third Department, who minuted that discontent was most widespread among 17 to 25-year-olds, who were 'enamoured of liberty which they do not understand in the least but which they take to mean the absence of subordination'.

Reading Deutscher's account of Trotsky's Odessa life, one of David's bookcase milestones, I was already speculating from the coincidence of age, place and family background that my grandfather must have come across the man who might have led Russia. Then in Trotsky's own autobiography I spotted the real possibility that they had indeed met. Trotsky wrote that when he came back to Odessa in 1896 – he was a precocious seventeen, David eighteen – he was, like David on the smoke-filled railway station, confused about his future and trying to find himself. 'I made casual acquaintances among workers, obtained illegal literature, tutored some private pupils, *gave surreptitious lessons to the older boys of the trade school* [my italics] . . .' This is not proof, to be sure, but it seems almost certain that it was the views of Trotsky and his circle – those 'agitators living in Odessa', in the words of the police file – that led David down the long road of dissent to Siberia. It would be intriguing to know whether my grandfather or Trotsky came across yet another Odessa activist, four years David's senior: Sidney Reilly, the British secret agent operating in Russia during the Revolution, and later fictionalised as the 'Ace of Spies'. He was christened Sigmund Rosenblum, was the illegitimate son of a Jewish doctor, and spent time in Odessa jail for 'carrying messages for a Marxist group', before setting out on his far more publicised career.

As we lift the next layer off the doll, the images of David the Student and David the Metalworker give way to what was for me an equally improbable persona: David the Soldier. And not just a soldier, but serving in the Tsar's army, whose attitude to Jews faithfully reflected that of its supreme commander. In 1827 Nicholas I allowed Jews to serve in the army, but saw it not as part of their rights and obligations as citizens but as a crude attempt at social engineering: 'The chief benefit to be derived from the drafting of Jews is that it will move them most effectively to change their religion.'

In 1856, Jews were allowed to serve in the ranks of the elite guards units and as non-commissioned officers in the other regiments, though they could usually rise no further. One account tells us that throughout the entire nineteenth century the Russian army had only one Jewish officer, Herzl Ysak Tsam, who had joined as a seventeen-year-old conscript and took forty-one years to rise to the rank of captain; despite constant pressure, he never converted to Christianity. (Other sources believe that there may have been a handful of others, but the mere fact that researchers comment on it at all underscores the singularity of the achievement.) A more peculiar form of exclusion was the regulation that no more than one third of the players in a military band could be Jews. Since the piano and the violin were more the instruments of choice in the Jewish community than the trombone or bass drum, in practice this may not have been a major barrier. Jewish recruits took a theologically muddled oath to perform their duties faithfully and to obey their superiors as if they fought for 'the salvation of our own land and our Holy Torah. But if I should sin either of my own will or persuaded by someone else and violate the oath which I am taking today faithfully to serve in the army, I together with my family shall be excommunicated in this world and the next. Amen.'

Across the Russian Empire as a whole, the prospect of conscription into a hostile military environment had become one of the factors driving Jewish emigration to the United States. In the remoter Jewish villages the months leading up to the conscription period each year were a 'time of desolation'. It was less, one young man wrote later, a distaste for the idea of military service as such than a profound fear, fanned by their wailing mothers and grandmothers, of becoming part of a very visible underclass in a brutal gentile system in which prejudice would be naked and unashamed, and in which alienated from their community and their religion they would have to eat pork, work on the Sabbath and generally prove the Tsar right in his prognosis. Some cut off a finger, some starved themselves close to death, some jumped off roofs or lifted huge logs to induce hernias. Others sheltered behind the false identities of infants who had died at birth but whose deaths had not been registered.

The system (feared just as much by non-Jews) allowed for many exemptions, not that different from those granted to young men liable for British National Service in the 1950s. Doctors and clergy were excused, and conscripts could also seek to opt out for 'family' or health reasons (many doctors were happy to issue certificates in return for a small fee), or the need to finish a course of education. The eldest son of infirm parents was only called on to serve four weeks a year, creating further scope for imaginative or commercially motivated medical certifications. So, David could clearly have avoided or deferred the draft. Maybe he did not want to emigrate. Maybe it was 'I'll show them' pride, or patriotism, or because he felt or was told that, despite all the odds, he could best serve the revolution from inside a barracks.

Men became liable for service on 1 January of the year they reached twenty. At what point in 1898 David actually arrived apprehensively at Odessa's Light Artillery Depot we do not know. Enlistment was a two-stage process, probably, like anything else in Russia, susceptible to bribery. Names were drawn allegedly at random to determine who would actually serve in the army itself; the others went into the militia, a form of territorial reserve with less likelihood of being put 'in harm's way' and less exposure to the day-to-day rigours of army life, though most of the conscripts were peasants and unskilled workers to whom barracks life offered far better living standards than their hovels at home. Many were so malnourished that they were given extra rations in their first few weeks of service. Almost all the officers came from the aristocracy. Their penchant for idleness, gambling, drinking, duelling and whoring was to some degree counterbalanced by a senior layer of generals of German origin from the Baltic states, many of whose names – Todtleben, von Rennekampf, von Stackelberg, von Gobsberg, Meller-Zakomelsky – sound as though they were confected by Central Casting to cast a chill over enemy hearts; we shall meet some of them later. (Writing about one of the major pogroms, Alexander Solzhenitsyn remarked that it was 'one of the Empire's ironies' that if a reader simply looked down the list of names of the officers and police officials involved, he would be hard put to it to know that it had happened in Russia.)

Of the 294,902 conscripts in 1900, 151,490 were illiterate. Though landowning officers were no longer able to use their men as personal serfs on their estates, or in a flash of temper order men to run the regimental gauntlet of 1,000 stick-wielding soldiers, they still ruled largely by fear and enjoyed several feudal privileges such as being able to supply grain from their estates to the army without formal contracts, an unwritten licence to print money. By the time David became liable, the period of service had been reduced to four years with the colours and up to thirteen in the Reserve, though the more education a conscript had, the shorter the period of service, with boys from secondary schools serving only two years and university graduates six months. Assuming the Odessa Trade School qualified as what the regulations termed a 'technical school', David faced three years' service.

Parading that first day on the depot's barracks square, David was not joining a second-rate outfit, some Bessarabian equivalent of the British Army's former Pioneer Corps. According to a Victorian-era British officer, the Russian artillery was 'very good . . . Especially the [Light, or] Horse artillery . . . they consider it their best arm and perhaps the best in the world.' David's hair would have been shaved to leave a patch about the size and shape of a bristle broom head running from ear to ear. The new recruits would then have tried to march, barked at by an NCO, to the stores to be issued with their badly fitting thick woollen uniforms and heavy leather boots. Many peasant lads had spent their childhood barefoot, or in bast sandals or felt overshoes, and found it hard to get used to the unaccustomed weight, stumbling around for days like deep-sea divers out of water.

Like Redstone the locksmith, my grandfather in uniform is hard to imagine; let alone tending the Putilov 3" Rapid Fire Field Gun used by the Light Artillery, with its 'panoramic sights, recoil-less mechanism and 24 grooved uniform twist barrel'. Nor, notwithstanding his voracious reading appetite, do I see him studying the *Drill Rules for Light and Horse Batteries* with any marked interest. Did he and any other non-Christian recruits really give full-throated support in singing the National Anthem (not all that different *mutatis mutandis* in melody and patriotic sentiment from Britain's) calling on a white-bearded Semitic God who, most Russians were convinced, dwelled within easy reach of St Petersburg, to save 'The Russian Orthodox Tsar' and 'first in its majesty, Orthodox Russia . . .'?

David is more likely to have been engaged and enraged by one of the 479 tracts in the 'Soldiers' Library' series. Sold for a few kopecks, their stories sought to shape recruits' minds on topics such as alcoholism, superstition, theft and the blandishments of women. Others discussed in simple language Russian history and military successes, and even more complex issues such as national minorities and foreign lands. Russia being Russia, many were xenophobic and anti-Semitic. The tone of a story about Jews in a garrison town in Poland was one of 'scorn and demonisation'.

Nor do I know how long he had served before he was 'dishonourably discharged'. There are two versions of what happened. The first is the one in the police dossier: he had underground literature and associated with troublemakers, making him a troublemaker too. So he was wheeled off to jail, in the army phrase, 'so fast his feet didn't even touch the floor'.

Edgar Nathan's far more circumstantial account oddly makes no mention of David's underground connections. One can overdo the conjecture; memories may again be out of alignment and David may well have been seeking, for some of the reasons we have speculated about, to play down his revolutionary side. That Edgar's version is not cited in the summary dossier does not mean it did not happen. It is a storyline worthy of the writer Joseph Roth. 'The officer in charge of the Commissariat', Edgar wrote, 'found that David had a good knowledge of arithmetic and accounts. He was promoted to NCO and put in charge of the books relating to the regiment's catering . . . the books were kept methodically. As so often happened in those times when young members of the aristocracy entered the army for want of having anything better to do or as a matter of tradition, the young officer in charge of catering spent much of the time enjoying the pleasures of the nearby town. He gradually developed into an inveterate gambler and his losses mounted from day to day. How was he to recoup them? He worked out a scheme by which he could take monies from the regimental funds in the middle of the month and replace them when the central payments came to hand at the end of the next month. The scheme worked well enough until the inevitable happened.' There was a surprise audit and the 'black hole' was discovered. The young gambler had 'good friends among his fellow officers who were of his class and background and they decided that for the honour of the regiment no charge should be brought . . . However, the accountant insisted that a culprit must be found and who better than the young Jew who had been in charge of writing up the account books. The officer clique were delighted at this suggestion and . . . in due course David faced a court martial of which the young officer was a member.' He was found guilty and sentenced to two years in a penal settlement.

Trying to tie together the 'agitation' and 'peculation' versions of how David got into trouble, it is quite likely that, knowing him to be a revolutionary and finding themselves short of hard evidence (unlike the police, the military had more difficulty with unsubstantiated 'administrative arrests'), the regiment took deft advantage of an opportunity to save one of their own while trumping up charges that would enable them to hand David over to the gendarmes and make sure he got a severe sentence. It does not matter how it was orchestrated; the reality was that he was in serious trouble.

The dossier tells us that he spent fifteen months in prison. While this may have been in a penal settlement, I believe it far more likely – based on other exiles' experiences – that he began the long road north in Odessa jail. There, typically, he would have been locked up in 'a large but gloomy cell at ground level with a worn paved floor, a low stone-arched roof, a double iron door . . . whose huge bolts had a heavy padlock that the warder opened with a huge key from a bunch hanging from his belt . . . and an unglazed window barred with an iron grille.'

At least the 'politicals' had their cells mopped down by one of the criminals, and they were already communicating with their neighbours in a primitive form of text messaging by knocking on their cell walls in simple code, so many taps per letter, in the laborious technique remembered by David in reminiscing with Edgar Nathan and described by Koestler in *Darkness at Noon*, another of David's bookcase mementoes. Attempts to talk through the unglazed windows were met with yells from the sentries in the yard to 'keep your mouths shut, there', and threats to shoot. Locks and threats did not prevent a steady flow of secret messages into and out of the jail, scribbled in code on tiny scraps of paper, and carried by bribed or sympathetic warders.

If David were following the regular routine, he would have left for a holding period in Moscow to wait his turn for Siberia. (Though Trotsky was arrested in Nikolayev, his later sequence of spells in the jails in Odessa and Moscow and the exile transfer prisons in Siberia was almost exactly the same as my grandfather's – and, of course, thousands of others). At some stage David was in solitary confinement and allowed only two books; he claimed to Edgar Nathan that he chose the Bible and Euclid's *Theorems*. His mother tried to visit him but was turned away at the jailhouse gate.

The administrative wheels creaked round; the dossiers passed from hand to hand, and a weary senior official signed another pile of forms. One clerk won a bet by putting in front of a regional governor, who was signing like an automaton, a neatly written copy of The Lord's Prayer, on which the great panjandrum duly scribbled approval.

The exiles sat in their cells, defiant or dejected according to their personalities, staring at the doleful graffiti of earlier generations and the blood-red smears of squashed bedbugs on the rough plastered walls; did the smell evoke for those from the south the bouquet of Bessarabian wines? Out of the blue, a warder would bang on the door and tell them to get ready to leave on the next stage of their trek to the unknown.

Many passed on from the provincial jails to Moscow's Butyrki prison. It lies on what was once the highway from Moscow to St Petersburg, near to the Petrovsky Park, whose chateau was said to be the closest Napoleon came to the heart of Moscow. About half of the 1,300 convicts in Butyrki at the turn of the century were 'politicals'. Their communal cells, twelve paces long by five wide, lined by wooden sleeping platforms, held twenty-five prisoners. To the 'house spirits' of the Butyrki and to its generations of warders, a scratching, hawking, feverish prisoner was just another number, whether murderer, revolutionary, poet or peasant; the roster of those who passed through its gates over the centuries is the story of Russia. Some found inspiration. In his first published verse, the futurist poet Vladimir Mayakovsky, a troublesome sixteen-year-old prisoner whose cell window gave him a sobering view of an undertaker's parlour, wrote in 1909 after several months in solitary confinement:

> I learned to love
> In Butyrki
> Who cares about the Bois de Boulogne?
> Who sighs over seascapes?
> You know I fell in love with a 'funeral establishment'
> Through the peephole of Cell 103.

Mayakovsky was lucky to get out with his health unaffected. Since prisoners were given only a few minutes each day in the open air, it was no wonder that sickness was rife. The straw in the pillows was changed only once a year and the authorities supplied no mattresses or blankets. George Kennan noted that a special meeting of the Committee of Moscow's Sanitary Inspectors was told that in one ten-day spell at least seventy men in Butyrki had gone down with typhus. The warders had spread the disease to a nearby barracks, where ten soldiers had died.

It is hard to decide which link in the conveyor belt into exile was the worst: the arrest and interrogation, the long wait in jail for an unknown penalty, the journey itself, or the years of frost-bitten monotony. It was like few other journeys in the world. At least David, that adolescent footplate-rider, could do most of it by train.

7

Out of Sight, Out of Mind

For all its cruelties Siberia was not yet the Gulag. Stalin and his secret police henchmen, Yezhov, Yagoda and Beria, had still to build their pyramid of hundreds of thousands of informers, interrogators, executioners, torturers, guards, engine drivers and bureaucrats. They were all co-conspirators in the massive crime against humanity, connived at by generations of Western 'fellow travellers' and gullible liberals, that the Gulag represented, but they did not invent the exile and hard labour system any more than they did the secret police or censorship. Most understood only too well the advantages of the system to an authoritarian state, having been in jail and exile themselves.

The system which now swallowed David Redstone was as much a part of the Russian heritage as transportation had been in the British Empire. Put in place by the Empress Elizabeth in 1760, it had replaced the death penalty and grotesque physical mutilation as an efficient way to provide the labour to exploit Siberia's resources while ridding Russian society of criminals, the 'politically unreliable', religious dissidents, prisoners of war and, in earlier periods, almost any misfit (including homosexuals and heretics) whose community elders felt did not belong. It was outside the formal judicial system and thus open to every sort of abuse, and the widespread use of catch-all charges such as *'brodyazhnichestvo'* ('vagrancy') and *'durnoye povedeniye'* ('vile behaviour'). In the system's early years, every serf a landowner exiled to Siberia meant that they had to provide one less able-bodied conscript from their estate for military service.

One distortion of history of which we too are going to be guilty is to view the tsarist exile system as though its victims were largely political offenders. Though the 'politicals' have always taken centre stage in any account of the Russian system, they were in fact only a small, if voluble, publicity-conscious and later famous part of the whole doleful equation – by one account rarely more than 2 per cent. The balance were society's outcasts, religious dissidents and the 'conventional' motley crew of criminals – thieves, rapists, forgers and the like that plague any society. Though some authors have addressed the wider spectrum in the Soviet era, it fitted the politically correct view of the Revolution and its heroes to concentrate on the political personalities. Today's Russian intelligentsia would not find this at all odd. What possible interest could there be in what happened to criminals? After all, they would say with a contemptuous curl of the lip, 'They had no ideas.'

That exile could be imposed by the police outside the judicial system, by what were called 'administrative measures', made it a very handy tool for shipping the politically unreliable to places so remote that in theory they were removed from the dissident currents and would no longer be a threat to the fraying fabric of society. As we shall see, in the case of David and the Romanovka the theory did not work. It is one of the many ironies of history that the tsarist courts, maligned by all revolutionaries as cruel and corrupt pawns of government, were still independent enough to demand real evidence. When it came to political charges, judges had been known to acquit unless the police produced as a witness the informant on whose testimony the allegation was based. Reluctant to do so for fear of exposing their undercover sources and also the flimsy nature of most of such charges, it well suited the police to be able to operate 'administratively'.

Until the end of the nineteenth century, exiles had reached Siberia in 'convoy' parties, most of them on foot, the richer ones or the seriously ill in carts, staying overnight in the log-built *étapes*, or 'staging prisons', stretching in a grim necklace across the breadth of

Russia. When they were on the move in the summer, the cloud of dust, which enveloped the parties as they trudged wearily away from hope and home, could be seen for miles across the countryside.

But industrial progress meant that my grandfather and those who were to coalesce into the Romanovka group were able to travel as far as Irkutsk by rail on the newly laid Trans-Siberian Railway, a prodigious feat of engineering and management first conceived by the American Perry Collins in 1859 and implemented out of grand political and commercial ambition; it opened up Siberia and gave Russia access to the Pacific as well as a route to ship troops for expansionist adventures. At the peak of its construction, its brilliant engineers and designers orchestrated 90,000 vodka-sodden navvies, Chinese coolies and convicts, who hacked halfway around the world with picks and shovels backed up by the latest in international construction machinery. Many of the Trans-Siberian feats, especially the tunnels and bridges, were masterpieces. One of the bridge tests involved driving five locomotives one after the other to stand buffer to buffer on a newly completed span to see if it would buckle; driver no. 5 must have been quite stout-hearted or well insulated with vodka. The railway engineers advanced like an invading army, building its encampments – the stations and their surrounding settlements – ahead of the line itself, each with workshops, water towers, a handful of houses, barracks for the workers, a medical centre, a church, a school and a library, many of which still stand today. A recent railway history claims proudly that 'the first train on a new stretch always drew in to a completed station'. (The magnificence of the engineering meant little to a superstitious peasantry, whose horizons were bounded by forests and whose ideas of locomotion were based on the rutted tracks through the forests, the horse, the ox and the sledge. To the first few who had glimpsed it, its red-hot coals and clouds of steam suggested an invention of the devil. In one tiny hamlet, goggle-eyed villagers paid two kopecks to listen to a travelling entertainer imitate the sound the railway made – the eldritch shriek of the whistle, the puffing crescendo of the engine and the clickety-clack of its wheels.)

The grandiose project cost far more than the country could afford, a gap met by foreign borrowing. One of the reasons that even today travellers on the Siberian section of the line comment on the slow speeds and the way the carriages rock is that to save money as costs mounted, the builders reduced the width of the earth bed under the tracks, thinned the ballast layer, laid lighter rails and used fewer sleepers. Every pound of steel in the rails began in the never-ending incandescent flow from the roaring Bessemer furnaces of Yuzovka. A quirk of the Russian railway system was that it was built to a broader gauge than the rest of Europe. Though this was later claimed to have been intended as a deterrent to invading armies who would not be able to smash their trains across the frontiers, it actually reflected a debate that had begun in England, with the pioneer Brunel favouring 7 feet as promoting a steadier ride, only to be eventually out-lobbied by contractors who could lay track more cheaply if the width was reduced to just under 5 feet. In Russia, the most tangible effect was an interminable wait for passengers at border stations while carriages were winched off one set of bogies and dropped onto Russian-width wheels.

The railway reduced the time it took to cross Russia somewhat closer to a comprehensible human dimension, though for the exiles facing stiffer sentences, there were still thousands of miles to travel even when this nine-day leg had been completed. They spent the time in prison compartments with only two windows, looking more like mail vans, attached to the Sunday night 'fast' train from Moscow. A soldier stood sentry at each end of the carriage, bayonet fixed.

The train's departure was heralded by one blast of the steam whistle fifteen minutes ahead of time and a double blast five minutes before; the final triplet signalled that the wheels were about to turn 'and big men with swords kissed each other fervently'. Depending on the mood of the authorities and whether one had the money, a few such as Lenin, helped by a handout from his doting mother, were able to travel the 5,108 kilometres to Irkutsk in the normal carriages, with a plain-clothes police escort, paying 75 roubles 60 kopecks, which at the exchange rate then was some £8, though bed linen, changed every three days, was extra. The exiled hoi polloi were a long way physically and psychologically from the luxuries of first class, let alone the de luxe 'country house drawing rooms' in miniature operated by the International Sleeping Car Company. The regular first class carriages, their electricity supplied from a Swedish turbine, had an early version of air conditioning, a fan blowing over blocks of ice in a tank on the roof, and a nurse and a hairdresser were on call. In the dining car, white-whiskered waiters swayed like ballet dancers to keep their balance as they served the finest food. Next to the dining car was the library, an intellectual's oasis with heavy curtains to shut out tedious stretches of landscape, a mahogany bookcase, and an ivory chess set, elaborately tasselled chairs, and even fitted silver holders for the engraved glasses from which most upper class Russians drank tea. Since most of the political exiles did not believe in God, or if they did, followed other creeds, they were probably not too distressed to be excluded from the hushed mysteries of the carriage which served as a travelling Russian Orthodox church, heavy with the incense odour of Slavonic sanctity, the altar screens a sumptuous tribute in red paint and gold leaf, two bells outside tucked under the gable of its roof, its windows arched; even the exterior walls had elaborate fretwork patterns.

From Moscow the trains crossed the endless plains, cut through the Ural mountains (whose vaunted grandeur 'could not hold a pine knot to the Tyrol or the Grampians', as one disappointed English traveller complained) and puffed across frail-looking metal bridges over Russia's mightiest rivers – the Volga, the Irtysh, the Ob and the Yenisei, passing on its way the 25-foot-high stone obelisk that marked the notional dividing line between Europe and Asia. The route has been 'tweaked' over the years and the midpoint between Moscow and Vladivostok is now the village of Uk, unmemorable other than for its name and a nearby waterfall. There were eighty-nine stations along the route (each of their platform clocks arrogantly all set to St Petersburg time), but the fast train stopped at only thirty before puffing into Irkutsk. Though the big cities had stone-built stations, most of the halts were wooden structures, with twin gables intricately carved. Alongside were a water tower, fire station and a store house, and on the wide board platform, fenced by palisades, a pair of wooden pointers rather like Indian totem poles indicating on a semicircular 'clock face' the next arrival and departure times. A gaggle of old ladies in a circle, cheerful but aggressive in white kerchiefs, long skirts and felt boots, offered bread, birchwood jugs of honey, cutlets, chicken, game and duck spit-roasted over charcoal braziers, smoked pike, sterlet and perch, and in-season fruit, melons and berries. The self-important stationmaster checked his fob watch. There was always a handful of soldiers lounging somewhere on the scene. A bunch of silent peasants in rough-cut sheepskins looked on impassively. Though the landscape had its impressive moments, as the days passed and they chugged interminably on through Siberia, most passengers found the trip increasingly boring, trundling at 20 mph across 'this ice bound land, inconceivably remote, a few miserable lonely towns . . . wooden houses grey with age . . . white churches with green roofs', interrupting otherwise endless vistas of bog, birches, larch, cedars, pines, cattle, corn, haystacks, stubble, windmills and muddy tracks leading nowhere in particular. How much deeper the feelings of the exiles, who had few views and fewer hopes? (As we shall see, the exile experience varied with the mood of the regime and the severity of the offence. What David Redstone faced as he jolted eastwards was far grimmer than the early exile years of Stalin, Lenin and other future leaders, characterised by Simon Sebag Montefiore as 'almost reading holidays in a distant Siberian village with one part-time gendarme on duty'. When they chose to get tough, the authorities could wield more power than the few 'inept policemen' who kept a desultory eye on Lenin.)

To the regular passengers easing themselves out of the train, cramped and jaded after eight days, eleven hours and thirteen minutes if it was on time, Irkutsk station was a bourgeois oasis and may have seemed like a mirage. Behind the long glass-topped tea counter in the buffet a brass samovar bubbled, and chefs in starched white linen stood at attention behind a row of steaming silver dishes of meat and vegetables. If it was evening, the room was softened by the glow of electric chandeliers draped with red muslin.

The town, too, was designed to impress. Prominently sited on the Angara River where it joins the Irkut, it had 57,000 inhabitants, was the second largest city in Siberia and bore itself proudly. It was a seat of government and a major manufacturing, trading and banking centre. The arcaded bulk of the Sukachev House was home to the various courts that sat at the hub of the Siberian legal system, in one of which David and his fellow exiles would put on a bravura performance in the time ahead. It gloried in its five-domed cathedral, its array of ecumenical buildings (including two synagogues and a mosque) and a fine collection of libraries, museums and learned societies. Among them was the imposing baroque bulk of the Civic Theatre on Bol'shaya Ulitsa (Grand Street); designed by the architect Schröter, it would not have been out of place in Vienna or Berlin. The first book had come off an Irkutsk press in 1785 and by 1900 there were ten printing works in the city. The six display windows, canopied in summer, of the impressive Makushkin and Posokhin bookstore offered not only literature but also many foreign and Russian newspapers and periodicals. Though it is not clear how many of them overlapped, between 1856 and 1917 some 156 journals and newspapers were published locally. The *Guide to the Great Siberian Railway* thought it 'one of the finest and best organised towns in Siberia', even though 'the streets are unpaved and badly lit'. A newspaper of the time reported that the mud could be two feet deep in places and that two small boys crossing the street would have drowned one wet morning if a coachman had not been alert. Like Manya's Nerchinsk, its institutions – schools, orphanages, hospitals, galleries, museums – had been funded by wealthy nineteenth-century locals; in twenty-first century Russia, city websites and guidebooks make much of the generosity of this once reviled class, perhaps to imply that wealth, even on an oligarchic scale, is not intrinsically evil provided some of it is judiciously channelled for the public good. The *Guide* recommended The Deko Hotel (perhaps another Napoleonic legacy as a transliteration of 'Decaux') as the best in town. Its newspaper advertisements suggest a different rhythm to the Siberian day. The main meal was served each day from 2 p.m. to 6 p.m., the five courses (including 'Roast Beef, Moscow style') interspersed with singers, ballerinas 'in magnificent costumes', gypsy musicians, a 'mimic-clown' and a comedian.

What catches a traveller's eye is always a surprise. One British visitor of the time commented that he would 'be at a loss' to know where to go in London to find a selection of telephones for sale as extensive as the store in Irkutsk. It is so close to China that it is hardly a surprise to find another traveller noting 'hundreds of Chinese' milling in the town, and even a flavour of Chinese building style in the long stretches of high grey-brown timber walls broken by heavy gates, which lined the residential streets.

There were other parallels, for instance with the American Wild West. For all its prosperity, Irkutsk was a city with a crime rate 'that would be considered excessive in a new mining camp', in the words of John Foster Fraser, who had seen both. Bradshaw's guide, *Through Routes to the Cities of the World*, cited by Harmon Tupper, warned a few years later that 'The police are few, escaped convicts and ticket of leave men many.' Banks, the mail vans which carried gold dust in from the mines for smelting, and even churches were regularly robbed, and 'no respectable citizen would dream of passing alone through its suburbs at night'. Some householders would fire a pistol shot or two in the air before locking up for the night, to scare off loitering marauders. The Russian equivalent of outlaws – gangs of escaped or time-expired convicts – roamed the forests and robbed unwary travellers. Unlike Texas, there were no lanky sheriffs walking tall to gun them down; the gendarmes and even the Cossacks usually gave them a wide berth. It was little use complaining; the American traveller Michael Shoemaker observed with a shrug that if a victim wanted the police to investigate a crime, he needed to pay them fifteen roubles straight away, and much more to follow. He reported that there was an average of one murder every day.

None of this Irkutsk travelogue would have meant anything to David Redstone and his unwashed, scratching train companions. They arrived in winter and were immediately prodded into sledges, which slithered them out of the public eye; an escort clattered alongside, over the River Angara and the hills to the exile transfer prison forty miles away at Aleksandrovsk. It had been built in the 1870s on the site of a former distillery. Given the gargantuan Russian thirst for alcohol, for which the official unit of measurement was a *vedro*, literally a 'bucket', or twenty-one pints, it can only have been decommissioned in favour of some newer plant with even greater capacity nearby. (The alcohol was often sold 'pure', each bottle to be diluted with two-and-a-half bottles of water to produce a vodka closer to being fit for drinking rather than blindness; needless to say this step was often omitted in the interests of an even faster descent into oblivion.) Distilling had become a state monopoly in most of Russia by 1901 in what was piously proclaimed as a bid to reduce consumption of crude home brew, minimise price-gouging (since several of the larger distillers were Jewish-owned, this could be seen as another anti-Semitic swipe) and even – a forlorn hope – reduce consumption.

The prison, later to be the stage for one of the boldest episodes in the Romanovka saga, was a large, tin-roofed building around a courtyard, with nearly sixty *kamery*, or large communal cells, ten solitary-confinement cells and five so-called 'secret' cells, where particularly important or dangerous prisoners could be kept out of sight and sound of the world.

In summer by boat and in winter by sledge on the ice, the exile parties followed the same route from the transfer prison to Yakutsk along the River Lena, 'the great waterway of the exiled', which rises near Lake Baikal and which in the brief summer swirls and eddies northwards into the Arctic. Only the Mississippi and the Amazon Rivers are longer.

Prisoners in the transfer prison were usually told only the evening before that they were about to set out, and where they were going to be 'settled'. Anyone daring to ask beforehand would be brusquely told that where they would end up was a matter for the Governor of Yakutsk, and they set off without being able to leave word of their destination for family and friends. The year before David got there, 'Iron' Felix Dzerzhinsky, creator of the Soviet version of the secret police, had led a major sit-in in the transfer jail demanding that the exiles be given much more warning.

8

The Great North Road

David was one of a 'winter party'. Before they set out, he would have jostled in the throng clamouring for the limited allocation of fur coats, wraps and hats provided by the genteel ladies of the Irkutsk Red Cross. But most had to make do with the official handouts, off-cuts of stinking half-cured sheepskins which the exiles had to sew clumsily together during their last night in jail to create some minimal protection. One of my grandfather's travelling companions boasted of his home-made coat with a collar 'like a stovepipe' that protected his entire face and head. Some had quilted coats, all had thick, wadded felt boots and none wore socks. Instead they carefully wound round their feet the traditional Russian *portyanki*, cloth strips probably synonymous with the Anglo-Saxon 'toe-rag'. Wool was regarded as useless for underwear. It did nothing against the cold and was uncomfortably hot as soon as the wearer went into the usually superheated Russian building.

From the jail David and his comrades jolted in a small convoy of sledges from one grimy *étape* and post-station, where the sturdy horses, their hair as thick as bears' fur, were changed, to the next, firstly across the hills and then over the rutted ice of the Lena, which was so thick that it still serves – a few mishaps apart – as a roadbed for heavy lorries. This was not Manya's Siberia. They were headed towards the Arctic Circle, where there were no cities, no colourful fairs, no family, no social fabric, where life was lived at the whim of a dictator governor and the caprice of petty local policemen. One exile wrote of that winter journey: 'Only those who made the trip could appreciate what real cold meant. Hour after hour in the deepest frost, perhaps 40 degrees below huddled under the canvas hood of the sledge. If it had blinds you tried to keep them tightly shut to keep out the wind. Even so you had to wrap your face in a hood and grip your collar. In a second it would be coated with icicles and every hair on your face would freeze. You tried to keep your eyes open to stop your eyelids freezing together. However deep down you burrowed when you set off, the cold would stab at you like a knife and with every hummock in the snow the corner of a wicker basket or someone's suitcase would jab you spitefully in the back.

'You could curl into a ball like a hibernating hedgehog but then one of the escorts, just as cold as you were, would push against your legs as he tried to dig himself deeper. You felt you were frozen to the marrow. Even your soul was frozen solid. Then the driver would mutter that he had caught the first glimpse of the next *étape*. The horses would break into a trot at the thought of fodder and warm stables. No matter how filthy it was, the *étape* hut was bliss, with its tiled stove radiating heat in the middle of the room. The joy of unwrapping, unfreezing, having a glass of tea, hanging your shawl on the rope in front of the stove to dry. . .'

Like the calculation of wind-chill factor, the effect of the savage climate was multiplied by the staggering distance – from Irkutsk to Yakutsk, where David was due to wait until it was time for him to go even further into the wilderness, was some 1,200 miles, at least fifteen days' travel and often much longer. Two prisoners were jammed into each sledge, slithering and bouncing along the frozen river, '*u chyorta na kulichkakh*', an untranslatable Russian phrase combining the sense of 'to the end of the earth' with 'in the devil's own country'. Some food – if they were lucky, meat cutlets, yak tongues and dumplings – was carried in the sledges. There was no risk of it spoiling in a world that was a giant deep-freeze. Even vodka sometimes froze. The food was taken into the post-station at the next change of horses, to be melted and eaten in the brief interval allowed by the escorts before they hurried their charges on. One traveller remembers soup which had been cooked in a mould, flash-frozen by being put outside the door for a minute, and carried in the sledge wrapped in sawdust 'like a piece of green glass sculpture'.

The term 'summer parties' suggests the sunny, salt-sprayed cruises of the Black Sea Yacht Club. Though in fact they lacked any redeeming recreational value, they were so much less severe than the winter runs that it is fair to speculate whether the timing of an exile's journey was in part determined by whether the authorities wanted to add to his or her punishment by scheduling their journey in the ice and snow. The summer groups were driven by cart from Irkutsk to wherever the river began to be navigable that season. They covered the first shallows in a convoy of small birch-bark or tarpaulin-covered *shitiki*, or punts, until they reached the deeper waters in which the ferry steamers plied. Some exiles travelled on the steamers themselves, but by Kennan's account most were confined in 220-feet-long triple-decker iron barges, operated by local contractors. The usual Russian blend of venality, administrative chaos and indifference to suffering meant that while the barges could sometimes be half full, they could also be crammed to suffocating point. Usually towed by a steamer but sometimes left to run with the current, and guided by the rudder and a pair of massive oars, with blades some 8 feet long, they carried both criminals and political prisoners, men, women and children, the average load recorded by Kennan being around five hundred. Some of the women were exiles in their own right. Others were voluntarily following their men into exile, with their children alongside. The exiles had their own dormitory, and the top deck of the barge had separate wire-mesh cages known as 'hen houses' in which the men and women could get some air. There were also 'cells for the privileged class and nobility' next to the escort officer's quarters and the medical dispensary on the top deck.

The river-runs to Yakutsk – there were twenty round trips each summer – took about a month. Most of the later Bolshevik leaders had traversed at least part of the route into their own exile, and one story – almost certainly a myth – has it that Lenin, born Ulyanov, took the last of his aliases from the River Lena. At each little settlement where the barges moored ('nests of the banished', to quote Trotsky again), the exiles sentenced to spend their time there shuffled off to find their quarters. When St Petersburg was in one of its more relaxed moods, the others would be allowed to disembark, buy food, and mix with their comrades who had already put down roots. These stopovers were a psychologically important part of a stressful process. Both the bored and out-of-touch exiles in place and the nervous newcomers, many of whom knew each other or had mutual friends, had the chance to gossip and exchange news. A shift in policy which sought to prevent contact, by force if necessary, was a significant factor in the build-up of tensions leading to the Romanovka stand-off.

An earlier exile wrote of a summer trip that seems to have been shorter than the average: 'For three weeks we drifted slowly down the . . . mighty stream [which] grew wider and wider each day. Its banks were dotted with wild berry blossoms. Forests of larch, cedar and fir rose along them like green walls.' But it was not always an easy run. The escorting guards were a rough lot; the photographs we have show most of them as seedy and dishevelled even by Russian military standards. They were recruited from the army itself and may have been a dumping ground for the sort of soldiers commanding officers all over the world are anxious to slough off to other units. Armed and organised into fourteen military companies, two of them con-centrating on the river traffic, they shuttled to and fro across Russia as indifferent to the human beings they were guarding as the warders of the Butyrki. Their officers were often even rougher, free with their fists, drunkenly assaulting women and, on the river-run, pocketing most of the official allowance for food and palming the exiles off with hunks of meat going green at the edges and weevil-studded bread.

There are many accounts of the river trip. The story of Officer Sikorsky, told later in the exile journal, combines violence, retribu-tion and also coincidence since the prisoners involved came from the small colony in Ust'-Kut, where they had known Trotsky before his escape. They had been brusquely told that because of their 'attitude', the colony was to be wound up and those left were to be shipped downriver to Yakutsk and then further north. Part of the 'attitude' problem was their connivance at Trotsky's disappearance. They had also managed to offend the government, even from a distance. When

1. 'It won't be a stylish marriage...' David and Manya after their wedding in Irkutsk, Christmas Day 1905.

2. A sketch of an Irkutsk Prison cell by George Frost.

cell in Irkutsk Prison

An unlikely setting for love at first sight: Irkutsk Prison, where David and Manya met, August 1905.

4. Odessa's Cathedral Square, c. 1900, as David would have seen it: 'a bouillabaisse of races'.

5. The faces of Manya's childhood in Siberia, as drawn by George Frost.

6. A one-way ticket, the train to Siberia:
'the prison without a roof', here crossing the Volga.

7. Exiles and a guard on the train to Siberia.

8. Political and criminal prisoners being herded on to a steamer to travel down the Lena, 'the great waterway of the exiles'.

9. Some of the protestors crammed inside the Romanovka. David Redstone is second from left in the front row.

10. The Cossacks must have seemed terrifying to the
Romanovka group.

11. The siege as dramatised by a contemporary artist.

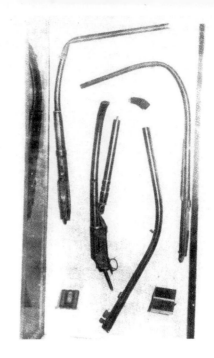

12. Romanovka 'Marksman' and veteran Bolshevik fighter, Victor Kurnatovsky.

13. Weapons destroyed by the defenders before surrender.

14. The protestors with their lawyers as they await trial.
David Redstone is second from the right, underneath the window.

15. Those of the Romanovka group who chose to face hard labour.

16. One of the Siberian silver mines, where many prisoners were worked to death.

17. Leapfrog and stilts in the Yakutsk Prison yard.

18. Another jailhouse wedding: the dashing Anton Kostyushko-Valyuzhanich, one of the inner Romanovka group, and his radiant bride, Tanya Zhmurkina.

war with Japan broke out in 1904, some bright spark in the Exile Administration in St Petersburg took it into his head to send the exile communities 'urgent telegrams' suggesting that they 'expiate their guilt before the Throne' by volunteering to fight in Manchuria. In return their sentences would be quashed, though quite when is not clear. In Ust'-Kut as elsewhere the appeal was 'universally' rejected by the recipients in written submissions couched 'in harsh language'.

When the Ust'-Kut group set off, the river was running high and their three barges simply drifted downstream with the powerful current, without a steamer pulling fussily ahead. The barges were tethered together, a hundred criminals in one, thirty exiles and six religious dissidents in the second. The third housed the escort commander Sikorsky, a former railway clerk, his stores, his cronies and a stock of vodka, which he sold to the convicts. The guards splashed between the slow-moving barges in rowboats. Sikorsky made it clear from the outset that he would react violently to any trouble and at one stopping point ordered his guards to fire over the exiles' heads when they got too close to their comrades on the shore. He spent most of the days and nights drunk, and it did not take long for his bloodshot eyes to fix on 18-year-old Rebekka Veinerman, one of six women housed in a curtained-off section of the exiles' barge. Rebekka was pretty; she was also there by cruel error, something she bore with remarkable cheerfulness. The daughter of rich parents, she had the misfortune to be related to a prominent woman activist in the Bund, who was on the 'wanted' list. When the gendarmes could not find her, they snatched Rebekka instead and, as she drifted down the Lena, her parents were frantically pulling every string they could to get her back. One evening Sikorksy ordered a pair of guards to bring her to his cabin, where he locked the door and made 'filthy proposals'. Though he even tried to tie her up, she managed to get away, as he groped and stumbled drunkenly around the cabin, and persuaded the escorts to row her back to her lighter. The exiles were determined to keep her out of the clutches of the vodka-sodden captain. At 4 a.m., as the sun began to turn the river mists pink and orange, they cut the ties, took the oars and struck out downstream, hoping to reach a village where there would be a policeman (another example of their inherited faith in a legal system most were determined to overthrow) and from where they could cable Irkutsk for help. Had the situation not been inherently terrifying – adrift on a river in the middle of nowhere with a deranged escort captain and his trigger-happy troops – it would have been almost comical, a Mad Hatter's boat race as the furious Sikorsky urged his men to bend to the oars and give chase. The exiles drew ahead and reached the village first, with just enough time to explain to the elderly village constable what was happening. He would do no more than tell Sikorsky, when the latter splashed ashore in a fury, that the convoy would be under his protection until it passed out of his jurisdiction, and he solemnly rowed alongside them until that point.

That night the exiles knew there would be trouble. The next village was twenty miles away and there was no way out along the banks, which merged into thousands of miles of impenetrable forest. The exiles had one Browning pistol, smuggled out of the transfer jail, a couple of knives and a can of paraffin. The women prepared 'poisons' from the medicine chest, though whether to use on themselves or to hurl at the guards is unclear. As the sun rose again oars creaked and splashed, voices boomed and Sikorsky appeared swaying, at the hatch, wrapped in a felt cloak and armed with a revolver and a whip, with a dagger and a sabre in his belt. His guards glowered menacingly behind him. As he stepped down into the sleeping space, Mark Minsky, a Tomsk student, took the Browning and shot him dead. The guards fired back, killing one exile and slightly wounding Minsky. They were on the point of shooting the rest out of hand when an NCO appeared, restored order and had the lighters moved to the shore. Not long afterwards, Rebekka's parents secured her release, and Minsky was sent for trial; we shall meet him again briefly later.

A hundred miles or so from Yakutsk, travellers floated through the Lena Pillars, whose jagged rocks, some 300 feet high, towered like a fantasy fortress over the water. When the 37-year-old St Petersburg attorney Berenshtam made the voyage on his way to argue the defence case in the Romanovka trial, he had already travelled through much of Europe, including Switzerland. But he thought even the Alps had nothing quite like those honey-coloured limestone buttresses. First, there was 'one towering stone pillar, with a sharp tip on which balanced a big round boulder'. Behind were more rocks of all shapes and sizes, 'some like ruined castles in which giants had once made their homes . . . cliffs which seemed to have doors and windows carved in them . . . ravines, some sparkling with streams and waterfalls, some dark and gloomy . . . the steep slopes littered with slabs of rock that looked like grey, black and yellow fish scales . . .' Even after the river was in full spring flood, the water's edge was still spiked with the last chunks of winter ice, its dirty crust underlain by a layer of dazzling azure blue. The crew on Berenshtam's boat had great fun telling him the story of the Convent of the Blessed Shroud which had been built a few years before, high up in the crags. Everything was ready for the nuns to begin a life of cloistered contemplation in their new home. The Mother Superior had been chosen, the nuns had been allocated their whitewashed cells and their housekeeping chores. A date had been fixed for the Bishop, the Governor and other local worthies to make their ceremonial visit. The news that all the nuns, 'with the Mother Superior at their head', had whisked off their wimples and decamped into the forests with a group of 'randy mining prospectors' thus came as something of a social shock.

Berenshtam's description of the Yakutsk skyline is about as close as we can come to seeing it through the eyes of my grandfather and the Romanovka group: 'A tiny little provincial town.' Its most impressive building was the State Liquor Monopoly, which was surrounded by mainly single-storey wooden houses, none of them painted; and there were the towers of ancient churches, two of which conducted their Orthodox services in Yakut. 'Occasionally you actually came across a Yakut mud hut tucked inside one of the inside courtyards. The streets were unpaved and largely unlit. The dust was frightful . . . The pavements were just wooden planks laid down on the mud in a terrible state, full of holes.'

Berenshtam was puzzled to see that a rich range of furs, shotguns, revolvers and ammunition was freely on sale in a town so prone to trouble – as a City-bred lawyer he did not realise that, as most meat had to be shot or trapped, these weapons were essentials rather than a social menace. And he was struck by the high price of other essentials, like candles and paraffin, all of which had to be imported. Then, as now, vodka and furs were about the only real bargains.

For a few, Yakutsk was not the end of the road. David Redstone was one of those destined for Kolyma, later to become almost synonymous with the Gulag itself, of which prisoners said grimly, 'Kolyma zhnachit smert' ('Kolyma means death'), or if they had any sense of humour left, 'Wonderful place, Kolyma – twelve months of winter and the rest one long summer.' The journey northwards into oblivion from Yakutsk was even more perilous and was almost always undertaken in winter since there were no rivers and only a few barely discernible rocky tracks through the forests and over the Verkhoyansk mountains. It was easier therefore for the Cossacks to deliver their human cargo across the Arctic Circle by sledge and horseback, the ponies sometimes sinking to their ears in the drifts. The journey had been known to take a couple of months. That any exiles survived the outward-bound trip is remarkable. That some actually found their way back after years in an exile of unimaginable loneliness and savage weather is unbelievable, but they did.

9

The Land of 'Endless Snow'

Even in Yakutsk, David Redstone found himself in a land where winter could last perhaps 240 days, with the sun unseen for weeks on end and temperatures falling to −30 degrees and −40 degrees C; Verkhoyansk and Oymyakon are the coldest places in the northern hemisphere, recording temperatures as low as −71 degrees C. In the words of one exile, 'It was as though nature had created the Yakut region to allow the Tsar to settle scores with his most dangerous enemies.' Another wrote: 'The ferocity of the horrible cold is impossible to describe in words: to understand it you have to experience it. The mercury in the thermometer has frozen long ago, so now one can make bullets out of it, or cut and shape it as if it was lead. Iron gets fragile and breaks into pieces like glass if you hit it . . . The sounds of someone walking are heard far away; the huge trees of a century-old forest are cracking one by one; and fissures in the ice and frozen soil resonate in response.'

Yakutsk today is the capital of the Republic of Sakha, whose diamond and gold resources add a high degree of self-confidence, even feistiness, to its relationship with Moscow. Confusingly for outsiders, 'Sakha' is the name the Yakuts actually use to describe themselves in their own dialect; 'Yakut' was adapted by colonising Russians from a name given to the Sakha by a neighbouring tribe.

The town's roots lay in a little stockade hammered into the hard earth on the banks of the Lena by Pyotr Beketov and his Cossacks in 1632. The grinding weeks it took the later exiles to head into oblivion by train, boat and sledge must have seemed an eternity but were nothing compared to the trip of the Tsar's first appointee as mayor, Peter Golovin, who left Moscow in 1638 with 395 Cossacks and five priests and arrived in Yakutsk in 1641.

By the time David got there, Yakutsk had a population of some 7,000. To them it was home; harsh, humble, sometimes a trap from which they could not escape, sometimes a source of a good living, and often a military or civil service post with a decent salary. The 150 or so exiles saw it differently, and the locals too saw their unwelcome guests through less than rose-tinted glasses: troublemakers, Jews, criminals, who were without money to spend. A first glimpse moved one of my grandfather's generation to write: 'There were no walls around us, we weren't harried by malevolent guards, but it was a grave, this endless snow, lashing at us from every direction, every step we took bringing death closer. It was a prison without fences or padlocks, torture without a torturer, the remorseless elements making a mockery of the passions and hopes of those who though theoretically still living were in reality powerless and buried alive . . .'

Between the extremes of Kolyma and Verkhoyansk and Yakutsk itself lay another gradation of punishment, known as 'banishment to the *ulusy*', or native settlements, where conditions were reminiscent of the Stone Age. One exile told Kennan: 'The Cossacks who had brought me from the town of Yakutsk to my destination soon returned, and I was left alone among Yakuts who do not understand a word of Russian. They watch me constantly, for fear that if I escape they will have to answer for it to the Russian authorities. If I go out of the close atmosphere of the solitary *yurt* [the cone-shaped native 'house' built from branches, covered with animal hides and mud] to walk, I am followed by a suspicious Yakut . . . I return, and before the fireplace I see a Yakut who has stripped himself naked and is hunting for lice in his clothing – a pleasant picture! The Yakuts live in winter in the same buildings with their cattle, frequently without any dividing partition. The excrement of cattle and of the children; the inconceivable disorder and filth; the rotting straw and rags; the myriads of vermin in the bedding; the foul, oppressive air, and the impossibility of speaking a word of Russian – all these things taken together are positively enough to drive one insane. The food of the Yakuts can hardly be eaten . . . often of tainted materials, and the unaccustomed stomach rejects it with nausea. I have no separate dishes or clothing of my own; there are no facilities for bathing, and during the whole winter – eight months – I am as dirty as a Yakut. I cannot go anywhere – least of all to the town, which is two hundred kilometres away. I live with the Yakuts by turns – staying with one family for six weeks, and then going for the same length of time to another. I have nothing to read, neither books nor newspapers – and I know nothing of what is going on in the world.'

He also complained bitterly about the diet, not perhaps surprising since horsemeat and mares' milk were staples, though it is hard to complain about cows' milk mixed with fruit and berries and frozen into slabs for a winter dessert. Another exile moaned that the Yakuts 'never wash a plate, they just lick it clean,' and left us a graphic account of how the men dealt with dirt in the winter: 'They pull their shirts over their heads and sit with their backs to the fire until they are beet-red. Then they call over one of their young sons who scrapes their back with a knife and the dirt falls onto the floor in strips . . .' The exiles learned by bitter experience the truth of the succinct advice Captain Cochrane had offered his English audience many years earlier on how to get the best out of the locals: 'The more a Yakut is beaten, the more he will work. Touch a Tungus and no work will be got from him.'

One of the Romanovka group, Naum Kagan, a 29-year-old journalist, had worked abroad as a newspaper correspondent but had fallen foul of the police for his suspicious connections and his work for an underground paper in Russia. Sent into exile, he took his wife and children but left them in Yakutsk when he was moved to a remote settlement to serve his five-year stretch. There he was offered the stark choice of an 'abandoned bathhouse' or a roofless shack with just its four walls. Even after he spent what little cash he had to buy the timber to cover it, there were months in which every night the walls were covered with a sheet of ice – on the inside.

Others pointed out that no other area of Russia had so few doctors or nurses, and those who might venture out into the *taiga* (the swampy pine forests) were given a hostile reception by the Yakuts, who preferred shamanistic remedies. Though the exiles did try spreading their various political gospels among the Yakuts, their lack of success must in part be attributable to their attitude of amazed condescension at the Yakuts' savagery. 'Wild men' is a phrase that recurs. In fact, given their liberal and socialist leanings, sympathy seems to have been rather lacking for the plight of a people whose nomadic life had been challenged as colonisation inexorably depleted their hunting and farming lands in the forests. They grew poorer and less self-reliant, and like simple people in other lands they found themselves ever more deeply in thrall to rapacious merchants, many Russian but some Yakuts. While one can expect alcohol and tobacco to create addictions and debt, it is curiously sad that their intro-duction to bread, which became a staple part of the Yakut diet, increased their dependence and financial hardship since grain supplies were in the hands of Russian traders.

The exiles' reaction to the nomads' living conditions underscored their essentially middle-class roots. They had clearly not even spent much time inside the average Russian peasant hut, which, though built of wood with plank floors and hempen mats, intricately fretworked shutters and beautifully carved door locks, was usually not more than two rooms, divided by a corridor which quite often doubled as a pigsty or cowshed. One room was for storage, the other for communal living and sleeping, dominated by a high, tiled brick stove and a sleeping bench shared by the entire family. Instead of the nomads' amulets and shamanistic emblems, there would be a picture, usually torn from a newspaper, of the Tsar and at least one icon: the Mother of God, St George slaying the dragon, a pantheon of bearded saints, or biblical episodes, in predominant tones of red and gold – in front of which a little oil lamp flickered day and night. There was often no chimney; plumbing and sanitation were not even dreamt of.

As they scoffed at the shamans and their rituals, did any of the Jewish exiles who grew up in the Pale of Settlement remember what they had learned from their teachers about the seventeenth-century Rabbi Baal Shem Tov, the founder of the Hassidic ('the pious ones') form of Judaism? He had started down his spiritual path as a magician and Kabbalist, blending theosophy, mysticism and belief in miracle-working, and healing the sick by incantations, herbs and prayer. His movement's deep belief in the presence of God in all aspects of existence and the interlinkage between the past, the here and the hereafter created what one sympathetic observer called 'some marvellous and impressive superstitions and rites'.

My grandfather and others en route to Kolyma had arrived in Yakutsk at a time when there was already a crowd of exiles in town facing the same ordeal, having been transferred as a punishment from less harsh settlements nearer Irkutsk. The influx was greater than the limited number of sledges and guards could handle and a backlog had built up. It is hard to describe the delay as a stroke of luck, but had David gone to Kolyma he might not have returned. On the other hand he was now to get drawn into a dangerous and desperate escapade that could cost him his life or even more years of his liberty.

IO

The Governor Gets a Grip

If any one event can be said to have a cause in a chain of history as complex as Russia's, we might trace the day in 1904 when the Romanovka exploded back to the assassination in April 1902 of the Interior Minister Sipyagin. In his place the Tsar appointed Police Chief Vyacheslav Plehve, a subtle spymaster and a hardliner who believed that head-on confrontation was the only way to deal with unrest, and who laid many of the foundations of the modern police state. (Some writers ascribe to Plehve the honorific 'von' – usually to play up the fact that though his background is obscure, he is generally thought to have been of a German origin – but it seems nowadays to be generally omitted.)

Plehve was adroit in penetrating the various underground organisations, though what was perhaps his major accomplishment turned out to be 'too clever by half'. Once he had his targets and suspects in the net, exile remained his main retaliatory tool, but he concluded that it was losing its deterrent value and that conditions should be tightened up. The rules by which the political exiles lived, and often died, were prescribed in calf-bound volumes of carefully drafted statutes whose draftsmen, like their later counterparts in the Nazi and Soviet eras, preferred to use euphemisms for the more unpleasant words; their titles included 'Personal Detention as a Police Measure to Ensure Public Safety' and the Himmleresque 'Statutes Relating to the Anticipative Prevention and Frustration of Crime'.

However, written regulations were one thing, the degree to which they were enforced was another, and reflected the swing of the pendulum of oppression and reaction in the capital. To some degree a relaxed approach had suited all the apparently conflicting parties – the government, who hoped to 'tame' the exiles; the local authorities, who wanted a quiet life; and the older exiles, many of whom, if they were not in the harsher sites, rapidly became adjusted to being simply 'out of circulation' for a while, reading, writing, reshaping the world in their dreams and recharging their mental batteries. 'Convalescents' and 'milksops' were two insults flung at them later by their more aggressive brethren.

Plehve saw things differently. He became concerned by the increasing number of escapes by exiles and reports that they were 'agitating' among the Siberian community, and as the first step to his vision of the new order he replaced the Governor-General of Eastern Siberia, Panteleyev, whom he suspected of being too sympathetic to his charges, with 64-year-old Count Pavel Ippolitovich Kutaisov, who, as a descendant of the hero of the battle of Borodino, would obey orders from the centre and not be too sensitive in the process. The Governor of Yakutsk itself was also fired. Kutaisov wasted no time in issuing hectoring 'secret' circulars to the pyramid of town governors, police commissioners and local station officers, the Corps of Gendarmes, and the civilian 'political supervisors', who were the structure's eyes, ears and, if needed, fists. To borrow a phrase from the next century, they were told to 'get a grip'. He actually dictated his first sharp missive, No. 942 of 16 August 1903, while still in the birchwood-panelled, private carriage of the train bringing him through Siberia, drawing town governors' attention to the lack of supervision over exiles he had been concerned to see at various stations en route to Irkutsk. 'His Excellency noted that [this] allowed them to mix with those already there, exchange letters and money and make altogether undesirable contacts.' Had they lived to see the day, Plehve and Kutaisov might have smiled (or more prudently hidden a smile behind their hands) to hear Stalin admonishing the Central Committee in 1937 in much the same terms: '. . . the prison regime for enemies of Soviet Power . . . is intolerable. The prisons resemble nothing so much as compulsory rest homes. [The prisoners] are allowed to socialise, they can write letters to each other at will, receive parcels and so on.'

The convoy escorts began to use boots, rifle butts and handcuffs to stop incoming parties mingling with exiles in place. In the 'liberal' period, though exiles had been barred from some jobs (teaching in public schools was forbidden as likely to be inflammatory, but giving private tuition was permitted), many found work as librarians, museum curators, chemists, dentists, and so on. To the previous administrations, mindful of what idle hands and minds might get up to, this was a pragmatic diversion, and also gave the exiles extra pocket money to augment the meagre government living allowance. Kutaisov abruptly banned exiles from taking work of any kind. There had also been tacit acceptance by the authorities that 'banishment to the *ulusy*' was tough. Before they set out, exiles had been allowed to spend time in Yakutsk buying supplies and clothes to equip themselves for the hard times ahead; that these supplies included shotguns and rifles for hunting, though exiles were supposedly not allowed to buy handguns, explains some of what was about to happen. Now Kutaisov told the police to move the exiles out to the *ulusy* as fast as possible, and tried unsuccessfully to insist that they be held in jail during the waiting period. The police had also become inclined to turn a blind eye when *ulusy* exiles drifted back into town for a few days to visit a doctor, stock up with supplies or just catch up with friends. Kutaisov ordered a clampdown on this too and told his gendarmes that exiles were forbidden to leave the narrow limits of their settlement without written permission. In their Catch 22 world, this meant that there was virtually no chance of getting permission; requests had to be delivered in writing, the exiles were forbidden to move and the Yakuts were uncertain and unreliable postmen.

Now if the exiles were found 'absent without leave', they risked being hauled away by the Cossacks to even more remote areas such as Kolyma. Some even had their term of exile arbitrarily extended by as much as a year. Censorship of mail, always a sore point, was intensified. Exiles were justifiably upset when a crude supervisor would make a crack about something in an incoming letter he had sniffed and chortled over, but which they had not yet seen. Letters were sometimes just thrown away, or arrived with phrases inked or cut out, or with pages scorched to illegibility because the letter had been held over a candle to bring out any traces of invisible ink.

Bullying supervisors began to appear on exiles' doorsteps unannounced at all hours of the day and night, armed with a questionnaire personally drafted by Kutaisov on which they laboriously noted the names of anyone they found there, what reason any visitors gave for being there, what the exile had been doing at various times of day, whom he or she had seen, and what they had discussed.

Discontent grew, as did the number of exiles in Yakutsk, because of the delay in shipping them north and because more exiles from the 'softer' settlements 'upriver' were being punished by being shipped there. Adding fuel to the mix was an unintended consequence of Plehve's policy. Many of those now being exiled as the result of his 'get tough' line were younger and more militant, ready for more action than spending their exile poring over Plekhanov or musing over Marx. In an odd concatenation of interests, the new, harsher regime suited the hard-line exiles as much as it satisfied hard-line Plehve, since it gave them more to be militant about.

The level of anxiety rose sharply when word spread that on orders from Plehve via Kutaisov, the new Yakutsk Governor Bulatov was making difficulties about finding the money for exiles to return home at the end of their term, even though this was specifically provided for in the exile regulations. He even refused to pay the horse and sledge hire costs of two men who, against the odds, had survived Kolyma and were due to return to Yakutsk. First he claimed that there was no money in his budget; then he argued that it was not a legal requirement and finally insisted that he could not act without permission. Though this particular wrangle was settled, the possibility of arbitrary government action shutting off that final escape hatch was unsettling.

When all this came to a head, David Redstone was one of fifty-seven men and women – the tally varies slightly because people came and went as the drama unfolded – who shared the rendezvous with death at the disputed barricade of the Romanovka. Who were these people? Like David, they were young, mainly in their twenties, hot-headed, many of them naive and swayed more than they realised by at least one experienced and calculating mind. To judge from their names, half were Jewish, and several key voices were members of the Jewish Socialist Bund, of which Rozental had been a founding member. Others, like David, were Social Democrats who later, when the term began to mean something, became Mensheviks.

Wherever they felt they belonged politically, the Romanovka group had been exiled for offences that are indicative of the malign capriciousness of the system. None had thrown a bomb, assassinated a minister or blown up a train. From the files, at least, the closest any of the younger exiles seem to have come to real terrorism was 21-year-old Misha Logovsky, a man of good family, who was serving five years for 'providing his brother the financial means' in 1901 to buy a ticket to St Petersburg to make an unsuccessful attempt to kill the uncompromising Pobedonostsev; a later account suggests that he was rather more closely involved.

The youngest, Stefanida Zhmurkina, known as Tanya, a 20-year-old peasant girl from the Orlov district, was serving five years, after more than a year in jail, for 'joining the crowd in a street demon-stration . . . carrying a red flag and shouting "Down with autocracy".' Autocracy was to have its revenge on her. At 22, Meyer Tsuker ran her close, all the more since he had been in jail and exile since he was 16 for attempting 'to change the economic order of the Empire' via stoppages and strikes, and he volunteered for the Romanovka even though his five-year term was close to an end. Others risking their lives alongside them in the little house on Pokrovskaya Street included a vet, an actor, a doctor, a seminarian, a couple of engineers, a chemistry graduate, three Georgian peasants who spoke almost no Russian, a tea-packer, a Brussels-trained artist, a hair-dresser, a ladies' tailor, a photographer, a surveyor, a jeweller, two midwives and a seamstress. Other than idealism a common denominator is hard to find.

The smoky soirées, which were a staple of exile society, usually focused on politics, literature or just life – this was, after all, Russia. In January 1904, just around the time David arrived, they began to debate these alarming new pressures and ask, '*Chto delat?*' ('What is to be done?'), to borrow Lenin's famous question. As Russians, they were voluble and argumentative by nature; all the more so as they were political animals and for the most part members of the intelligentsia, with the additional spur of sharply opposing views. Though there were 160 exiles in the town, there must have been 260 different opinions about what to do at any point. Outside it was 40 degrees below. Inside, in the yellow glow of the kerosene lamps, the heat beat out from the tiled stove. They argued, hands waving, the men's beards wagging, the girls' eyes flashing, through the grey spirals of tobacco smoke and the steam of the hissing samovar.

I can see the young David Redstone, in a high-necked shirt, debating vehemently with the rest of them about the various ways to make a meaningful protest. The references to him in the two books, his role with pistol and dagger on the guard squad, his vote at the end of the affair and his later adventures, suggest that while certainly not an advocate of terror, he was rather closer to the militant end of the spectrum than his later persona suggested.

To take arms against a sea of Cossacks and police was playing for high stakes. A similar bravura protest in the town back in 1889 had ended with seven exiles shot and three more swinging from the gibbet, and was still very much part of local folklore. Anton Kostushko-Valyuzhanich, one of the Romanovka's leading lights, was a charismatic militant whose dossier noted that he was 'a member of the nobility' and son of an army officer. ('Nobleman' did not necessarily equate to an English Whig grandee. Though Russia had many princes and aristocrats with ancient lineage, huge fortunes and estates, there were many more well-born families living on the genteel Chekhovian edge of poverty; 'nobility' itself had fourteen ranks and included many layers of officials down to a humble college registrar.)

Kostushko-Valyuzhanich argued at a meeting in early February that they should simply take over the town. Kostyushko, as he was known, had been a rebel from early days. When he finished officer cadet school, he had a 'glittering career' open to him in the Guards, but, as a friend of his wrote later, he chose a less showy regiment, though even there he chafed at the stupidity of his fellow officers. In his diary for 1897 Kostyushko tells us how he broke his rule of trying to stay out of trouble in the mess by keeping his mouth shut. 'A corpulent captain' harrumphed about how much he agreed with a newspaper article, arguing that wars were essential for mankind to curb population growth, 'otherwise we'd all be standing on top of each other'. Kostyushko wrote, 'I just couldn't help it. I said rather too loudly that if he was worried about there being too many people on the planet, the best thing would be to spread the Plague across Russia, and kill two birds with one stone – it would solve the space problem and would be a blessing for the government too, since it wouldn't have to waste money on an army and running quarantine hospitals.' This was not the sort of comment junior officers were expected to make to their elders and betters, and Kostyushko soon resigned his commission to study at an agricultural college, only to be expelled a year later for taking part in 'student disorders'. His wedding photograph gives us a sense of his attractive personality, but does not really convey the restless spirit of a man who also had a spell 'going to the people' as foreman on a bridge-building crew before enrolling at the Yekaterinoslav Mining Institute. He only lasted a year there before being arrested for orchestrating demonstrations in the town and a nearby village. He was exiled for five years for his role, which included 'singing revolutionary songs', yelling 'Down with autocracy' and 'Let's pull down the House of Romanov', and resisting arrest.

Kostyushko told the open-mouthed exile group that the entire Yakutsk garrison was only 150 strong, about half of them escorts rather than trained regular soldiers. 'We could get a combat squad together, grab some guns, take them by surprise and take control of the town in two to three hours.' It would light the fires of revolution all across Russia. He was crestfallen when the general reaction was hoots of laughter. What would they do then? Troops would be sent up from Irkutsk and his 'little kingdom' would be overwhelmed. In another place at another time, with David Redstone hovering in the wings, Kostyushko (who had been part of the Dzerzhinsky-led revolt at the Aleksandrovsk jail) had his chance to play out a similar script, but not now.

Naum Kagan talked excitedly of a general breakout and a trek of some 500 miles across the *taiga* (pine forests) to the port of Ayan, on the Sea of Okhotsk opposite the northern tip of Sakhalin. There the group would persuade the Japanese to take them back to Japan, a major propaganda triumph in the war that had just broken out with the surprise Japanese torpedo boat attack on the Russian fleet on the night of 8 February, anticipating Pearl Harbor by half a century.

Though Kagan's plan seems even more far-fetched than Kostyushko's, it was not laughed out of court. Nonetheless, saner heads pointed out that if such a daring scheme had any chance, which they doubted, it could only be pulled off in the summer; the fact that maps of the period show a 'rough track' leading all the way from the Lena down to the port suggests where Kagan got the idea.

On the moderate wing, some favoured simply handing in a petition seeking relief from the new inflictions. Others fell back on Marxist doctrine. There was little point in any political action since there was no local working class to 'energise', only the Yakut 'wild men' who were totally apathetic. At the other extreme, the left-wing Socialist Revolutionaries, whose Combat Organisation had so many lives to its debit, had no truck with this talk of mass action. There would be too many casualties. The surgical strike with bullet or bomb was the only way, what they called 'individual acts of terror' against Kutaisov and his subordinates.

II

A Small Siege in Siberia

Out of all this came a crowded meeting of eighty exiles on 14 February 1904, and a second meeting the following day, when sixty turned up to agree that a sit-in was the answer; by the time this meeting reconvened to start hammering out details, many had had second thoughts and only thirty-six arrived. The consensus was that they should barricade themselves in a house and refuse to come out until their demands for a relaxation of the harsh new system were met. They knew full well that this was an impossible outcome; violence and the use of force were inevitable. They moved fast, believing that they could escape police attention, but this was surely a delusion. Yakutsk was a small town, with a small town's prying eyes, and far more suspicious of the 'politicals' as disruptive elements than sympathetic to their plight. It was not only the townsfolk. The exiles were under close surveillance, including at least one secret informer (referred to in the records simply as *'shpion'* or 'spy'). The new Town Governor had, fortunately for him, gone on leave and control lay in the hands of 38-year-old Nikolai Chaplin, the Vice-Governor, who from the way he handled the weeks ahead was a cool and shrewd operator and who had probably decided to watch and wait as the reports and rumours found their way to his two-storeyed stockade.

The Romanovka, where David Redstone, Kostyushko and several others were already billeted, was chosen as the stage because it was far enough away (about a quarter of a mile) from the marketplace to

94

minimise the risk of injuries to civilians when trouble flared up, but still prominent enough for the townspeople to be able to watch what was going on at a distance, publicity being an important part of the strategy.

A teeming Yakut family occupied the ground floor but in tune with Russian attitudes to the 'wild men', even among the socialists and liberals, no one seems to have given a thought to what might happen to them. The house bore the name of its owner, Romanov, a Russian-born merchant. None of the commentators at the time or later, even Kostyushko, who had urged the crowds in Yekaterinoslav to 'Pull down the House of Romanov', thought it worth noting that their landlord shared the surname of the dynasty the exiles were determined to overthrow. The house stands today, and the photograph shows just what a strange site it was to choose for a siege – as if a tiger had deliberately tethered itself for its hunters in the middle of a well-trodden jungle track. A flight of steps led from the hallway to a veranda and a hallway, off which opened four bedrooms, a long dining room and a kitchen. There was no running water, no inside toilets and no bathroom. There was space for a family or a few exiles to live in under normal circumstances, but it was inconceivably small and ludicrously vulnerable for the exiles who would soon be besieged there.

The group formed an executive committee to discuss how the house should be stocked and prepared, and, as the days went by, defended. Its recommendations were put to a communal vote. It was headed by taciturn 28-year-old Nikolai Kudrin, a stocky mining engineer referred to by Rozental with admiration rather than criticism as 'deservedly our boss and our dictator'. A man with considerable underground experience, Kudrin had arrived in Yakutsk with David and, like him, was destined for Kolyma, in his case for eight years. It was not his first exile, nor the first time he had been to Yakutsk, though his earlier journey had been a clandestine mission rather than a punishment. He had been exiled in 1900 for 'criminal propaganda among the working classes' but had escaped, only to be rearrested several months later when he turned up in the Ukraine with a false passport and 150 pounds of 'anti-government' literature shipped in from abroad.

Also a member, and one whose biography as related in two abbreviated Soviet-era essays makes Kudrin look like a novice, was the dour, half-deaf, depressive Viktor Kurnatovsky; he too was from a 'noble' family and at 35 an even more case-hardened revolutionary now facing four years' exile after two and a half years in jail. His expulsion from St Petersburg University in 1887 had been the start of a 'career' in which spells of underground militancy were interspersed with longer and longer periods in prison and exile, including three years in the Arctic. He spent four years in Zurich after his first exile, combining university studies in chemistry with publishing and smuggling revolutionary literature.

When he tried to slip back into Russia in 1897, an alert border guard spotted his false papers and he was exiled to Shushenskoye on the Yenisei River. There one of his exile neighbours was Lenin, an old acquaintance from Zurich, dreaming dreams of the revolution to come and furiously dictating articles and letters, in between spells of hare-shooting. Lenin's wife, Krupskaya, describes Kurnatovsky, who was working in a nearby sugar refinery, as 'a good comrade' at that period, though the relationship cooled temporarily when Kurnatovsky strayed briefly into the Social-Democrat camp. After another short spell abroad, he returned to Russia, this time to Tiflis, where in the summer of 1900 he met another future member of the Bolshevik pantheon, Josef Stalin, who had just started on his long transition from seminarist to revolutionary, bank robber and tyrant. He later remembered Kurnatovsky as an 'attractive personality'. Kurnatovsky was also effective, playing a larger role than the more hagiographic biographers of Stalin have conceded in orchestrating the street demonstrations and railway strikes which brought the Tiflis area to a standstill. Kurnatovsky was soon back behind bars, serving two years' hard labour in the forbidding military prison in Tiflis' Metexh Castle on the cliffs above the River Koura. He was exiled to Yakutsk in July 1903.

Also on the committee were: the first chronicler of the whole episode, Pavel Teplov, serving five years for the catch-all charge of 'political unreliability'; Naum Kagan, the journalist who had come in from the cold of his *ulus*; the fiery Kostyushko; and Lev Nikiforov, a veterinary surgeon exiled for three years, whose wife and two children had voluntarily joined him. He had been an early revolutionary, who, after escaping arrest in Moscow, had also made contact with Lenin and the Iskra group in Zurich, and was active in their underground distribution chain until the police caught up with him in 1901. He had actually volunteered for Yakutsk in preference over a 'softer' exile further upriver, when he was offered what at first sight seems the slightly improbable post of town vet. But since horses and dogs were the lifeblood of Yakutsk commerce and its links with the briefly green, mainly glaring white, wilderness around it, the job was rather important. Teplov and others depict the bulky Nikiforov as a histrionic and self-important man, who was unreliable under pressure and who took an early opportunity to sidle out of the Romanovka trap.

Alerted by a note scribbled in French (on the reasonable assumption that if it were intercepted the police would not be able to make head or tail of it), Rozental and his wife arrived in town by sledge from their home in the *Skoptsy* village of Magan (much of it now buried under the tarmac of Yakutsk airport) on 18 February. The Romanovka was 'a giant anthill': a human chain of exiles passing from hand to hand logs, planks, heavy wire, nails and tools to make barricades, to serve as a lining of 'armour plate' inside the walls overlooking the street, and to build a small observation platform in the hall above the front door. There also had to be food – meat (some of it the local staple, horseflesh), a calf's head, fish, flour, sugar and jugs of frozen milk and blocks of ice, which together with snow scraped from the yard were the only source of water, and of course the black bricks of tea. There was also an arsenal of weapons, which sounds formidable but which was no more than a handful of peashooters compared to the resources ranged against them: six Browning automatics, seven revolvers, three double-barrelled shotguns (one a pump-action Colt) and five single-barrelled shotguns, two Berdan rifles (the nine-shot weapon made by Colt of the US and phased out by the Russian army in the 1870s), daggers, knives and axes. (A few days later a new arrival, lacking only a wide brimmed hat pulled low over his eyes to complete the revolutionary stereotype, smuggled in under his sweeping fur cloak 'an oval-shaped shell wrapped in a coil of heavy wire and evidently filled with gunpowder', which thankfully for the exiles and the wider community was never put to the test.)

'Inside the house everyone was in a fever of excitement. Some were busy sorting out where everyone was to sleep' – at that point there were forty-two exiles crammed inside but, as the next two days unfolded, their number would grow to fifty-seven. Others dry-fired, then loaded the guns. As Teplov remembered, 'We agreed the signals we would use to communicate with those whose job was to stay in the town and support us as a "reserve". . . we locked and barred the front doors, and barricaded the back door . . . boarded up most of the windows, leaving enough space for us to fire out if necessary . . . We stretched wire across the steps . . . the house shook with the noise of saws and hammers . . .' Several steps were yanked out of the stairway up to the front door to make it almost impossible to climb. The Yakuts downstairs complained to their landlord Romanov, who sent a boy with a message to the exiles saying that he had rented the rooms for them to live in, not as a carpenter's shop. Romanov himself scurried off to the Governor's office to report, hat in hand, 'may it please your most distinguished Honour', that the exiles were up to some sort of mischief.

One of the protestors crunched off through the snow to the Governor's office to deliver a petition declaring that they would stay where they were until Kutaisov's measures were rescinded. The rest set about writing letters to their families and loved ones, which were taken into town for mailing by one of the 'reserve' party. To quote Rozental again: 'We poured out our hearts . . . by the time the letters reached their destination the whole thing would be over one way or another.'

It never crossed their minds that none of the letters would get anywhere. Chaplin had anticipated them and shrewdly held all outgoing mail at the post office. One of his concerns was to delay news of the sit-in getting back to Russia; however, the exile communications network was as always resourceful and surprisingly fast, and it was not long before news of what was happening in Yakutsk reached not just Russia but the major European capitals. A more subtle benefit for Chaplin, Rozental speculated years later, was that having all those 'uninhibited' letters also gave him a good understanding of the protestors' readiness to die if it came to it, an insight which might have led him to decide against an immediate assault on the house and to work for a non-violent solution.

We can only speculate about whether the seven women in the group were any more apprehensive about the dangers ahead than the men; probably not. Or whether they were more squeamish about the conditions into which they were moving: no room to turn, the only toilet the yard or buckets, only melted ice or snow to wash in, and no privacy. Four of them at least had someone to hold on to and, if they were to die, they would not die alone. Olga Viker, aged 28, had followed her husband David into exile voluntarily, though she had revolutionary leanings herself, having served five months in jail in 1898. Anna Rozental, also 28, had been charged with the same offence as her author husband, and like him been handed a six-year term. Also sharing her husband's sentence and the pressures of the Romanovka was the 24-year-old Odessa girl Yekaterina Roizman, while Tanya Zhmurkina, the baby of the group, was the partner of Kostyushko, whom she later married. We know little about twenty-two-year-old Marianna Aizenberg, a midwife, in Siberia for four years for being a member of the Bund, or Rebekka Rubinchik, part of the Iskra distribution network and on her way to five years in an *ulus*. Pesya Shriftshteilik, a 26-year-old seamstress, has one of the longest dossier entries to justify her five-year exile, which took into account an earlier six months' prison sentence for distributing 'propaganda' in Odessa. Her main offence was to have 'headed a criminal society . . . in Kishinyov whose members sought by means of demonstrations to urge the general public to disobey the established authorities . . .'

Eva Broido, who had followed her husband Mordukh (later Mark) into his eight-year exile – they were both to become prominent Mensheviks – had a 2-year-old daughter to worry about and care for and, expecting her second child, did not join him in the Romanovka. As the later unfolding of the story shows, family concerns were more often subordinated to the calls of the Cause. (It verges on the bizarre to think that over eighty years later I sat and reminisced with that as-yet unborn child, Vera, then a gracious elderly lady, half a world away in a Hertfordshire garden.)

Chaplin surprised the group by his first response, which was to knock politely at the barricaded front door, accompanied only by the Police Chief Beryozkin. Displaying *sangfroid* (literally and figuratively; they cautiously refused to come in and stood on the doorstep in a temperature of −37 degrees), Chaplin said that he had passed the exiles' demands to Irkutsk and St Petersburg as he did not have the authority to deal with them. They would have to wait. The group might have been less comforted had they known that the next day the Public Prosecutor in Irkutsk telegraphed succinctly to his superiors in St Petersburg: 'Political exiles who came into Yakutsk without permission from outlying areas, plus some recent arrivals, total fifty or so, barricaded themselves yesterday in private house. They are armed. Refused orders of local authorities to disperse. Presented various demands intended improve their conditions. If resistance continues, administration intends use force.' Chaplin slung a loose cordon some distance around the house, mainly police huddled into their greatcoats and stamping their feet to keep their circulation going in the Arctic wind that sawed at their faces like a blunt razor, with orders that, while any of the protestors was free to leave, no one was to be allowed in.

Inside, 'sentries' were changed every two hours, while those who could sleep uneasily in sheepskins and scraps of blanket and cloth lay on the floors. In the yard outside more 'sentries' – David Redstone to the fore with a pistol in his hand and a dagger in his belt – kept watch when the women went out to collect buckets of snow to melt into washing water. Food was also a concern. Rozental described how, 'every morning and evening we got a glass of tea and a slice of bread and for lunch a bowl of buckwheat porridge and a small chunk of meat.'

It fits the surreal air in those first few days that the exiles' main messenger to and from their supporters in the town was an elderly sledge dog. 'Needles', hardy veteran of several Arctic scientific expeditions, would lollop innocently to and fro as needed, with notes tucked in his thick fur, tempted across the street by dangling chunks of raw carp.

At this point – the group dynamics shifted as events moved on – Kudrin's principal aide was Vladimir Bodnyevsky, 28-year-old son of an army major and a landowner mother; his brother served as a civil prosecutor. Bodnyevsky was a 2nd Lieutenant in the Army Reserve, who had fought in China; he was a poet, a depressive like Kurnatovsky, and suffering from what Rozental tersely calls the 'fatal affliction of the Russian male', alcohol. Bodnyevsky shared with my grandfather the dubious distinction of earning the maximum ten-year exile term, since he too had been hauled in while on military service. According to his dossier, he told his regimental NCOs that the Bible forbade murder and urged them to disobey orders to fire on demonstrators. His first job was to organise the building of 'armour plate'. It had not taken the group long to appreciate that while their primitive defences of wire, missing steps and barred doors might delay a direct attack, if Chaplin's men were simply to fire from a safe distance, they could riddle the wooden-walled house and all those inside. All the more since ranged against the exiles' amateur armoury, the troops outside had Mosin rifles (introduced in 1891) with a five-shot magazine and capable, if the soldiers were not frostbitten or drunk, of smashing 13.73 gram lead bullets into the Romanovka from a range of nearly 4,000 feet. A makeshift inner wall, about waist high, was crudely nailed together, parallel to the outside in the most vulnerable sections, the eighteen-inch gap filled with more logs, slabs of stone from the yard, and bucket after bucket of soil from the thick layer of earth which, as in all Siberian buildings, had been spread above the ceiling as insulation. As Rozental recalls, 'A pall of dust hung over the rooms all day and at night when people unrolled their sheepskins and blankets, it unleashed another choking wave sending everyone into paroxysms of coughing.'

After dark was the worst of times and the best of times. Worst because it was all too easy to imagine that the slightest noise on the snowy street outside was the jingle of a bridle or sword scabbard as the Cossacks shifted into position to attack; the Jewish exiles especially had vivid memories of what that meant. Best because they could at least relax and talk – how they loved to talk – and even sing. In the nervous quiet of a Yakutsk evening, the soldiers on the street must have been puzzled to hear not just revolutionary refrains but 'plaintive Polish melodies', the rhythmic stamp of the Georgians showing off their *Lezginka*, involving much whirling and pirouetting on tiptoe, and even the chanting of what Rozental called 'Armenian couplets', each singer trying to outdo the other in inventiveness:

> If it's rich you want to be,
> Eat spoons of jam as you sip your tea
> But if happiness is what you seek
> Stewed prunes for you, five days a week.

(Though he never became rich, my grandfather heeded both admonitions for the rest of his life, sipping his tea from a saucer with spoons of cherry jam – for Russians, digging your jam out of the jar with a knife sets social teeth on edge – eating prunes for breakfast and grimacing as he swallowed his ritual Friday night glass of Senna Pod extract for good measure.)

Another evening pastime in the Romanovka, recalled by Rozental, was a competition to see who could remember the largest number of stations at which the exile train had stopped on that long rattling journey into the unknown from Moscow. When I read this, my mind flashed again from images of Siberia to the Redstones' little London sitting room and I could hear my grandfather diverting his grandchildren with a rhythmic recitation of the stations on the last stretch. 'Omsk,' he would chant, 'Tomsk, Irkutsk, Chita.' We would mouth the mantra along with him, without any idea of what meaning it had for him. To us they were just the songwriter's 'far away places with strange sounding names', far more exciting than the sequence of shabby Southern Railway stations – Purley, South and East Croydon, Norwood, Clapham Junction and Victoria – through which we passed so often across the great divide from the meat and two vegetables of Surrey to the buckwheat porridge, pickled herring, boiled carp, cold fried fish, cabbage and egg pie of Golders Green – all far more delicious from Manya's hands than this menu listing suggests. But as Rozental also tells us, despite the endless talk, by unspoken common agreement the revolutionaries stuck to 'konspiratsiya', the cardinal rule of their dangerous world. In English it translates best not as 'conspiracy' but rather 'security conscious-ness', 'keeping one's mouth shut', 'tradecraft' and the 'need to know principle': '. . . we wanted to know nothing about each others' history, what part they had played in the underground, why and where they had been arrested, or even what we were all thinking. Even though we were facing death, asking questions was just not something we did . . . even so we spent a lot of time talking and arguing about politics . . .'

As Yekaterina Roizman wrote after it was all over: 'We fought our fight and did what we had to do, in silence, and though we all expected to be killed, we never thought we needed to say anything to each other about what we were doing. The act itself spoke louder than any words.' She remembered a late-night talk with Yuri Matlakhov, the tubercular 24-year-old son of a Ukrainian peasant, whose health had not been improved by being beaten to a pulp by the police after his last arrest in Odessa. He had been a militant spreading the revolutionary gospel in the factories and docks, but was actually picked up for yelling the ubiquitous 'Down with autocracy' and throwing leaflets from the gallery of a theatre. He was, Roizman remembered, the conscientious 'boss' of the guard system, changing the sentries every two hours and constantly checking to see they were awake. 'Night-time. Outside it's frosty; inside it is cold, terribly cold. I'm at my post by the window looking out at the white snowy street dotted with the black shapes of soldiers and Cossacks. It's quiet; everyone except the sentries is asleep. Yuri comes up and whispers, "Everything OK? The soldiers aren't moving?"

'"Doesn't look like it."

'Yuri moves off to check on the next sentry . . . When my shift ended, I didn't feel like sleeping. Yuri went and sat on the floor in the corner and I tucked down next to him. The room was in semi-darkness and you could just make out the shapes of our comrades sleeping in rows on the floor wrapped in scraps of cloth. Yuri whispered that what we were going through, the hunger, the cold, nowhere to wash, was extraordinary, all the more since we were all still "pumped up", full of self-confidence, and ready to fight back at a moment's notice.

"'You know, Katya, if any of us live through this, we'll never be able to do it justice in words because you can't describe it." He told Rozental, "This place is out of this world. Here we don't speak, we feel."'

What did they feel? Bravado, terror, isolation, physical discomfort, hunger, fear of being wounded rather than killed outright and being dragged off to years of solitary confinement or hard labour. For three women, the threat of rape and humiliation. For all, the shadow of the noose, the memory of family, the conviction that they were doing the right thing and concern not to appear weak-kneed in front of their comrades.

It is impossible to work out who knew whom before it all began, though there was a high proportion of Oddessites – Matlahkov, David Redstone, a frail-looking photographer named Orezhovsky, Leib Rudavsky, who had actually been at the Odessa Trade School, but who had ended up working as a tea-packer, the Roizmans, Pesya Shriftshteilik and Lev Tesler. Some of them must have been among the Trotsky-touched 'agitators living in Odessa' mentioned in David Redstone's dossier. And even if they had not already met, they would have had friends and memories in common to share at the darkest moments.

In the deepest watches of the night, when two or three of those on guard duty sat in the small pool of candlelight round the 'duty table', surrounded by a heap of snoring, shifting, scratching bodies, the veil would occasionally be lifted. 'Dictator' Kudrin, for instance, once let slip to Rozental that he had been in Yakutsk before, but not as an exile. He had arrived incognito on a 'party mission' to exfiltrate a senior Bolshevik. With grain sacks slung over their heads and shoulders as makeshift coats, the 'uniform' of the marauding, escaping or time-expired civil convicts, they were able to walk, hitch rides on carts and occasionally small ferry boats until they reached the Amur River and safety – albeit short-lived. Kudrin was now back as an exile.

12

Blood on the Snow

Inaction bred rumour, much of it reaching the house in terse notes tucked into Needles' fur. The police chief had dismounted the old and rusty smooth-bore cannon mounted in the bow of one of the river steamers to test-fire down by the Lena banks. Like the bomb, thankfully for the entire community, it failed to work. The garrison commander was claimed to have said that he was not going to attack the Romanovka head on, but would pick the protestors off using a squad of marksmen on the monastery wall, which ran to the rear of the house. This sparked even more intense work on the 'armour plate'. The rumour gained credence when soldiers were seen taking up positions on the wall. Yet another story was that Chaplin planned to freeze the protestors out by spraying the house with water from the local (British-made) fire pumps. As the sense of foreboding grew, one group made sure that everything in the house that could be used to strengthen the 'armour plate' was unscrewed, torn off, pulled up or chopped, while others were filling cartridges with gunpowder and casting bullets. The air was thick with candle smoke and the acrid smell of molten lead.

David Redstone's twenty-sixth birthday, 22 February, passed uneventfully. Three days later, Chaplin, still playing out the string, sent a senior exile who was not part of the group in an unsuccessful bid to broker a settlement on the basis that only 'the ringleaders' would be punished. The emissary went away, taken aback, as Rozental tells us, by the vehemence of the refusal.

As eight tense days and nights passed in what was clearly a test of nerves, the mood started to shift. This was hardly surprising; the mental wear and tear and the sheer physical discomfort must have begun to affect even the stoutest of hearts and, according to Rozental, some of those on the committee and others in the wider group were very highly strung and others verged on the hysterical. But before hysterics came democracy, and the group voted, by a very narrow margin, to allow the committee to 'take offensive measures'. Since the mandate for action was obviously less than resounding, the committee acted cautiously, its first step being to raise a red flag on the roof at dawn each day and haul it down at 6 p.m., hardly the most aggressive of moves but one which provoked the soldiers in the street, when the shadow of the flag was briefly cast on the snow, into stamping on it and then gathering round to hawk and spit. As one of those in the Romanovka noted wryly, it was likely to be the only house in Russia over which a red flag was fluttering without the police crashing in to tear it down.

Though the group had its reserve of supporters outside, the town as a whole was not happy; it was increasingly nervous about what might happen if shooting started, and the merchants especially were upset by the loss of trade. Alarmed by the false rumour that twenty-five of their fellow tribesmen had been shot for helping to supply the house, the Yakuts stayed away, so no fish, game or horsemeat was reaching the town, and as their barter business dried up, so too did the merchants' takings. The troops were angry too. Not only were they on constant, freezing alert but many were from the escort contingent and without the diversion of the Romanovka would long since have been heading home.

The group's next move was to send Chaplin a provocative declaration that the blockade was an attempt at 'bloodless murder'. Death in battle was better than starvation and, unless the blockade was lifted, they would have to take 'extreme measures' to render it ineffective. The first definition of 'extreme' was less dangerous than it was farcical, as well as being embarrassing for Chaplin. On the evening of 28 February Bodnyevsky and 31-year-old Misha Lurya, a typesetter, slipped out of the Romanovka wrapped in white cloth, 'like the ghost of Hamlet's father', to merge with the snow. Their mission was to get supplies and news. With careful planning and the cordon taken by surprise, they were able to gallop headlong back into the courtyard the next day – one of the Cossacks later said that he thought the devil was coming – driving a pair of hired horse-drawn sledges piled with bread, sugar, tobacco, meat and two flagons of vodka.

Their surprise sortie was the end of the phoney war. On 2 March Chaplin moved his men forward. Some twenty soldiers took over the house next door, a ring of sentries closed in on the Romanovka, setting up makeshift shelters, and one was actually posted just inside the courtyard gates. They hacked holes in the fence through which the soldiers could keep watch and, if it came to it, shoot from comparative safety. The soldiers began to point their guns, clicking their tongues to simulate the sound of bolts being drawn, and to yell obscenities when they caught sight of one of the women.

The fateful decision came on 3 March, when the group met again and, after another heated debate, gave the committee the power to shoot first, without waiting for the troops to do so. Everyone was overwrought. Feelings ran high. The Rubicon lay at their felt-booted feet. Those in favour of firing first pointed out that the house was surrounded, the cordon was obviously now hostile, and an attack could be launched at any time of day or night. To sit down at that point and have a discussion about the rules of engagement was ludicrous. Lives would be lost needlessly. The group worked itself into what Rozental described as 'a state of temporary insanity' and, though many wavered initially, the majority voted in favour. But even so, he felt somehow that the mood had changed. Those inside had known that there was likely to be bloodshed. Now it was fast becoming a reality, many of those crammed into the fetid space, where dust still hung heavy from the building of the 'armour plate' – and where many had wracking coughs as a result, compounded by a wave of flu that had swept the house – 'found it hard to rekindle the mood of reckless fatalism' of the first days. Whatever the shades of opinion, it was clear that 'once it was agreed we could fire the first shot, we would inevitably do so'.

Rozental was right. Teplov's account of what happened on 4 March is more circumspect than Rozental's, but both attempt to

portray subsequent events as a justified response to intense provocation. However, although there was provocation, it is not clear
that the response from the protestors was justified. It seems to have
been more a mix of semi-hysterical passion and the dispassionate
seizing of an opportunity to escalate the affair irreversibly. What we
know from the record is that Chaplin's soldiers swarmed into the
yard carrying long poles which they used to slam the shutters closed.
This set off a wave of panic; maybe this was intended to 'blind' those
inside as the prelude to a surprise attack. The protestors broke the
mica-glazed windowpanes and wrestled the shutters back open,
snapping off the fastenings in the process to stop them being shut
again. They yelled down into the yard that if the soldiers tried again,
the protestors would shoot. The next morning, Teplov records, he
was on guard duty when the house was shaken by loud noises from
the floor below as if a crew of heavyweight poltergeists were hurling
the furniture around. Outside the police could be seen dragging
planks into the yard and piling them under the windows, perhaps to
be used as makeshift ladders to get to the first floor.

At 3 p.m. on 5 March, those in the main room heard footsteps
pounding through the dining room and into the kitchen. There were
hoarse shouts, then two shots, fired by someone in the Romanovka,
that in the small space sounded like bombs. Everyone dived for the
floor, huddling as close as they could to the 'armour plate', except for
Matlakhov, who stayed up on the platform above the front door,
which, cobbled together from planks, served as a rudimentary look-out
post. For a few moments there was silence, the collective suspension of
breath. Then their introverted, committed world erupted into gunfire,
the thump of bullets, shattering glass, flying chips of wood, screams and
shouts. Even above the din they heard a heavyweight fall like a
carcass slipping its hook in the abattoir and saw Matlakhov on the
floor, arms outstretched, his rifle clattering alongside him. Rozental
crawled over to him. Matlakhov was dead, a bullet through the brain.

While everyone else tried to squeeze between the cracks in the
floorboards, shaking with fear and praying to whatever deities they
held dear, Bodnyevsky sat cheerfully upright in the centre of the
room, swigging vodka. To its targets, the firing seemed to go on

forever, though, as Rozental later estimated coolly, it was not much more than five minutes – long enough by any measure. When it stopped, the sudden stillness of the room was filled with sobbing, bewildered murmurs and anxious questions about who was hurt. They began to sit up, cry and pray over Matlakhov's corpse, and ask themselves, 'What next?'

The question was answered in a way that yet again was breath-takingly anti-climactic. There was another knock at the door. Chaplin shouted that he was there with only Beryozkin as an escort. Those two shots from the protestors had killed one of his soldiers and mortally wounded another. They had no option now but to surrender and stand in the dock. The group's spokesman told him rather equivocally that they would not fire again 'unless it was self defence against further provocation'. Chaplin and the police chief walked with dignity back out through the yard, though the hairs on the nape of their necks must have been prickling at the thought that a trigger-happy zealot might be tempted to shoot them in the back. No one did. Nor does hostage-taking seem to have crossed the protestors' minds; those were innocent times.

So what had happened? The spirit of *konspiratsiya* that governed the protestors' dealings with each other was even stronger when it came to the authorities, and neither in the police investigation nor in the trials which followed, nor for many years afterwards, did the identity of the Romanovka shooter become known. For now we can call him 'The Marksman', not too overblown a title for someone who managed to kill two men with two successive shots, firing an antiquated rifle under stress at an awkward downward angle. The soldiers had come back and tried again to close the shutters, this time over the kitchen window. When one of the men inside, probably Mark Broido, had pushed them open, he had been hit on the hand by a stone thrown by one of the soldiers. The Marksman, who had been in the dining room, rushed forward – his were the running feet the others had heard – snatched up a rifle and scrambled towards the window, yelling to those around him, 'Shall I shoot?' 'Shoot,' someone alongside him replied. Another stone bounced off the wall. The Marksman fired twice. The men and women in the Romanovka were on their way perhaps to death and certainly to jail, and the little house and its fairytale fretwork shutters had earned its footnote in history.

After a night of fear and cold, the sense of terror was intensified by the complete absence of a response, the total silence outside and the police presence, which was closer and greater. At 2 p.m. the next day, as those inside went through their daily routines like robots, with voices muted and faces drawn – and Matlakhov lying in a crudely nailed pine bier with his feet pointed at the door according to Russian tradition so that his soul would not be tempted to wander back – a single shot cracked out. Even as they stared open-mouthed at one another, wondering what was going on now, answering volleys sprayed the house and everyone dived for the floor. Rozental found himself huddled against the usually undemonstrative Kurnatovsky, who reached over and pressed his hand.

A few terse questions confirmed that no one in the house had fired. So who had? There was only one plausible answer. Whether or not acting under orders, or with a nod and a wink from Chaplin, or perhaps simply out of frustration, a soldier on one side of the house had deliberately fired in the air over the roof, to give the itchy-fingered squads poised in Pokrovskaya Street an excuse to return the supposedly 'hostile fire'. The drink-sodden Bodnyevsky plunged into one of his mood swings and became 'totally apathetic'. The others had a quick council of war. David Redstone's fellow Odessite, Lev Tesler, was sent out into the snow under a white flag carrying an 'open letter' to Chaplin asserting that the shot had not come from the house. Chaplin hinted that he was well aware of this, and his men had been given orders to fire only if the protestors came out on to the street carrying weapons.

Tesler had only been back a few minutes when Anna Rozental, keeping watch from an upstairs window, saw a rifle muzzle prodding through one of the holes in the fence. As she jumped back, the soldier fired. The bullet shattered the windowpane, whistled past her head and smashed into what was left of the stove. Again the soldiers on the Pokrovskaya side took this as their cue to open up, with what to the overwrought men and women inside seemed far greater intensity, though most of the shots were absorbed by the 'armour plate'.

When the firing finally stopped, Bodnyevsky was the first to crack, lurching half drunk to his feet and screaming, 'God knows what's happening. We've got to surrender.' Once the 'S-word' had been spoken, it could not be taken back. Despondency deepened when it was seen that Kostyushko had taken a bullet dangerously close to his spine. Tanya Zhmurkina cradled his head while Rozental bandaged him as best he could. The group needed time to think and the indomitable Tesler was sent back out to ask Chaplin for just that. Again Chaplin told him his men had fired only in response to a shot from the house and even that had been against his orders. But no doubt sensing the way things were going and breathing a private sigh of relief, he gave the group six hours to reflect.

The last 'general meeting' began at 4 p.m. Revolutionaries well out of harm's way obviously criticised the group's decision, since not long afterwards Olga Viker felt it appropriate to write at length in Lenin's newspaper *Iskra* about the arguments for and against that those desperate and bone-weary men and women tossed to and fro in their shattered rooms. 'The least understood aspect of the Romanovka affair was why we surrendered – the most tragic episode in the entire saga.' She described the group as 'shell-shocked and supine'.

That did not stop them arguing. Nothing short of death could. There was a strong though by no means unanimous view that things could not go on as they were, even though there was enough food to hold out for a while longer. In Viker's painful self-analysis, 'To die, guns in hand defending ourselves, that was why we had barricaded ourselves in . . . but to be shot like fish in a barrel, just waiting for the bullet with your name on it, or to watch helplessly when the comrade lying next to you took a bullet, made absolutely no sense.' As in the earlier debates, some of the views were extreme, made more so by the ordeal. Some suggested collective suicide. Others thought that the group should simply charge out on to the street, knowing full well, according to Viker, that this was just a bolder version of suicide since they would immediately be mown down. Cooler counsel and subtler arguments began to prevail. For them all to die would serve no real purpose except martyrdom. The group was there to fight and, as one adroit mind argued, the only way to go on fighting was to surrender. To stay put would mean staying dead, silenced forever. If they surrendered, they would have their day in court to ventilate their grievances and set the record straight about who fired, when and why. Rozental argued for delay. Every day they held out was another victory, so why give in today? The Romanovka already had its place in the history books. Why spoil it with an 'inglorious end' before every resource had been exhausted? In the end, democracy prevailed and they took a vote, which Rozental carefully tallied: thirty-two voted to surrender, twenty-two voted against, and one abstained. The dejected Bodnyevsky, the two Vikers, Teplov and Tesler (who had seen for himself the forces massed outside, and had taken the measure of Chaplin's resolve) were among those in favour. Those set against surrender included David Redstone, Kurnatovsky, the wounded but conscious Kostyushko, and the two Rozentals. That night, as Teplov records, 'None of us closed our eyes. We wandered around like the living dead. There were tears and anger at the thought of what the morning would bring.' At least it did not bring Kurnatovsky's suicide, since the guns were broken up during the night, except for the Brownings, which were hidden in the chimney stack for outside exiles to retrieve later.

Tesler negotiated the final terms and at 7 a.m. on 7 March Chaplin took the by now well-trodden path through the slush to the front yard. This time he had an escort of local troops, the latter a stipulation of the protestors who were worried that the Cossacks and convoy guards might seek revenge. In the first of several moral victories and one major physical triumph that were to follow in the months ahead, they also refused to have Matlakhov's corpse and the two wounded taken directly to the hospital. Instead the victims had pride of place, the plank coffin carried by a group of the men, the two wounded hauled on a sledge. The sad procession slithered and splashed its way to the jail. Though it was early and the cold bitter, word of what was to happen had spread quickly and the wide street was lined with groups of exiles and townspeople. As Teplov wrote, 'By the harsh light of day the tormented, dust-streaked faces of the group were a terrible sight. Their eyes dulled by sadness and despair. They trudged in silence as though on their way to execution.'

13

Defiance from the Dock

The mortal threat of a summary court martial remained all too real. The moment he learned of the surrender, Plehve had cabled Kutaisov in Irkutsk urging him to have the protestors tried by a military tribunal, 'as was done in the similar case in 1898'. Excited tongues in the town wagged that Chaplin already had a list of those to be executed.

But first there was police procedure. The group was searched, and their personal details and descriptions laboriously noted by semi-literate officials until after many hours they were moved into the stockaded prison. They were given one entire wing to themselves with three large dormitories, three single cells and a separate room for the women close to the guard house, whose occupants soon got tired of whistling and cat-calling every time they spotted one of the women. The men from Odessa took one dormitory, the 'Caucasian Suite' was occupied by those from the south, and the third, soon known as 'The Cop Shop', was where Kudrin and other 'hard cases' held sway, discouraging visitors, no doubt because they were plotting their next moves. But the dormitories pooled their food (the minimal prison rations were augmented by supplies sent in by their supporters in the town) and set up a roster, shared by men and women, to do the cooking and the communal laundry. The group took turns sleeping in the single cells for a night free of talking, hawking, smoking and snoring.

When the Chief Investigator arrived at the jail on 15 March to question them, he seemed almost relieved to find that he had less work to do than he had expected, since every one of the group refused to say a word. They had decided this at the outset, in part to save what they had to say for the public forum of the courtroom, but also to deny the authorities any opportunity of evidence that might help them separate the 'sheep' from the 'goats'. In particular they needed to conceal the identity of The Marksman, forcing the court to find all of them guilty. The investigator was nonetheless thorough, and by 23 March had taken statements from 108 witnesses: fifty-six of them soldiers and police, landlords, shopkeepers, sledge-drivers, three passers-by who claimed they had seen something of what happened, even though at a distance, and the anonymous *shpion* ('informer', literally 'spy').

While the group took every opportunity to sneer at the legal system that they despised as a cornerstone of the edifice of autocracy, this did not stop them from using all the procedural avenues the system offered from the day they learned with relief – even 'The Cop Shop' hard cases – that they would be tried in the Yakutsk Civil Court and not by court martial.

When in the years ahead some of them – Eva Broido is a prime example – fell foul of the Socialist legality they had helped to create in place of the vilified autocracy of the Tsars, one wonders what went through their minds. In the Soviet Union, and just as surely in today's Russia, an incident such as the Romanovka would have been snuffed out in a flash and any survivors shot on the spot.

We do not know why Plehve's orders were disregarded. The government was already reeling from its defeats at the hands of the Japanese, and wrong-footed by the publicity the Romanovka affair had already received in the west (compounded by growing reports of suicide among other despairing exile communities), and had – for the moment – become concerned about its 'image'. The exiles' links with the outside world were remarkable; Rozental tells us that several participants maintained 'close and uninterrupted communications with their organisations' outside, and that messages and documents were sent back to Russia and from there to the west, slipping swiftly through the network of interception and censorship. However it was done (the bulk of those moving in and out of Siberia were bona fide private and commercial travellers and would not have been searched), it worked. In a real sense it had to, since the aim was to fan the flame of reaction – within Siberia, in Russia and amongst the international community – which could be whipped relatively easily into a frenzy of meetings, press articles and even fund-raising, and thus put St Petersburg under even greater pressure. The exile press in Europe and some European papers carried surprisingly up-to-date reports, exile letters and the texts of strident supporting resolutions passed by Socialist and Jewish organisations across Europe. In London, *The Times* had a slightly garbled story about the Romanovka, which was picked up a few days later by the *New York Times*. A surprising 4,000 people crammed into the 'Wonderland Hall' on Whitechapel Road in London's East End for a meeting organised by the Bund and backed by other movements, where they were harangued in Russian, Yiddish, Polish, German and English about the bravery of the protestors and the iniquities of the tsarist regime. (The hall, now long gone, was better known as a boxing venue, site of the last bare-knuckle bouts in London, and for its variety shows; histrionic political debaters from Eastern Europe were thus not entirely out of place.)

In Yakutsk, Governor Kutaisov was already back-pedalling, telling everyone who would listen that his circulars had been 'misinterpreted' by his minions, but the prisoners' first priority was to retain defence lawyers. Here, as with communications, the exiles' ability to reach out and pay for top-flight talent was remarkable. Though there were fund-raising appeals in Europe, these cannot have met more than a fraction of the cost. Where the rest came from we do not know. The Bolsheviks and presumably also the Bund had a network of wealthy supporters, and the Bolsheviks were soon to embark on what they called 'expropriations', in ordinary language 'bank robberies', in which Stalin was a leading light, to fill the clandestine coffers. In one sophisticated coup they contrived a marriage between one of their activists and a sympathetic heiress so that the revolutionaries could get their hands on her inheritance.

Whoever was writing the cheques – the Chief Rabbi of Moscow

commented in later years that 'the Trotskys made the revolution, but the Bronsteins paid for it' – the group was able to retain two leading lights of the Russian bar. Aleksandr Sergeyevich Zarudny and Vladimir Berenshtam arrived in Yakutsk towards the end of June. Zarudny was the son of the distinguished jurist and legislative draftsman M. I. Zarudny, who ironically had played a leading role in reforming the tsarist legislative system on enlightened European lines. In the process someone had adroitly slipped through a key footnote, which allowed the authorities to take powers at their discretion to 'prevent and limit the consequences of felonies and misdemeanours', a provision relied on by the Ministry of the Interior to justify the quasi-legalities of the exile system which the younger Zarudny was about to assail.

Zarudny was one of a cadre of top-flight attornies, many but not all Jewish, who specialised in defending victims of pogroms, political trials and workmen's compensation cases. Today they might be headlined as 'prominent human rights lawyers'. The grandfather of the Soviet era dissident Andrei Sakharov is said to have 'made his name and fortune' in this way; we have to assume that the others too made an adequate living, which again raises the question of who paid the bills. The Bureau of Jewish Defence in St Petersburg, which was backed by some of the community's wealthiest members and overseas sympathisers, often instructed Zarudny and others not just as defence attorneys but to take on 'watching briefs' in some of the more high profile cases; Zarudny's forte was to commission detailed on-the-spot investigations of his own into the local police evidence, quite often with powerful results. As so many of the Romanovka group were Jewish, it would have been natural for the Bureau to back them, and we can only assume that this help was extended to others who stood defiantly in the dock.

As Kostyushko later wrote to his parents, the 41-year-old Zarudny 'was highly talented, a man of conviction and though by education, character and to some extent those same convictions he is cut from rather different cloth than us, every single one of us has taken to him very much. Berenshtam is a nice, cheerful, even flippant guy, a bit tubby. He was quicker to get in tune with us and understand what we were driving at, but didn't command quite the same degree of respect from us as Zarudny, who is an extremely gifted lawyer.' Zarudny was identified as an 'extreme left-winger' but apparently without any party allegiance, though his brother Sergei had been exiled to Siberia for his role in an attempt on the Tsar's life in 1887 for which Lenin's brother was executed. At first sight he was unimpressive, a small, self-effacing man, with a tendency to mumble, but one who seemed to grow in physical stature and presence as he unleashed his formidable speaking powers on courtrooms across Russia. He was a 'game-keeper turned poacher', having spent most of his early career as a prosecutor.

Kostyushko may have underestimated Berenshtam, then 33, whose memoirs show him to be sophisticated and perceptive. One of his stories might have come from the Russian version of *Rumpole of the Bailey*. Zarudny had already taken a couple of rooms for them. Since they were in the 'most expensive house in Yakutsk', Berenshtam was taken aback on his first evening – they were sharing a bedroom and had just lit their lamps – when Zarudny handed him a 'heavy tin' of insect powder. 'I got this just for you,' he said.

'You must be joking,' Berenshtam recoiled. 'This isn't one of those fleapit jails.'

'Take a look, dear boy,' Zarudny smiled, waving at the wall. 'It's alive!'

Berenshtam gasped. 'I had never seen anything like it in my life. The walls were seething. Drawn to the flickering light, bedbugs were coming out of every crack, milling unhurriedly over the walls like bees on a hive.'

The two night-shirted attorneys tugged their beds away from the walls and sprinkled the powder liberally around them in circles much like frightened Transylvanian travellers might have laid out saucers of holy water and bunches of garlic to ward off vampires. They even heaped powder on the bedclothes, with the result that while the bugs stayed at a distance, the two men were kept awake all night by Zarudny's sneezing.

'Is it going to be like this every night?' Berenshtam asked plaintively.

'It certainly will,' Zarudny assured him gloomily, trumpeting another violent blast into his handkerchief. Little wonder that in the subtitle to his memoirs, Berenshtam described what he had seen in and around Yakutsk as 'the Godforsaken Places'.

Berenshtam had been far closer than his senior colleague to the crackling flame of revolution. Though he later claimed that he never joined any of the political parties, he and his brother had been kicked out of St Petersburg University for a time for their part in 'student disorders', and even after he became a quasi-respectable qualified lawyer he remained involved in 'anti-government activity'. He was arrested in 1897 and again the following year, and questioned about his alleged participation in spreading 'revolutionary propaganda'. He was under unremitting police surveillance, a fact which earns him another appearance in our story.

Plehve's appointment as Interior Minister had signalled the start of the repressive regime that had brought the Romanovka to the boil. With the grim symmetry of a Greek tragedy, it was the abrupt ending of his life that proved to be another turning point – short-lived but crucial for the Romanovka group – in the government's ultimately fatal vacillations between sabres and soft words. The manner of it would justify the description 'hoist on his own petard', since one of Plehve's most adroit manoeuvres backfired. He ran the operation from a secret police base in the house on the Moika Canal – such is the coincidental iconography of Russia – where Pushkin died after his duel with d'Anthes in 1837. Since the day he took office, Plehve had been a prime target of the Socialist Revolution's terrorist arm, the Combat Organisation. He felt that he had taken out a personal insurance policy by placing one of his own agents, Yevno Azef, in the heart of the Organisation and would thus be warned of any danger. But after several of its assassination attempts had failed, *konspiratsiya*-tuned noses in the Organisation twitched and some began to question where Azef's loyalty lay. To save his reputation and more importantly his life, he was forced to orchestrate another assassination bid himself, with Plehve as its target. The Combat Organisation used young men pretending to sell cigarettes from trays slung round their necks, other plotters masquerading as hackney carriage drivers, delivery boys and 'courting couples' to watch Plehve's movements until they found the right moment to strike.

As they schemed and watched, we come across another of those points where one of the background figures in our story reappears in a context in which coincidence strains credulity. So it is with Plehve's assassination and the expensive apartment in St Petersburg, which was the plotters 'safe house'. It had been rented by the revolutionary Boris Savinkov, who was running the operation under Azef's control and passing himself off rather quaintly as the sales representative of a British bicycle manufacturer. It is absurd to feel sympathy or admiration for a group that was plotting to kill and maim in the name of a 'cause', but it must have been hard for them not to crack under the strain of several bungled attempts, a bomb whose sweating dynamite exploded and killed its amateur maker, and the twenty-four-hour-a-day dread of the police hammering at the door. The petite raven-haired Dora Brilliant, 'with huge dark eyes', was playing the part of Savinkov's mistress, a music-hall singer 'between engage-ments', while two other plotters rounded out the phoney household as 'cook' and 'handyman'. Azef himself was in the apartment when, as Savinkov recorded in his chillingly unambiguous *Memoirs of a Terrorist*, they spotted the unmistakable – to even a half-baked conspirator – shabby suits and semi-furtive air of several plain-clothes policemen loitering in the street outside. The next day Savinkov was shocked to see the dapper Berenshtam getting out of a hansom cab outside. Through a discreetly pulled curtain, they saw a detective scurrying into the building behind him. Was this the beginning of the end? If so, why was Berenshtam there? Doors opened and closed, footsteps clicked on the stairs and bells tinkled faintly. After what must have seemed a very long wait indeed, there were muffled farewells, more footsteps, the thud of the heavy front door and then a yell for *'Izvozschik'* as Berenshtam hailed a passing hansom cab. The detective got into the one behind and trotted off down the street in the lawyer's wake. Savinkov's discreet quizzing of the concierge satisfied him that the police surveillance target was not his clandestine 'cell'. Berenshtam and another attorney who lived one flight up, on whom Berenshtam had apparently been paying a purely social call, were both under surveillance, the latter for having frequent 'student' visitors with whom he 'discussed books'. (The tsarist police archives show that Berenshtam was the subject of 'special dossiers' from 1901 to 1907, an honour accorded to Zarudny only from the time of the Romanovka trial.) Savinkov does not tell us how he recognised Berenshtam in the first place, but all said and done the incident, which must have happened only a few days before Berenshtam set off for Siberia, was probably no more than happenstance.

Azef kept his silence and the plot drove inexorably on to 'success' on 15 July. Plehve set off to take the train to Tsarskoye Selo to report to his imperial master. However, the only report the Tsar heard that day was the news brought by a flustered aide de camp that Yegor Sazonov had ruined the sunny afternoon by tossing a bomb into the Minister's carriage. Plehve and his coachman were spread in an egalitarian steak tartare of bloody body parts and fragments of varnished wood across the cobble-stoned forecourt of St Petersburg's Warsaw Station. The Socialist Revolutionaries told the world that 'Plehve has paid with his life for the hunger, the want, the robbery, the torture, the groans and the deaths of millions of working people.'

While the assassination did not prevent the exiles' trial opening as scheduled on 30 July, the political shifts that followed certainly tipped the scales in the group's favour. (They also helped young Mark Minsky, who had shot Sikorsky on the 'boat ride from hell' and who had been brought to Yakutsk for trial. Around the same time as the Romanovka hearing, he was brought before the District Court and, to general surprise, was acquitted on the grounds that the shooting had been in self-defence.)

Escorted by rifle-carrying soldiers with white pipe-clayed belts, the procession of prisoners, led by Police Superintendent Olesov and watched by clusters of clapping exiles whom the police had not managed to keep out of the town, walked over to the courthouse, heads now held high. One account claims, improbably, that Berenshtam had told the men to appear unshaven and unwashed, apparently in a bid to suggest to the court that they were all simple peasants at heart. A three-man bench, headed by Senior Judge I. G. Budzelyevich, was waiting, as was another small moral victory. The defence pointed out that the law stipulated that each defendant was allowed to have three relatives or friends present in court. That would mean over 160 people had the legal right to be crammed into a courtroom designed to accommodate perhaps a dozen spectators. After much head-scratching on the bench and tough negotiation, it was agreed that ten wives or fiancées would be allowed in. The hearings ran to a timetable that must have been dictated by the burning heat and the twenty hours of daylight of the brief Siberian summer. They started at 11 a.m., running on to a three-hour 'dinner break' at 4 or 5 p.m., and then reconvening until 11 p.m. or midnight. The two defence attorneys did a good job of tearing apart the fabricated evidence of the police and soldiers about who fired when, and in attacking the legal basis of the charges. Their long speeches and arguments were followed by fiery closing remarks from most of the defendants explaining why they had done what they did.

The most difficult moment came as The Marksman rose to take his turn. Rozental tells us that 'he was wrapped in his own internal drama and we lived every twist and turn with him'. One witness had claimed that Mark Broido had fired the two fatal shots and The Marksman had told his co-defendants that if the court pursued this, he would have to confess his own responsibility. The others watched him anxiously. It would do no one any good if he were singled out, since a cornerstone of their defence was that no single individual was to blame and several of the charges were therefore invalid. When The Marksman rose slowly to his feet, the group's collective heartbeat stopped as he began to speak: 'In the name of the truth that the president of the court holds in such low regard –' Budzelyevich angrily cut him short, telling him to stick to the point, but The Marksman ploughed on: 'I can affirm that there were only two shots and that the killing of the two soldiers, whom we regard as working men just like ourselves but who happened to be in uniform, could never have been and never was any part of our plan . . .' At this point Budzelyevich lost his temper and ordered him to sit down and shut up. The moment of danger passed.

Even though they had expected the worst (and despite the cold comfort of a dissenting opinion from one of the judges, who agreed with Zarudny on a point of law, and a passionate closing speech by the defence lawyer that in one defendant's memory brought the entire courtroom to tears), the sentences on 23 August must have struck even the hardest members of the group like a punch in the belly: twelve years' hard labour for all except Nikiforov, who had left the house ostensibly to forage for food before the shooting started and had promptly been arrested (Eva Broido later jeered that he had 'simply wanted out') and who was sentenced to twelve months on a chain gang. It was only a matter of days before *Iskra* and other journals spread the news round Europe, pointing out that at over 600 years, the aggregate sentences were the highest total from one trial since the Decembrists.

Kostyushko, who was recovering from his wound, later wrote to his parents in a bid to cheer them up that the sentences would not stand, because times in Russia were changing; Plehve had been replaced as Interior Minister on 25 August by Prince Pyotr Svyatopolk Mirsky, a strong opponent of his methods, who believed in 'trust' in society and talked of the coming of a 'spring' in social relationships. Trying to find a silver lining to the cloud, Kostyushko also told his parents that he had heard that hard labour sentences were calculated in 'years' consisting of ten and sometimes as few as eight months. He did not tell them that the conditions in the mines were so severe that many did not survive even an attenuated sentence, nor that the calculation of the shorter year began only after the prisoner had served several full years of a 'probationary period'. As for his bullet wound, there was no need to worry; he could now walk and had given his crutches to a 'sick Yakut'. In a throwaway postscript he added that he and Tanya Zhmurkina were going to get married the next day. Despite the jail walls, an even grimmer backdrop than a Soviet-era registry office, the life force in their wedding photograph leaps off the page.

The group was now due to put Yakutsk behind them and return as prisoners rather than exiles to Irkutsk. There they would split up. Those who had exercised their right of appeal – yet another avenue provided by the maligned 'autocratic' system – would sit in jail there to await another hearing. A more recalcitrant cadre had decided that appeal was unworthy of a revolutionary and that the sentences were in any event so harsh that the government would be forced to react. This group would be sent off to the mines to begin their sentences. David Redstone and a majority of others chose to appeal. Those who set their faces against it included Kudrin, Kurnatovsky, Bodnyevsky, Kostyushko, Mark Broido, Tanya Zhmurkina and two of the other women.

On 23 August, accompanied to the Lena wharf by the usual heavy escort and a buzz of exiles defiantly singing the *Marseillaise*, the prisoners and their families (including Eva Broido and her two children, but not the nimble-witted Nikiforov, who somehow wangled himself a berth on the steamer) filed down the gangplank on to a barge which was taken in tow by the *Count Ignatiyev*. Bodnyevsky and a few of his cronies squatted with their belongings on the roof of the barge and spent most of the time roaring drunk. At Ust'-Kut the water was too low for the steamer and they transferred to horse-drawn barges and then bone-shaking carts.

The long journey back was marked by both tragedy and triumph. With hindsight, Rozental reproached himself bitterly that he should have seen that Bodnyevsky was cracking up. He also remembered bitterly that in Yakutsk the poet had once asked him innocently to point out just where his heart was in his chest, and that they had secreted the three Brownings in the Romanovka chimney. All of this came together in a tiny village on the river when, shortly after being hauled back by the guards from an abortive escape bid, Bodnyevsky shot himself with one of the supposedly hidden Brownings. It was just before dawn, that terrible period for all depressives when black thoughts crowd sleep and hope from the half-awake brain. An exile in Yakutsk slipped him one of the hidden Brownings on the way to the boat and he remembered where his heart was. The group buried him 'far from the Motherland' in a hastily dug grave in the forest, a red ribbon on the pine-branch wreath, while they sang the revolutionary hymn, 'You fell a hero in the fateful fight . . . the time is here and the people watch, colossal and powerful and free . . .'

The triumphs were a series of escapes, which demonstrated not just the exiles' courage in taking off into the wilds but their ability to put the cause ahead of family. Yekaterina Roizman, and separately

Olga Viker, took advantage of the fact that the women were less closely watched. Each in her own way said *au revoir* to her husband, both hoping it was not 'farewell', and vanished into the night, certainly with some outside help. Mark Broido also slipped away, leaving his wife Eva with their two children. The next to go was Naum Kagan. The latter had the distinction of being guided out of Russia into Latvia by Maxim Vallakh, alias 'Daddy', then an active underground operator and Party money-launderer, later known as Maxim Litvinov, Soviet Commissar of Foreign Affairs.

The embarrassment of the officer in charge of their escort when he had to report this on arrival at the Aleksandrovsk Exile Transfer Jail outside Irkutsk, on 23 September, was deep. It was nothing compared to the mortification the remaining group was to cause the jail administration.

14

Digging for Victory

Taking no chances, Kutaisov had ordered the prisoners to be shut away in a separate building, with iron-barred windows and heavy door locks. A 14-foot-high palisade of fir tree trunks with pointed ends, like a row of giant crayons, so high that it cut out the sun, was built around it, with sentries, whom the prisoners derisively called 'parrots' or 'little priests', as they peered suspiciously down as if from bird cages or pulpits from their watchtowers at each corner. Three supervisors patrolled the narrow muddy space between the fence and the building, and guards roamed outside the fence. Kutaisov had also decreed that, appeal or no appeal, the prisoners were now hard labour convicts and were to be kept strictly isolated. When the exiles were led out for exercise into the larger yard next door, the regular prisoners were first removed. Again the men divided themselves much as they had done back in Yakutsk. The women were in a separate dormitory, and they were only allowed to mix for a brief period in the evening.

Escape tunnels are indelibly associated with Second World War prisoner-of-war camps in Silesia, cheery RAF officers in polo-necked sweaters setting up dummy vaulting horses over the tunnel mouth under the noses of the gullible German 'goons'. But there is nothing new about them – they have a history as old as prisons themselves.

The Irkutsk tunnel jailbreak was the biggest moral and physical triumph the group scored, after the bravado of the sit-in itself. It was the brainchild of Kudrin, who had trained as a mining engineer, and his fellow hard cases in The 'Cop Shop', whose habit of discouraging visitors to their room and conspiratorial aloofness meant that the project was kept from others in the group, except it seems Rozental. It was a classic of its kind. Floorboard nails were pulled up and replaced only with their heads to show no sign that the floor had been disturbed. Teams divided into 'tunnellers', who had to be small and nimble to get between the joists and who worked four-hour shifts, and 'rammers', whose job it was to tamp the excavated spoil under the width of the building. Improvised tools were used: a carving knife whose blade had been serrated into a saw, a handful of long 'ships' nails, obtained from heaven knows where, to pick away at the cement screed the edgy Kutaisov had ordered the prison adminis-tration to lay below the floorboards, and a frying pan handle, the end of which had been sharpened into a makeshift trenching tool. For once the climate was an advantage. Further north, as in Yakutsk, the permanently frozen Siberian soil was just a few feet beneath the surface, and sometimes hundreds of feet deep. Here it was thin enough to cut through, but solid enough to provide a firm roof for the tunnel, though chipping through the cement took a week in itself. Barring a couple of men who were sick and who were posted as lookouts, the entire 'Cop Shop' took turns at the work.

The tunnel ran along the barrack wall, then under the wall of the prison itself at a depth of about 4 feet out towards a little copse of firs. The further the tunnel ran – it ended up more than 300 feet long – the harder the job of pulling out the spoil became, and Kudrin devised a system of pulleys, levers and handles to move the sacks. When the work was at its peak, there were usually four men underground, all wrapped in makeshift overalls that they left underground when they popped out of the hole blinking and wheezing at the end of their shift.

When the soft thud of the tools was suddenly replaced by the sound of knocking on wood, they knew that they had reached the outer fence. As the earth was scraped away, the tunnellers saw the bases of the wooden posts outlined like the bottom of a long-buried medieval portcullis. The engineers advised that rather than try to tunnel underneath, it would be easier to saw hunks off the bottom of three of the posts. Some skilful 'metalworker' cobbled together a makeshift but serviceable drill, and the diggers bored holes in each post until the ends could be broken off. To muffle the noise of drilling and the cracking of the wood, a group of exiles stood by the fence, lustily singing revolutionary songs – again anticipating the Second World War. Two of the stumps were left underground to be used as roof props, but a problem arose when the third was dragged back down the tunnel to be burned in the 'Cop Shop' stove. The wood was damp, took hours to smoulder away, and the stump protruded from the stove door like an accusing hand until late into the night. Luckily the warders left them undisturbed.

Work under such difficult and tense conditions took its toll. It was a miserable coincidence that this was just the time – we do not know why – that the trickle of money from friends and family temporarily dried up, leaving the prisoners dependent on the meagre prison diet and deprived of their one last late-night treat, toasted black bread smeared with dripping, which they mordantly nicknamed 'grouse'. (*Force majeure* must have compelled even the more observant Jews in the group to be flexible about their dietary disciplines.) The tunnellers let the group's 'housekeeper' in on their secret and he managed to slip them a few extra potatoes and the occasional dab of fat.

November brought a setback. When the group first reached the Transfer Jail in September, several of the 'hard men' had been appalled at the cramped and stuffy quarters – 'not even enough space to hawk on the floor when you wake up', as one put it straight-forwardly – and had put in for a transfer to the main jail in Irkutsk, where most of the 'politicals' were allocated single cells. As the weeks passed they assumed that like most such requests it had vanished into the waste-paper basket, and they were taken aback when the warders bustled into their building to tell them to get their things together and move. They included Kudrin and several other tunnellers, who decided that to refuse to move now would look suspicious, even though it meant missing out on the escape if the project reached its end. The work had to go on and others were let in on the secret. It was slow-going – chipping painfully away at a large boulder added days to the effort.

However, by the end of December the tunnel was 150 feet beyond the fence. The breakout was scheduled for New Year's Eve, when the guards would be distracted by rowdy celebrations. But two days before, as anticipation mounted and escape clothes and papers were being put together, a troop of mounted gendarmes galloped into the prison's compound jail to tell the prison governor that they had been tipped off by an informer that a large-scale escape was being planned. When or how, they did not know, but something was up. Though apparently unconvinced that anything major could be happening without his hearing rumours of it, the governor took the warning seriously enough to double the number of guards patrolling outside the walls and ordered them to carry their rifles with a bullet in the breech.

When this news reached the escapers via the prison grapevine, they put off the breakout until 16 January, a week after the 'Bloody Sunday' massacre of peaceful demonstrators in St Petersburg had raised the fervour and the stakes in the revolutionary process to new heights. When the tunnel began, the group had decided that while it would be ideal from a publicity and exile-morale point of view for everyone to make the attempt, a winter escape made this too risky. Every additional body worming out into the snow increased the risk of a guard spotting something, and the terrible weather, and the difficulty of getting hold of enough horses and 'safe houses', all added to the problem. So only those directly involved would make the attempt. The crust of earth and snow above the tunnel mouth was carefully cut away, and a circle of night sky appeared: a vision of freedom. One by one, wrapped in white sheets to make them harder to spot, fifteen men clambered out and floundered through the drifts to the copse. They had left straw-stuffed bolsters in their bunks to try to fool any warder peeking through the door grille. Glancing apprehensively behind them as they headed away, they could see the guards ambling unsuspecting along the outside of the fence walls; they spotted nothing.

Once free, they were dependent on the efforts of exiles outside and on the operation of the maxim that if anything can go wrong, it will. One group was held at gunpoint by local villagers, who had mistaken them for horse thieves who had been plaguing the area. Three more travelling by a sledge that had been left hidden for them were stopped by a watchman and detained when they could not produce a receipt for the horses. The trains and stations were alerted and Senior Supervisor Zveryev, armed with a stack of dossiers and detailed personal descriptions, shuttled between Irkutsk and Verkhneudinsk on the train, picking up another five escapers over the next few days.

In the end, five made it back to Russia and two made it all the way abroad; not a bad score and, in terms of the shocked reaction of the authorities, and the lifting of revolutionary morale, a major triumph. Bureaucratic hell broke loose. A braided flurry of government officials descended on the hapless governor, who was dismissed. Fires were lit above the tunnel to melt the top layer of earth, and it was then dug up and filled in; one of the convicts detailed to undo the escapers' handiwork commented that he had worked in various mines himself but would not have gone down a rat hole like that for all the money in the world.

The prosecutor toyed with charging those who had stayed behind as accomplices, but in the end was left shaking his head and wondering why they had not all taken the chance to escape. There were in fact no reprisals or punishments, because Count Kutaisov was already easing restrictions, trying quietly to undo the damage his circulars had caused, and did not want to call attention to another security lapse on his watch.

On 28 January reality overtook euphoria as those who had not appealed and who were thus due to start their hard labour sentences were taken over to the criminal wing singly or in twos to have their physical features minutely noted for the files. They had almost convinced themselves that they would never actually have to go; that their fate would be suspended until the appeal was heard, at which point everyone would be bound to have their sentences reduced if not eliminated. Now hope ebbed. War traffic had disrupted the normal pattern of sending two groups off to the mines each week and they could not extract a firm date from the prison administration, but that the date would come was now certain.

On 21 February, a week after the anniversary of the start of the

Romanovka Protest (celebrated by the 'housekeeper' digging into his dwindling stores and giving each of them a hunk of what he swore was Dutch cheese, an extra slice of white bread and two cups of coffee), news came that the appeal would be heard on 5 April in Irkutsk. A cable to Zarudny asking him to act on their behalf again produced a belated and demoralising response: 'delayed by constant and nerve-wracking pressure of work, which has left me totally distracted . . . Regret cannot come to Irkutsk as have to be in Baku. But main reason is that I don't have the strength to reopen a case once it has ended in failure. There will be defence lawyers there; the Moscow people [sic] have promised to send one. Berenshtam will cable his name from Petersburg. Please stick to same line of defence.' They cabled back begging him to reconsider.

No reply came and time hung heavy until the next blow fell on 10 March, when the hard-labour party were told that they were to leave the next day for what George Kennan called the 'famous and dreaded' silver mine at Akatui, of which Kennan recorded: 'I had never seen a place so lonely, so cheerless, so isolated from the living world.' Its central jail was described by one exile as being designed by an architect inspired by Dante's vision of the 'Inferno', while another reported that the air was so polluted by the mine workings that not a single bird was to be seen for miles around.

The mental and physical courage of the women in the group was remarkable, but if volunteering for the Romanovka took guts, to turn your back on an appeal and face the mines on a point of principle was bravery or foolhardiness of a high order. The mines were punishment on a totally different level, akin to the later Gulag. Unremitting physical labour in the worst of conditions was overseen by brutal guards, who could and did hand out terrible punishments for the mildest supposed breach of discipline; prisoners could be forced to wear the 'heavy grade' of 12-pound fetters for a year, chained to a heavy log which they would have to drag around while they worked, ate and slept, or were simply and cruelly flogged. So Marianna Aizenberg and Yekaterina Roizman (recaptured after her escape attempt) must have been exceptional.

In the blurred photograph of the hard-labour group just before it set off, the men's fetters can just be seen – these were the 'light version' at 6½ pounds, chains that ran round the waist, between the legs and round each ankle. The women's coats are too long to show whether they too were shackled, though Rozental refers to 'screams' as the first dull clink of the chains was heard. In a strange concession to kindness, the regime supplied the convicts with leather anklets to stop the fetters from chafing their legs. Curious in another way, but typical of a hide-bound hierarchical system, was the fact that Kurnatovsky was not sent with them. Though he was the toughest and most militant of the bunch, he had nobleman's rank and noblemen could only be sent to hard labour if the Tsar gave his personal consent. This earned him only a few days' respite since a clever civil servant soon worked out that the easiest thing was simply to deprive him of his rank and remove the problem.

This was perhaps one of the lowest moments. Those left behind felt a little better on the 15th when Berenshtam cabled that he was on his way. On the heels of this came a terse but comforting note from Baku: 'Coming. Zarudny.'

At 5 a.m. on 30 March, the warders woke those who were left in the Transfer Jail – David Redstone among them. They formally wished them luck with their appeal and at 7.30 a.m. allocated them to a line of carts which would take them over the hills to Irkutsk. The day stuck in Rozental's mind above all because it was the third anniversary of his arrest back home in Bialystok. He also remembered the weather: It was 'a nice day and a touch of morning frost meant that the ground would not be too muddy for a while at least'. The escorting soldiers marched alongside with their young commanding officer on horseback at the head. He had only been commissioned for two months and responsibility for this crowd of troublemakers sat uneasily on his young shoulders; he told one of them that he would have preferred to be an artist. After an escape-free night in a 'gloomy and dirty' house converted into an étape, they crested the hill on another bright morning to see Irkutsk spread out below them, the splendid skyline of blue-and-gold domes and spires set off by plumes of steam from the engines in Innokentovsky Station and a view of the pontoon bridge that led into the city.

The exiles' convoy was routed around the edge of the town to avoid too much public attention, then headed towards the centre down Znamensky Street, over which towered the cupolas of the Kazanskii and Bogoyavlenskii cathedrals. They clattered past the gates and wooden walls of the women's prison, behind which loomed the imposing bulk of their destination. George Kennan took a photograph of the jail, which he remembered as 'a large brick building, two storeys in height, with its front façade just opposite the long bridge over the Ushakofka brook. As you cross the bridge the building has quite a beautiful appearance, and the idea that it is a prison does not at first enter your head. But it is not beautiful within. You enter the long vaulted gateway, and notice at once a heavy odour; but it is not very bad, as there is plenty of air. From this gateway there are two entrances; one on the right, leading to the guardroom, and the other, on the left, to the chapel and the hospital which is where the stench comes from. Beyond these entrances there are more iron gates, and on the other side of them is the court. The courtyard is clean, but the odour in the cells is murderous . . . On the left extends a low building with twelve or thirteen windows. In it are the secret *kameras* where they keep particularly important criminals. Here it is comparatively clean and neat – better than in any other part of the prison, not excepting the so-called "office of the warden". The bath-house is too small for such a prison, where the number of prisoners sometimes reaches 2,000, and the common cells and the hospital are incredibly dirty and stinking.' The prison held on average 1,280 prisoners, of whom on any given day nearly 200 were in hospital, almost one in ten of them suffering from typhus. As Kennan scribbled notes, Frost took the opportunity to sketch his impression of the inside of a cell, leaving us in the process a lasting image of the setting for David and Manya's first meeting.

On 9 April the group was spilt into parties of seven, and each, surrounded by ten guards, was led off to the Appeal Court in the Sukhachev House. Each party took a different route via side streets, but crowds still gathered and the courtroom was packed with their supporters, some of whom were dragged out after greeting an impassioned speech by Rozental with loud yells of 'Long live the

Revolution'. This did not stop sympathisers from putting on a show of support outside the courthouse during the lunch break, handing out leaflets across the city centre, and organising a meeting that evening at the Civic Theatre. It stood just a block away from the governor's mansion, where Kutaisov was worrying about where all this was headed. He may have had a quiet word with the judges about what verdict might allow the system to 'square the circle', with the court's dignity upheld while not allowing the exiles another opportunity to parade themselves in the 'Victims of Tyranny' cloak and create yet another focus for public disorder. Squads of Cossacks had been moved into the city to back up the police.

Although the appeal judges had refused to allow the defence to call Kutaisov as a witness, Berenshtam tabled three new circulars which he claimed showed that the governor was trying to shift the blame for what he admitted were 'mindless acts of repression' on to his subordinates and the lower ranks of the police, who, he claimed, had misunderstood his earlier orders.

The prosecutor had clearly been given a brief that reflected the changing political winds. He conceded that the sit-in itself had not been a criminal act and stunned the group by conceding that the Kutaisov circulars were illegal and that the two soldiers had not been killed 'with malice aforethought'. What had happened in Yakutsk was a direct consequence of the harsh conditions of exile life, which had been exacerbated by the circulars. In conclusion, he argued that the court had no alternative but to confirm the sentences and dismiss the appeals. However, while as a formal matter the sentence of the Yakutsk court had been lawful, it had been manifestly unfair. The answer was for the Appeal Court to request 'The All-Highest' to exercise his discretion and reduce the sentences, in other words the buck was to be passed back to St Petersburg.

When the court rose at noon, the prisoners were taken back to the jail in one group surrounded – the authorities were taking no chances – by some 300 soldiers, a company of infantry, and a Cossack squadron, supplemented by a throng of police and political supervisors. At 6 p.m. they trudged back. Rozental tells us that the townsfolk complained that the clatter and bustle of the cortège disturbed their after-lunch siesta.

The court then announced that the sentences were confirmed but that, despite a closing speech in which Zarudny had made clear that the defendants unanimously rejected the idea, the case should be referred to the Tsar through the Ministry of the Interior with the recommendation that the penalty be commuted to two years' fortress imprisonment without loss of civil rights. The presiding judge had hardly finished before the shouting began from the dock: 'We don't want the Tsar's mercy!', 'We refuse', 'This is a kangaroo court'. From the public benches came a supporting chorus of 'Three cheers for the Romanovtsy', 'Down with the Court's Court', and the favourite battle cry, 'Down with autocracy'. Visibly shaken, the judges glanced around nervously, grabbed their papers and scuttled out as fast as dignity allowed. Undeterred by the wall of troops, police and cavalry that surrounded them as they emerged, with supervisors yelling at them to keep quiet, the group burst into the revolutionary song 'Hostile whirlwinds . . .', which they insisted on singing through to the end before they left the forecourt. All the side streets had been cordoned off, and in front of them Cossacks trotted in line across the street to clear spectators out of the way. As Teplov noted with satisfaction, the group's behaviour in Irkutsk 'made a good impression. It drew even more attention to what had happened in Yakutsk not only from those in the court but also from the locals and the soldiers.' Some enterprising local merchants even offered a special discount to 'our Romanovtsy', whose heavy guard did not seem to stop them popping into stores on the way to stock up with sugar and bread for their next stay in jail, where they were to await the written judgment. Even that was not the final step available; they had the right to appeal to the Senate's Court of Cassation, a concept Zarudny's father had modelled on the British Privy Council. The group were also honoured in absentia at a public dinner organised in their support by local exiles and townspeople.

The groundswell of local sympathy prompted the authorities to decide that the group was a potential menace and that they should be moved back to Aleksandrovsk Jail straightaway. They and the attorneys argued that they had a right under court procedures to stay in Irkutsk until the judgment was actually delivered in writing. The governor rejected the argument out of hand, but the group managed to negotiate, as Rozental tells us, so that they could leave behind 'the people who really needed to be there'. They urged that the prison doctor (who may well have been a sympathiser) should be called to certify who was fit to travel and who was not, and in the event succeeded in maintaining a 'stay-behind' party of ten, which included the still-ailing Kostyushko, Tanya Zhmurkina, who was eight months pregnant, the two Rozentals and David Redstone. This may explain the shorthand version of events given to the family all those years later that Manya 'nursed him in the prison hospital', since, given what we know about conditions, sickness was always an odds-on bet. We also know from the two accounts that David had been a leading light in recording speeches and court proceedings, and it may have been useful to have him around anyway to make notes about the last few laps.

In yet another sign of the changing times, the Akatui hard-labour party was able to send a local newspaper, which felt bold enough to publish it, a farewell message from the 'gloomy mountain fastness of the Transbaikal' that they looked forward to seeing all their comrades soon 'in happier surroundings'.

David Redstone was in cell No. 9, down the hall from the fuggy 'common room'. On 17 April, the first day of Easter that year, the bells pealed triumphantly from every onion dome in the city and, in one of those quintessentially Russian gestures (Trotsky and Parvus had the same experience a year later in the Krestiy prison in St Petersburg), the warders came round to offer the prisoners the Russian Orthodox greeting, *Khristos Voskres* ('Christ is risen'), and the traditional gifts of brightly coloured eggs, *kulich* – a dry iced cake, the size and shape of an Orthodox priest's hat – and *paskha*, a sweet creamy cheese curd studded with raisins and shaped in a pyramid in a birchwood mould. (In another of those leaps back in time, when I read Rozental's account of this, I saw myself and my sisters sitting spellbound round the kitchen table, covered in a checked oilcloth, watching Manya dipping hard-boiled eggs into cochineal, saffron and iridescent green dyes and helping her pour the clotted milk through a muslin strainer into her *paskha* mould, carved with patterns of flowers and leaves by some Transbaikal village craftsman, and with the same *'Khristos Voskres'* injunction which had survived all those years and all those travels. I wonder now whether, when we sat down to those Easter meals, David thought back to that bizarre jail offering as he presided benignly over the family table, its delicate linen cloth laid with Noritake china on which were spread pies, carp, a range of *zakuski*, or appetizers, and on at least one occasion a haunch of venison given to him by a tobacconist in Scotland, an ecumenical alternative to the Paschal lamb.)

On 25 April those left in the jail were taken back to the court to hear the formal judgments read out. The prisoners continued to push their luck, exercising another of their many rights, this time to summon the Inspector of Prisoners, Zaitsev, to request that the men and women be allowed to walk together in the yard and that their cells be left unlocked until 9 p.m. Zaitsev reacted sympathetically, but the prison governor did not and sent word that if there was any more trouble, the prisoners would go back to Aleksandrovsk, sick or not. His mood was not improved the next day when Rebekka Rubinchik merged into a crowd of kerchiefed, long-skirted, virtually indistinguishable young women who had come to visit other exiles and, carrying one of their baskets and chattering insouciantly, slipped out with them under the eyes of the warders. She eventually made it to the United States. This good news for the group, though not for the harassed governor, was tempered by a report that Naum Kagan had been recaptured. When the governor retaliated by ordering that all their cells be searched, the prisoners reacted noisily, some smashing every stick of furniture, provoking him to carry out his threat to have them shipped out. But when the warders came to fetch them, the prisoners refused point blank to leave their cells, yelling that if they were to go, they would have to be dragged out. A little later, the warders were seen hurriedly sweeping and washing the corridor in preparation for some important visitor, and at 9 a.m. the City Prosecutor Fass arrived. He went into each cell, urging the prisoners to be sensible and go quietly. Rozental heard David Redstone bellow angrily that the escorting warder was 'going along with these dirty tricks for the sake of 50 roubles a month'. Others told Fass that the warders had beaten them up and demanded to see a doctor. Fass retired with dignity; he came back after a while to repeat that if they did not go voluntarily, they would be taken by force.

He then left again, saying that he would give them time to talk it over. But a group of officers, supervisors, escort guards and warders continued to mill around threateningly in the 'common room', waiting for the order to move in. When Fass came back an hour or so later, he announced in a mix of barely contained irritation and embarrassment that they could stay where they were for now; the protestors had scored again. Not only that, but an official was on his way over to look into the complaints of ill-treatment. Five minutes later, a foppish but amiable young man arrived to look at the damage and talk to those who had complained. We do not know what he reported, but the mere fact that he had been sent was yet another sign of the growing nervousness of the jail administration and Count Kutaisov at having these 'hot potatoes' on their hands as the Russian political landscape continued to glimpse through the clouds more shafts – however fleeting – of democratic sunlight.

The exile grapevine also bolstered the protestors' sense that what they had done was worth the risk and stress. Back in Yakutsk things had changed very much for the better. Restrictions on movement were lifted. Mail censorship had stopped, and many exiles left the Yakut *ulusy* (remote nomad settlements) and moved back into the towns.

Kutaisov's new-found liberalism had come too late to save his reputation. Issue No. 1 of the underground *Siberian Herald* declared around this time that, 'Your memorial will be a lamppost, you old rogue.'

A strike in the Irkutsk rail yard and street demonstrations on 16 August created a new influx of prisoners, some defiant, most disorientated. All the empty cells were filled, and the Romanovka group had to bunk in with each other. Almost the last to arrive that day, as Rozental remembers, were 'two young girls named Flegontova', who took over David Redstone's cell, and he moved in with his fellow-Oddessite Tessler. It is not clear how long Manya was locked up for. Rozental describes her stay as 'short-term', though it was long enough for her and David to fall in love.

A fortnight later, Tanya Zhmurkina came back to the cells with her new baby Igor. In another demonstration of the priorities of revolutionary life, Kostyushko, knowing that the warders would assume him to be totally absorbed and would not watch him too closely, sawed through the bars of his cell window and escaped into a night of pouring rain. Rozental commented approvingly that he was confident when he heard the news that, unlike those who had made it abroad, Kostyushko would stay in Russia and keep fighting the good fight. He was right.

There was a growing sense of a world turned upside down. It was the members of prison administration, now paralysed by indecision and hesitation, who seemed themselves to be almost prisoners of a fate yet to be determined. Rules for visitors were relaxed and some even smuggled in bottles of vodka. Rumours multiplied that the authorities were mulling over amnesties for some political prisoners and that Kutaisov was lobbying St Petersburg for the release of the Romanovka group.

The summer passed. Manya was released but, as disease and fever continued to rage in the jail, she volunteered to go back in to nurse the sick, David among them. By 12 October Russia was in a crisis, or, more accurately, back in a deeper state of crisis than usual. Civilians and even more the troops were demoralised by Russia's defeat at the hands of Japan, a disgrace ever more freely attributed to the short-comings of the Tsar himself – if he had all the power, intellectuals muttered, he should have to bear all the responsibility. Regular soldiers were reported to be increasingly 'infected' by the socialist views of the hundreds of thousands of conscripted reservists who had swollen their ranks. As so often when wriggling on the horns of a dilemma, St Petersburg made the wrong decision and added fuel to the smouldering discontent by delaying demobilisation, in a bid to reduce the risk of disaffected peasants returning to their villages with dangerous ideas. This led to confrontation in military depots, small-scale mutinies and even the killing of officers and NCOs. An emboldened press became less circumspect and the censors stayed their blue pencils and scissors. Trains (even the Trans-Siberian), telegraph offices, banks, schools and government offices were hit by lightning strikes. Doctors shut their surgery doors, and, even if a patient already had a prescription, pharmacists were refusing to dispense them. Peasants torched their landlords' crops and estate buildings. A French observer noted, characteristically, that 'even the *danseuses* of the Imperial Corps de Ballet refused to move a muscle'. Professionals found the courage to organise into 'unions' and trade associations aiming to seek a voice in whatever structure might emerge from what was seen as the impending chaos.

On 4 February, Azef and Boris Savinkov's team, flushed with their success in demolishing Plehve, assassinated the Tsar's uncle, Grand Duke Sergei, Governor of Moscow. The Odessites in the Irkutsk prison must have heard with satisfaction and apprehension in equal measure about the mutiny on the *Potemkin*; the police and military reaction to the subsequent rioting in Odessa left up to 1,000 dead and many more wounded. (However, the current guidebook to Odessa is at pains to point out that this did not involve blood, broken eyeglasses or bouncing perambulators on the Steps themselves, notwith-standing Eisenstein's film images. The authorities had closed off all the access roads and all the fighting took place along the Primorskaya Boulevard.) At one point both Moscow and St Petersburg were without rail connections, and on 30 May 'not one locomotive raised steam anywhere in Russia'. Even a concession intended to reopen the universities misfired when it became apparent that, rather than return to their books, many students were simply using the lecture halls as a new venue for political meetings.

The Imperial Court was in panic, to the point where senior officials began to think seriously about where the royal family might go if they had to seek refuge abroad. Whether it was a result of taking private soundings from various embassies, we do not know, but the conclusion was that this would be a problem because of the sheer size of the family; a move would be seen as translating an entire dynasty to a new centre, rather than finding a discreet home in some European castle where a discredited royal couple could grow old gracefully. In October, the Tsar gave in and took what he called 'the terrible decision', one of whose ripples was to float the Romanovka group out of jail. He wrote to his mother that, as he had no one at court to whom he could turn for support, 'the only thing left to do is cross myself and sign what they are clamouring for', the promise of constitutional reform known as The Manifesto.

Irkutsk itself had been shut down by another general strike, but the police simply stood back and watched as worried conversations between passing strangers coalesced into street meetings and leaflets passed from hand to hand. On Sunday the 16th, one of the supervisors whispered to Rozental that he and his colleagues had been called to the prison office at noon and issued with revolvers. A company of soldiers had arrived at the jail and the guards outside had been doubled. Mounted Cossacks were patrolling the streets. 'Why do I need all this?' he fretted. 'The pay's lousy and what use is a revolver? If you guys go for me, I'll be crushed like a cockroach between twenty cows,' he added in an earthy phrase worthy of that later son of the soil, Nikita Khrushchev. On 17 October, Kutaisov, torn between his responsibility and reality, issued a proclamation that was pasted up throughout the city. 'An insignificant handful of people, clearly siding with the enemies of the government, is calling on the people of the city to resort to force and create disorder on the streets. Stupid and patently untrue rumours are being spread. These people are confusing peaceful citizens and forcing them by threats to resort to criminal acts . . . I call on all subjects to be resolute and to hold firm to the oath they have sworn to Our Sovereign . . . Disorder in the streets will be put down by force, so I warn all peaceful citizens not to join the crowds as otherwise the innocent will suffer along with the guilty.' That evening a warder spoke gloomily of Jews being beaten by thugs from the anti-Semitic 'Black Hundreds'; fifteen were killed in the city.

At midnight on the 20th, the Romanovka group were woken and told brusquely to be ready at 5 a.m. to be moved back to the Aleksandrovsk. The warders were in no mood for resistance. Convict clothes were thrown into the cells and the prisoners were ordered to change out of their civilian gear. David Redstone shouted across to Rozental that one prisoner had been dragged out handcuffed to a guard and another pulled screaming out of his cell with his hands tied behind his back. After a cold and bumpy cart ride, the prisoners and their thirty-strong escort approached Aleksandrovsk on 21 October.

At this point they had no idea what lay ahead: more bullying, solitary confinement, the silver mines – anything was possible.

What a shock it must have been, as the high fence loomed up, to see a happy crowd of soldiers, hats and belts thrown off and tunics flapping despite the first sharp twinges of chilly weather, singing and dancing along the roadside with civilians in their Sunday best – white kerchiefs, embroidered shirts and ribbons – as an accordion wheezed folk songs. The prisoners' bewilderment was compounded when they were met outside the gate by a crowd of warders, who rather than standing menacingly with handcuffs at the ready were bursting with excitement. One of them was waving a sheet of paper. 'It's the Manifesto! They issued it on the 17th and we've just got it,' he yelled. He read it aloud in all its sonorous and, in the event hollow, majesty. The Tsar had declared his 'unwavering will to give the people the foundations of civil liberty'. For the newly arrived Romanovka group that fine sentiment was of less consequence than the statement that all political prisoners were to be freed. 'It is hard to describe how we felt,' Rozental wrote laconically. The group was ushered into the main hall for a celebratory lunch, and the married prisoners were at long last allowed to share a cell. For Anna and Pavel Rozental, even though 'with two of us in it there wasn't room to turn around, to us it felt like the plushest suite in a grand hotel'.

Three interminable days followed until the prison governor joined the group at lunch to announce, to cheers and the banging of mugs on the table, that the Public Prosecutor was on his way with their official release. The emotional roller-coaster ride was not over yet. Cheers gave way to a few boos, a few moments of stunned silence and then uproar as the Prosecutor, trying not to catch anyone's eye and shifting from one foot to another in a state of near-panic, muttered that while the amnesty had been extended to a broad range of exiles, it had not specifically cited offences covered by the two sections of the Criminal Code under which the Romanovka group had been charged. 'They just got missed out by accident,' he sought to reassure them. Though calmer voices said that this must be a simple clerical error that would not delay their release for long, the mood was understandably jittery.

It was not until 28 October, four long, fingernail-chewing days later, that Chief Warder Ledoshkovich read out a telegram from the Minister of Justice formally annulling the Romanovka sentences, restoring the prisoners' civil rights and freeing them of any obligation to remain in Siberia. They could go home.

There was much speculation as to why in the end they had won out. Some claimed it was Kutaisov's lobbying. Others, adding what may be a very Russian embellishment, claimed that Yakutsk's Deputy Governor Chaplin, stricken by a fatal illness shortly after the Romanovka trial, had asked his mother on his deathbed to make every effort to have the group released as the affair was weighing heavily on his conscience. Seeing her son's death as God's punishment, his mother had taken up the case herself with influential friends at court.

Red Cross officials came to see how the prisoners were, and prison and army officers surged around congratulating them. An army officer insisted on sweeping them away to his quarters for supper. Having lunched on jail food in the acrid prison mess hall, it must have been an almost out-of-body experience to sit perched on tasselled chairs and be plied with sweet wine, tea and hors d'oeuvres, making polite conversation, while their hostess tinkled Glinka at the piano. The next day, the 'heroes of the Romanovka' were hailed at a public meeting, and two days later they were all on their way home; Kutaisov, obviously delighted to see the back of them, had expedited the paperwork and provided the rail tickets. All were released except for those who had been sent to hard labour in Akatui, who had to wait another three weeks for the machinery of release, more used to shutting people away than letting them go, to fill in and stamp the paperwork and pass it through the clerical labyrinth.

David Redstone was another exception. For, as Rozental recalled with evident sympathy for this evidence that love laughs at locksmiths, David had now become engaged to Mariya Flegontova and 'decided to settle in Irkutsk'. There was no going back to Odessa. A summer of violence and rebellion there culminated in street savagery in October – at almost the same time as David was released – in which more than 400 of the approximately 500 dead were Jews;

hundreds more were left to crawl away beaten and bleeding. The bustling port was 'dead', street lights went out as the electricity system of which the city was so proud was shut down, bombs exploded in the darkened streets and, even in daylight, people going about their business were shaken down by young revolutionaries stridently demanding money for the 'cause'. *The Times* told its readers that 'the monied classes' were making a 'frenzied exit', by train and boat.

15

More of the Puzzle

Manya told my sister years later that she and David were married on 25 December. It is interesting but probably irrelevant that on an earlier Christmas Day, David had, as was required, reported to the police upon his arrival in Yakutsk.

Russian Orthodox rules would not have permitted a mixed marriage like theirs to be solemnised in church, but army and prison chaplains, who in their years in Siberia had seen the power of love and fear of death create even more contrasting permutations of background and belief, were known to be flexible about performing the ceremony on neutral ground. I like to think that my grandparents would have marked the occasion with something of the traditional Siberian Christmas meal, in fact more of a buffet that ran from mid morning to late evening when the last guests reeled cheerfully out into the sub-zero night. Wherever they were in Irkutsk on that happy day, the tables would have been covered by platters of the Baikal salmon *taimen'*, sturgeon, the fatty *nalym*, or burbot, cut-glass bowls brimming viscously with red and black caviar, platters of goose, smoked sausage, cold yak tongues, marrow bones, pies and pasties, then ice creams and two or three varieties of frozen wild berries, a reminder of the vanished summer. Tea bubbled in the charcoal-fuelled samovar, and vodka, maybe even a bottle of French champagne, would have flowed more freely than the icebound river, boosted by the Russian passion for endless toasts and speeches.

If David and Manya did settle in Irkutsk, it was not for long since our next sighting of them is in Chita, some 350 miles away as the hawk flies, but 500 by rail as the track winds round the southern end of Lake Baikal. It took me a while to find out what had brought them there. At one level I now know; at another, a puzzle remains.

Chita is the main city of the Transbaikal region, about 175 miles west of Manya's home town of Nerchinsk, and before the railway punched its way there, it was a provincial town of some charm with the Yablonnovy Mountains, claimed to be the birthplace of Ghengis Khan, towering between 3,000 and 7,000 feet as a majestic backdrop. Its climate is not as harsh as Yakutsk but can still surprise at 20 degrees C in the short summer, plunging to −24 degrees C in winter.

By some accounts the city gets its name from the Evenk word for 'clay', though rather more romantically the local dialect dictionary tells us that it means 'birch grove'. Its first exiles were the noble and wealthy Decembrist conspirators, many of whom were packed off there in 1825 after an abortive attempt at a regime change that left several of the main plotters swinging at the end of a rope. They had the energy and money to set about the first steps in town-planning, building smart wooden houses on the neatly grid-planned roads, still evident in the town plan today. One was the Damskaya, or Ladies' Street, named after the elegant Trubetskois, Volkonskys, Muravyovs and Naryshkins, who had accompanied their husbands on the long journey east. But it remained a backwater. A jaded turn-of-the-century newspaper correspondent complained, 'You cannot imagine what Chita looks like – dilapidated wooden houses, dirty unpaved streets with cattle and stray dogs wandering here and there. The only decent buildings are the Governor's house, the hotel and three churches.' (The city claims today to be matched only by Jerusalem in the ecumenical positioning of a mosque, a synagogue and an Orthodox church on the summit of a single hill, where the Inogoda and the Chita Rivers merge.)

All this changed with the coming of the railway, and the population quadrupled to over 400,000. Even so, the *Guide to the Great Siberian Railway* was honest enough to point out that while there were now two hotels, the Tokyo and the Bianchinsky, 'the rooms are very bad'; since they charged only 2 roubles (about 10 pence) a day, this may not be surprising. The streets were badly lit, though the town did have a telephone system and thirteen schools. More to the point for what was to follow, the town was a key marshalling yard and repair depot for the railway, the headquarters of the Transbaikal Military District, and a major supply depot and base for Cossack cavalry regiments and artillery units.

The straightforward version of why David and Manya went there is that Manya's brother, Pavel, a doctor, was preparing to open a medical practice in Chita, and his sister's qualification as a *feldsheritsa* – a combination of district nurse and midwife – could be put to good use, while David worked as a journalist. In fact her midwifery kept her so busy that she barely had time to rush back from helping a young mother give birth in order to bring her own vociferous Nina, her first born, into the world.

But life is not that simple. If we knew exactly when they went there, we could get a clearer picture. Maddeningly the only dates recorded are the birth of Nina on 19 March 1907 and a photograph of an unidentified woman in plain, formal dress, dated in David Redstone's unmistakable copperplate hand '24/4/07, Chita'. Where they were in 1906 is a mystery. If they were already in Chita, David would have been on the edge, at least, of another patch of trouble in which two of his Romanovka partners played the leading roles.

Immediately after his escape from Irkutsk jail, the unstoppable Kostyushko had found his way – or been ordered by the Party to go – to Chita, where, living under a false name, he was soon joined by Tanya and their baby son Igor. Another arrival in Chita right after being released from hard labour in the silver mines was the hard-case Kurnatovsky, who was increasingly frail and deaf but unrepentantly militant. This was a man who lived and fought for the Party so we have to assume that he was not in Chita by accident, or to see the sights. He was also a man who had killed, since he was the man we earlier knew as 'The Marksman', whose two deadly shots catapulted the Romanovka affair into a new dimension but whose secret his more than fifty companions kept for years in the best traditions of *konspiratsiya*.

They lost no time in making trouble. As early as November 1905,

Kostyushko had become 'Engineer Grigorevich', working as a draftsman in the strategically vital railway workshops, whose mechanics were a ready audience for revolutionary pyrotechnics. Soon after the local Buryats had failed in a short-lived bid to set up a regional government of their own with Japanese support, the workers of Chita, in the words of a Soviet-era writer, 'went on the offensive' under Kostyushko's leadership, starting with a daring night-time raid which he spearheaded on the armoury of the battalion guarding the railway. Seizing 800 rifles and crates of ammunition, they formed themselves into armed detachments and began to try to seize the centres of power. When the underground presses could not cope with the demand for leaflets to spread their message, Kostyushko led another after-dark raid on a commercial printing works, cut the phone lines to stop the printers calling for help and made them work till daybreak running off proclamations.

Kostyushko and his colleagues began to harangue not just the workers but also the Cossack cavalry, with some success, leading to the creation of the 'First Soviet of Cossack and Soldiers Deputies', in which Kostyushko was the leading light; even the town's governor 'subordinated himself to the authority of the revolutionary strikers'. The later writer of a brief biographical sketch depicts Kostyushko as spending nearly all his time in the barracks and at meetings, but still managing to help Kurnatovsky write, print and distribute a then clandestine broadsheet, *Zabaikal'skii Rabochii* (*The Transbaikal Worker*), whose smudged black-and-white pages evolved into a newspaper which will be a central theme in David's later story. Kurnatovsky also found time to travel back to the Akatui mines to secure the release of fifteen of the Potemkin mutineers who had just begun serving open-ended terms of hard labour.

In December 1905, the semi-military Corps of Gendarmes was disarmed and, for a brief and glorious moment, the Soviet felt it held the reins of power, all the more when on the 14th, 2,000 armed railway workers swarmed to a demonstration marking the eightieth anniversary of the Decembrist coup attempt. But this was also the watershed. The railway workers were solid, but support from the troops, who began to feel that if the troubles continued they might be stuck in the Far East for a long time, began to seep away, accelerated by sobering thoughts about the harsh consequences of mutiny. The old men in St Petersburg had taken another dose of whatever pills politicians use to stiffen their resolve and were now resolute in their determination to eradicate the problem, all the more since the railway had to be cleared to allow the demoralised and defeated troops to return home from the war with Japan.

By early 1906, the 'Chita Republic', as it had begun to style itself, found itself pincered between two punitive expeditions moving in along the railway from both west and east. As General Paul-Georg von Rennekampf's armoured train drew inexorably closer from Harbin to the south, and another juggernaut under the command of General Meller-Zakomelsky thundered in from European Russia to meet him in Chita, the town's courage crumbled. A last-minute appeal by Kostyushko on 19 January to 'man the barricades' fell on ears deafened by fright. On the 21st, Rennekampf took the city without a shot being fired. Kostyushko was arrested on 28 February and, after a summary trial in the Hall of the Military Academy, was executed, along with another three ringleaders, on 2 March at the foot of Titov Hill, after saying goodbye to Tanya and Igor (one report said that they had been forced to watch). Defiant to the last, he told the attending priest that the judges were 'murderers' and challenged him to show where in the Bible Christ blessed or even justified murder. The group refused the traditional blindfold and Kostyushko is claimed to have told the firing squad, as it formed up and took aim, 'Brother soldiers, we are dying in the struggle for freedom and a better future for the entire Russian people. I forgive you – your children will be living proof that I died for your sake. Long live the Revolution.' As another indication that this was planned as a serious coup, a third senior Bolshevik and an old friend of Lenin's from London and Zurich, I. V. Babushkin, was also on the scene. He was caught trying to take weapons up to Irkutsk, and shot out of hand standing over his freshly dug grave. Babushkin, who once told Lenin tartly after cleaning up his messy London rooms that, 'The Russian intellectual is so untidy – he needs a servant to tidy up for him, he can't do it himself,' has the consolation of having a street named after him in modern Chita. Many of the strikers were also put on trial, some defended by that Phineas Fogg of the Russian Bar, Zarudny.

As the city collapsed, Kurnatovsky found himself, like Kostyushko, in Rennekampf's clutches and, after being taken to see Kostyushko shot, was also sentenced to death. But at the last moment, he was slung into a special 'hostage coach' at the front of the armoured train; the general announced that if the train was attacked, or the track mined, the hostages would be the first to die. Kurnatovsky shuttled up and down the railway for two weeks until Rennekampf put him before a court martial, which sentenced him to hard labour for life. By then he was apparently so sick that he was sent first to a prison hospital, but he was not too sick to escape on 21 May 1906 – together with his guards, whom he had won over to the Bolshevik cause; nor too sick to prevent him walking all the way to Vladivostok in the guise of a shoe-peddler, where sympathetic merchant seamen hid him in a barrel in the hold of a tramp steamer and got him to Japan. He then went to Australia – that other land under whose stones so many exiles' bones are buried – to sewing buttonholes in a dress factory, wash up in a restaurant and to labour, clearing forests.

He was finally persuaded to go to Paris, where he arrived, an empty shell of a man, late in 1910. Lenin helped with money for medicine and doctors' bills, and even a bed in a nursing home, but in the end Kurnatovsky turned his hard-man's face to the wall in a tiny room on the Boulevard Montparnasse and died on 19 September 1912. When he was buried in the Père Lachaise cemetery, the single wreath had a note in an unidentified hand, probably from Krupskaya or even Lenin himself, saying goodbye 'To a dearly loved man who suffered much'.

Conspiracy theorists would salivate that this is all too much of a coincidence. Why should David turn up in a town where two of his revolutionary comrades-in-arms and other heavyweight trouble-makers were about to launch another even more dramatic adventure? However, his name does not figure in any of the accounts and I suspect that he was advancing even more rapidly from the kind of protest which brought death and mayhem, which he had just lived through, towards a liberal, Menshevik, democratic and family man's view of the world and how to fix it. On balance I think that in David's case, tempting though it is to see him at the centre of more strife, the simplest answer is the right one, that he and Manya moved to Chita only after the dust had settled and the Republic had collapsed.

But the coincidence nags all the more since sometime in the summer of 1907 the Redstones packed up and left. Ever the raconteur, David later claimed that it was simply that he could not stand the Siberian weather any more; maybe so. However, it was more likely a combination of his past record and his known links with Kurnatovsky and Kostyushko, whether or not he had actually been mixed up with them in the Chita troubles, which made him a likely target as the Russian cycle moved into another period of reprisal and repression. Like Plehve before him, Pyotr Stolypin, Chairman of the Council of Ministers and Interior Minister, was determined to meet violence with violence as 'a deplorable necessity'. The mobs came out to prey. In another of Trotsky's vivid descriptions, 'the petty shopkeeper, the beggar, the publican and his perennial clients, the janitor and the police spy, the professional thief, the amateur house-breaker, the petty artisan and the brothel doorkeeper' roamed the streets thirsting for revolutionary blood, 'waving the Tsar's portrait, a bottle of vodka and the red, white and blue flag'.

Stolypin imposed a system of summary military justice across Russia that from August 1906 to April 1907 sentenced over 1,000 people to death, behind closed doors, with no appeal, many of them hanged on gallows whose nooses were nicknamed 'Stolypin Neckties'. The entire 'Revolutionary Committee' in David's home town of Akkerman was thrown into jail. The tribunals worked so fast that by one account some alleged political assassins were executed before their victims had even been buried. The *Times* of the period has reports of Russian unrest almost every day, its index studded with references to 'mutiny', 'strikes', 'bombs', 'arms', 'Jews', 'martial law' and 'robbery'. The eminent historian of the Bolshevik era Richard Pipes cites an estimate that even after the tribunals were abolished, and terrorists and others accused of violent political crimes were again tried before civil courts, in 1908 and 1909 alone 16,440 people were convicted, of whom 3,682 were sentenced to death and 4,517 to hard labour. Not only were ten and even twelve-year sentences now the norm, but an exile term was always tacked on the end as extra punishment.

The same picture could be seen in the Siberian press on almost any day during that period. In the news columns the contrasting elements of the struggle are laid out in story after story without the editorial comment that would have brought the censor's intervention: a decree from the Tsar on 'The Essence of Supreme Autocratic Power'; houses to be festooned and lit up for the Tsarina's name day; and a general blown up in Moscow with a nail-filled bomb. Across the country May Day was marked by strikes and demonstrations; in the St Petersburg Ship Repair Navy an admiral was stabbed to death while urging the men to go back to work. In Chita thirty-four political prisoners being shipped to the Akatui mines spotted the unmistakable grey bulk of Rennekampf's own railway carriage, now thankfully empty and unguarded, in the station siding, broke away from their escort and stormed it. The carriage was soon surrounded by 'thousands' of cap, kerchief and umbrella-waving sympathisers, who joined the prisoners in singing the *Marseillaise*. Cossacks and police had to be brought in to break up the demonstration. Back in Irkutsh, Rennekampf had a lucky escape from a revolutionary bomb tossed at him when he was out for a stroll.

The Redstones read their papers thoughtfully, watched the city bubble around them and set off for England, where the veteran of the House of Romanov joined the House of Sobranie.

16

The House that Albert Built

To make sense of what happens next, we must go back again to Akkerman, and back again to the late 1870s; back too to David's family. The story begins a year or so after David was born, when his uncle, Albert Weinberg, left for London to set up in business making high-quality, hand-rolled cigarettes. What Albert's background was, his place in the family hierarchy, and why he left, are all unknowns. He was then thirty, a little older than usual for the tug of a young man's hunger for wider horizons. In his naturalisation application to the British Home Office many years later, Albert described himself as Romanian; given Akkerman's shifting allegiances, nationality must have been somewhat haphazard. Tobacco was a staple Bessarabian product, so some involvement in the trade probably gave him a pointer as to his future, but it must have taken courage and vision to believe that his homespun background could be translated into a business opportunity in faraway London – all the more since the London trade was tough to crack, with sixty or more small firms already competing in the 'quality' end of the market.

The long history of tobacco is not for us here, but one can sense its ancient roots by the fact that the Russian word for cigarettes, *papirosy*, comes from the Egyptian 'papyrus'. Cigars – 'tobacco wrapped in leaves' – had been brought to Britain by Wellington's soldiers returning from the Peninsula Wars, and it was again returning soldiers, this time after the Crimean War, who came home with the cigarette habit, which they had picked up from their French and

Turkish allies. The first recorded UK manufacturer, Robert Gloag, had served as a paymaster with the Turkish army in the Crimea and set up a factory in Walworth, producing cigarettes with cane tips, yellow paper and filled with Latakia tobacco from a funnel. Gloag was quick to spot the value of winning customer loyalty through brand names, and offered retailers the choice of 'Sultana', 'Rifle', 'Zetland', 'Opera' and 'Moscow' (the latter had a plug of wool in its mouthpiece, the first version of the filter tip).

As smoking and Britain developed, so did dress (the smoking jacket, and tasselled skull cap, to stop the clothes and hair becoming smoke-saturated) and etiquette. One early manual advised that 'a man may not smoke or ask to smoke in the company of the fair, on the street, in daylight or on a racecourse'. Sadly we are left to guess just what Victorian social undercurrents lay beneath the further admonition that it was the height of impoliteness to offer a cigar to a clergyman above the rank of curate. In the earlier days of the railway era, stations were no-smoking zones, as were trains themselves, until the more enterprising companies introduced 'divan cars' in which gentlemen could puff away in peace on their way to a long weekend at Blandings Castle.

In early stories about Sobranie, it was claimed to be chance that brought Albert to rent a room in London from a friend of the manager of Robert Lewis & Co., the patrician tobacco and cigar retailer, who gave him his start with an introduction. The Lewis shop, established in 1787 and housed in panelled aromatic splendour at 19 St James's, was the pinnacle of the trade, its customers including over the years practically every fruity branch of Queen Victoria's family tree, including Edward VIII both as Prince of Wales and, briefly, King. Lewis supplied cigars for his Surrey home, The Fort, in boxes marked 'Specially made for HM King Edward VIII'. Earlier notables on the ledgers had included Oscar Wilde, for whom Lewis produced cigarettes with 'Oscar' printed on them in red capitals, no doubt inspiring Wilde to write that, 'A cigarette is the perfect type of a perfect pleasure. It is exquisite. It leaves one unsatisfied, what more can one want?' The ability to pay the bills is one answer – he left Lewis unsatisfied to the tune of 43 pounds 17 shillings and 3 pence when he was bankrupted after his imprisonment. Another customer with many ledger pages to his name, the last ruled off neatly at his death, was Winston Churchill, who had been introduced to tobacco and to Lewis not by his father, a man with a range of bad habits, but by his American mother Jenny Jerome, who favoured Lewis's 'Alexandra' Balkan gold-tipped cigarettes.

Albert must have made a good impression, and he struck a deal with Lewis to supply them with Turkish cigarettes to be sold under their own 'Robert Lewis Yenidje' label. The second and third entries under Churchill in Lewis's calf-bound ledger for 1900 show him ordering from his 35 Great Cumberland Place home, '100 large Balkans' on 9 August and another 300 on the 24th. If, as seems very likely, these came from Albert's garret workshop, it is a nice thought that a young man from Bessarabia might have played an early role in shaping the medically unsound but clearly successful relaxation techniques of the man who saved the west from Hitler.

Nevertheless, for Albert from Akkerman to land a key account in St James's, based on no more than an introduction from his landlord, would have been a remarkable accomplishment. Even though the dates are hard to match, it is tempting to see somewhere in the picture, if not in the earliest days of the relationship then later, the over-sized entrepreneurial personality of the cigar and cigarette wholesaler who later took over Lewis. José de Sola Pinto was born in the East End, a Sephardi Jew, who broke with his family, through whom he claimed connections with Benjamin Disraeli, and with his religion. He had acquired a rich and elderly benefactor, Miss Samuda, when he married her companion. Miss Samuda was the daughter of a wealthy merchant whose family ran a large and successful London shipyard, and she was the source of the capital which propelled him through a full and successful life. His bloodlines were an emulsion of centuries of rabbinical scholarship and physicians from the de Sola side and the down-to-earth business skills of generations of Pintos. (The Sephardi community had long played a prominent role in the city's life. As far back as 1694, de Medina, da Costa, Fonseca, Henriques, Mendez, Nunes, Rodriguez and Texeira de Amatto, most of them merchants who had moved from Amsterdam as the centre of gravity of those early financial markets shifted, figured amongst the more substantial initial shareholders of the fledgling Bank of England.)

De Sola Pinto was described by someone who knew him well as 'a complete actor-manager . . . his expansive almost Falstaffian persona cramped into a too-small frame forever full of himself and nervous energy and as like as not at the drop of a hat to burst into music-hall song.' He was a man who deserves our apprehensive admiration. Though a diabetic, he balanced careful doses of insulin with 'a tumbler full of dry sherry in the morning, two bottles of wine at lunch and another couple at dinner, with quantities of good port afterwards'. He was also well read; a doting, generous and sagacious father, whose royal clientele would have been distinctly unamused to know that he muttered *Vive la République*' as he lumbered unwillingly to his feet when 'God Save the King' was played; a man who brought his cat to work with him in a hansom cab every morning and whose cable address was the cosy 'Intimidad, Piccadilly'. Although it was not until 1890 that he actually bought control of Lewis, his wholesaling business was already substantial and profitable, and it seems far more likely, simply on grounds of personality and background, that he would have listened to Albert at the urging of merchants back in Bessarabia or Bulgaria and maybe sent him on to Lewis. It was a bonus to find out that de Sola Pinto was one of the prime movers in organising the purchase for public enjoyment of the grounds of Golders Hill Park, close by his home, where forty years or so later I had my 'birds and bees' stroll with an embarrassed David Redstone.

Lewis's managers, who ran the shop from day to day, were very much of the West End trade; some of their characteristics are to be found not far from St James's even today. Charles Baxter and William Dodswell appear under the fictional names of 'Craven' and 'James' in the autobiography of de Sola Pinto's son Vivian, a brave First World War subaltern who served under Siegfried Sassoon and was later an eminent literary scholar. Dodswell, a short, heavily built man with glossy hair and 'a way with him' that appealed to the shop's upper-class 'carriage trade', had been 'a particular favourite' of Oscar Wilde. Vivian dismissed Baxter, with an adolescent's snobbery, as 'the type of suburban pseudo-gentleman of the period . . . copies of glossy snob periodicals such as The "Tatler" and "The Sporting and Dramatic" were usually lying around the [Baxter] home and represented, pretty well I think, the [Baxter] mentality.'

Whoever gave Weinberg the orders that launched Sobranie, we have to hope that they found him rather easier to deal with than another of the shop's connections, the aggressive Major Walter Clopton Wingfield, 'late of the 1st Dragoon Guards and a Member of The Honourable Corps of Gentlemen-At-Arms'. Wingfield was the inventor – he actually took out a patent – of a ball game he called 'Sphairistike', which later became more broadly accepted as 'lawn tennis'. He is deservedly less well known for his development of formation bicycling to the strains of Sousa marches, outlined in a book called *Bicycle Gymkhana and Musical Rides*, not a runaway bestseller. Among pipe-smokers however he did receive a certain éclat for his creation of 'Wingfield Tennis Smoking Mixture' pipe tobacco, which Lewis successfully retailed for many years.

Cigarette-smoking was still a taste rather than a habit – men preferred cigars and women hardly smoked at all – and smokers of luxury brands preferred the lighter Egyptian tobacco. But Albert rented a Soho attic, hired a small team of rollers – a trade much preferred by Jewish immigrants to the main alternative of tailoring since they did not have to kick back a percentage of their earnings to the foreman cutter – and was in business. There was one obstacle: buyers of Turkish cigarettes expected that if not actually shipped direct from Turkey, they would at least have come from somewhere abroad, rather than a garret behind Piccadilly Circus. Unfazed, Albert shipped his cigarettes to Belgium and then back to London, now bearing customs' stamps and seals that, if not Ottoman, were at least impressively foreign. In fact 'Turkish' seems to have been applied generically to tobacco grown in any part of the former Ottoman empire, and around the turn of the century Greek merchants had begun to export tobacco from Bulgaria 'under Turkish labels'. The key was in the blending since on its own much 'Turkish' tobacco is said by those who know to have a 'smell reminiscent of used horse bedding', with a nutty 'sweet and sour' flavour that for English palates was mixed with Latakia, a leaf which had been smoke-cured. Whether the customer knew what he was smoking, we can only guess.

In the late 1880s, Albert went home to Bessarabia – whether because he missed his family or to reinforce his tobacco connections, we do not know. When he came back in 1890, coinciding with de Sola Pinto's move into Lewis, it was with a new vision, the inspired choice of a new brand name and new thoughts on how to position and package the product. 'Sobranie' in its various spellings is one of those words which mean slightly different things in various Slavonic languages, though all with the same general sense of 'collection', 'assembly', 'association', 'meeting', even 'officers' mess'. In eighteenth-century Russia it had a distinctly aristocratic connotation. The *Rosiisskoye Blagorodnoye Sobranie*, or Russian Club of the Nobility, founded in 1783, was where the jeunesse dorée of St Petersburg danced and flirted under the beady eyes of their chaperones and parents. Albert actually took it from the title of the Bulgarian Parliament, a sketch of whose grand building appears in the background of some of the company's logos, and it went into smoking history, though language purists might regret that the final 'ie' lost its Slavonic final 'iye' sound and the word became simply 'Sobraahnee' when it was transmuted into tobacconists' English. Hector Monro was a war correspondent for the London *Morning Post* before he became better known as the humorous writer 'Saki'. He found himself observing the democratic process in the Sofia Sobranie one sunny day as, 'in leisurely fashion the members drift into their places, some clad in irreproachable mode, many in primitive and uncompromising peasant garb, and one political grouping affecting the red fez'.

Albert had designed a new package for his brand, a straw basket, but this proved difficult to print on and he turned instead to the porcelain boxes, which, for many of the older generation, remain the most stylish symbol of Sobranie. Several are still on display in Freddy Fox's Room, including three of the 'Jeroboam' of cigarette boxes, about 3 feet wide and 2 feet high, that held 1,000 cigarettes, the smaller 500 boxes, which might be called the 'magnum', and the 100s, which were those most usually seen. They reflect different habits of a time long gone when men did not 'pop down the road for a packet of Players' but bought in bulk, filling their monogrammed cigarette cases from the Sobranie boxes as their Woosterish day unfolded. The porcelain boxes looked and were expensive, and became collectors' items, but as business grew they proved too fragile for a trade that was expanding not just across the UK but also to the further reaches of the Empire, as it was then known, and dependent on the robust porters and stevedores of Carter Patterson, the goods trains and Peninsula and Orient Lines to hump their parcels around.

The image on the lid was evocatively recalled many years later by the journalist Frank Giles, a fan of Turkish cigarettes, as 'a scene of horse-drawn cigarette-laden wagons rolling through the mountains of Macedonia watched by two Balkan ladies in voluminous skirts and headdress, the whole picture redolent of Levantine languor and mystery'. So deep did the sense of mystery and intrigue run in that part of the world that even as the Ottoman empire crumbled to pieces in 1918, its last sultan still employed a eunuch to take the first puff of every cigarette in case it had been poisoned.

The images that excited Frank Giles survive in the UK Patent Office in two confusing formats. The first, registered in 1919, has by far the more detailed artwork but uses the English 'meeting' name. The actual Sobranie image filed in 1933, maybe because of reproduction problems, is far less stylised. The medium of choice became the elegantly printed tin and by 1900 the business was producing 40,000 cigarettes a week.

However, like so many entrepreneurs, Albert's life was becoming complicated. His Viennese wife greatly preferred her home town, still the glittering social and artistic hub of the Austro-Hungarian Empire, and his son also saw himself as Viennese rather than English and had no interest in the trade. So Albert sent down to Akkerman for David's younger brother Shaia, then sixteen, to join him in London and learn the business, and, if he proved himself, to take over the day-to-day management. Whether these included any labour difficulties is doubtful; Sobranie was too small and paternalistic. But the newly formed giant cigarette combines and their thousands of girl workers in the East End of London and Nottingham, who were paid a pittance in piecework, had long been a target of the increasingly militant British trades unions. In 1904, the same Wonderland Hall that was to echo a year later to speeches of support for the Romanovka protest was the venue for equally rowdy meetings by Imperial Tobacco workers, whom the company had 'locked out'.

The House of Sobranie in its early days was more like a mobile home, though Soho – conveniently close to Robert Lewis, who must have been able to order supplies almost on demand – remained its centre of gravity until the late 1930s. This was not the red-light Soho, or the nightclub Soho, or the Carnaby Street Soho of the 'swinging sixties', still less today's Soho of latex underwear and extreme sexual preferences. It was the Soho of artisans, artists, craftsmen, small businesses and cheap restaurants, an area which John Galsworthy found unacceptably un-Forsyte like, though his description evokes Puskhin's vignette of Odessa: 'Untidy, full of Greeks, ishmaelites, cats, Italians, tomatoes, restaurants, organs, coloured stuffs, queer names, people looking out of upstairs windows, it dwells remote from the British Body Politic.' The rash of blue plaques on the buildings today shows the traces of more distinguished figures, too, from Broadwood, the harpsichord and piano maker, via Canaletto, Mozart, Hazlitt and Theodore 'King of Corsica' to Zoffany and Dryden, whose rooms were above what is now the New Loon Fung Supermarket in Gerrard Street, Angelica Kaufman and Karl Marx. As yet, a plaque has still to mark the passing of Muriel Belcher, whose seedy Colony Room bar actually made a considerable if unusual contribution to post-war British culture by providing aid and comfort for so many drunken artists, writers and genuine eccentrics. Little remains now of the past, with a few notable exceptions such as Camisa, the Italian grocery, and the Algerian Coffee Stores, which was founded around the same time as Sobranie and which, in contradiction to its name but happily for those who want to see the real thing, displays on its wall a minutely detailed original 'brick' of compressed Chinese tea.

Sobranie's very first base was at 5 Swallow Street, which intersects Piccadilly almost at the Circus itself. Even in the nineteenth century it was only a stump of a once much longer road wiped away by John

Nash's grandiose Regent Street. In its day, though, it had housed a rather dilapidated inn called 'The Hog and Pound', a livery stable and churches for both the Scottish and Huguenot communities. Today it is a parade of tourist-oriented restaurants. By 1901, Albert had moved about 100 yards across Regent Street to 34 Glasshouse Street; the building is now submerged under the granite side western wall of The Regent Palace Hotel. The warren of rooms there also housed a supplier of trimmings, a fruit merchant, a cigar importer and 'Bat Mullin, Teacher of Boxing'. Just up the street was the London office of the Colt Firearms Company. The next move was to Great Pulteney Street, just a few yards away, where the neighbours were small businesses scratching a living – a silversmith, an engraver, an electroplater and a diamond mounter. According to Albert's British naturalisation papers, he lived for a while at No. 18, of which little is left but a Victorian warehouse façade and the memory that Haydn was recorded as lodging at the same address in 1791–2. Sobranie itself was somewhere in the attics of a row of Georgian houses from 33 to 35, the latter destroyed by a German bomb though its neighbours still stand. Outside No. 34 there is still a pair of brackets from which hang a quarter-scale metal penny-farthing cycle, the trade sign of the cycle shop which stood on the street for fifty years or more, originally providing small businesses with bikes for their delivery boys and mending the frequent punctures and slipped chains. I doubt that Albert, Shaia, or later on David, gave a second's thought to the history of their locale. Why on earth should they? For Sobranie, what mattered were quality and consistency, which meant profit, which meant staying alive. To borrow a catchphrase from a US advertising jingle sixty years later, 'It's the tobacco that counts.'

For his struggle with the Cossacks in Yakutsk, David had wrapped himself in sheepskins and a fur hat. For his own struggles with customers and suppliers, Shaia was given a bowler hat to embody his status as a representative of the House of Sobranie. That it did not fit was secondary; possession of the stiff black melon was nine points of dignity. He was paid eighteen shillings a week and told to learn every aspect of the trade. Albert deducted five shillings for clothing and insisted he put one shilling aside as savings. But frugality had commercial limits. When Albert heard that Shaia was lunching in a cheap chop house where he could get a good meal for three pence, he told him to upgrade to a restaurant where the lunch cost five pence. The food was not as good, but the fellow diners were 'a better class of person' and thus better contacts for the business. In that area the better restaurant could have been one of many, but it is likely that Albert directed Shaia a few steps round the corner to Lyons' Corner House, which had opened in 1895 on the site of what is now the Trocadero complex, once the site of a far seamier rendezvous known as the Argyll Rooms. The Corner House broke new ground, offering clerks and secretaries inexpensive food served by white-aproned waitresses known as 'nippies', against a background of mirrors, decoratively tiled walls and potted palms, while a string quartet battled valiantly to make light music heard over the clatter of plates. Lyons' statistics for its London chain of shops and eateries as a whole contradict the reputation of the British as a tea-drinking nation. They claimed to serve 400,000 cups of coffee a day and sell 600,000 slices of swiss roll a week.

Sobranie's status as what today would be called a 'niche player', a minnow in the ocean in which sharks and whales swam, meant it could sit on the sidelines while the large companies fought each other tooth-and-nail to dominate the mass market. As early as 1902, an attempt by the leading US manufacturer to establish a beachhead by buying up Ogden's, the Liverpool-based makers of 'Guinea Gold', led to a promotional stunt, reckless even by the low standards of such initiatives. They went out to the shopkeepers with the promise that those who committed to give preference to Ogden's brand would share the entire net profit of the company for the next four years, and, as if this was not enough, the pool would be topped up with an annual payment for the same period of £200,000. This was one war the British won. Imperial Tobacco was formed to unite the main UK makers, the American decamped, Ogdens passed into Imperial's hands and was smartly liquidated, making any share of profits rather academic and creating a field day for lawyers. Though the courts concluded that the retailers had a valid claim for the annual £200,000, the liquidator's lawyer F. E. Smith (later Lord Birkenhead), demonstrated great ingenuity – his tactics were later described as 'perhaps less than scrupulous' – by surreptitiously encouraging retailers to make claims. It seems not to have dawned on them that as a result the number sharing in the pool would be greater and each individual payout that much less. At the same time, the legal war of attrition and the cost of defending each new claim meant that the pool was being daily reduced by fees – a useful slice accruing to Smith himself. In the end, as so often happens after the lawyers feel they have taken out as much as the traffic will bear, the case was settled by compromise.

17

Foggy Days in London Town

We are now in late 1907, when David, Manya and baby Nina arrived in London from Chita. Although we know a lot about their later routes, here we have no clue, save that by inference, since their later Far Eastern experiences are obviously new ground for them, we can assume that they came overland across Russia and Germany, retched their way across the North Sea and steamed into Liverpool Street Station exhausted, uncertain but at least together, and with a brother and uncle waiting.

Despite the Home Office efforts – as Canute-like then as now – to push back the tide of immigrants, *Baedeker* records that passports were not required, at least for visitors. Whatever David produced, and whatever he claimed about his plans, it would be surprising if he was not questioned quite carefully when they arrived; he must have bobbed and weaved very skilfully to keep the conversation away from what had happened in Siberia. As early as 1904, as a prelude to the 1905 Aliens Act, the Home Office had pushed through new restrictions, aimed at stemming the tide of East European Jewish immigrants, which broadened the category of those aliens to be refused entry (among them prostitutes and people 'with infectious or loathsome diseases') to include anyone convicted in the previous five years of 'an extraditable crime'. To most minds, what he had been through would not have brought him into that net, but whether 'amnesty' was quite the same as 'innocent' was hardly a debate he wanted to have with officials. No doubt he was armed with a letter of support from his uncle to demonstrate that he at least had a job to go to, but it cannot have been easy.

Had the family arrived a little earlier in the year, they would have coincided with a gathering of most of the once and future icons of the Communist and socialist world, including Rosa Luxemburg, Lenin, Stalin (then still called Djugashvili but using the alias Ivanovich) and Trotsky, who were among the 350 delegates attending the Fifth Congress of the Russian Social Democratic Workers' Party. The choice of venue – the Brotherhood Socialist Church in Shoreditch – was a triumph of hope over subsequent experience; none of the Communist leaders rated 'fraternal feelings' high on their list of priorities in later years as they fought, argued and killed each other. If any of those attending had wanted to stock up for the next wave of the battle, they did not have to look far; among the nearby firms advertising in the *East London Observer* was Messrs H. Dorras, 'Carmen, Contractors, Dealers in Ammunition and Coal Merchants'. But they would have found it hard to slip away unnoticed, dogged as they were by a crowd of curious pressmen and a posse of British and Russian plain-clothes policemen, the latter shipped over by the Okhrana from Paris. It is unkind but tempting to wonder just how much misery the world would have been spared had some capitalist equivalent of the Combat Organisation blown the church to smithereens on the opening day.

Blood being thicker than water, David was taken into the family fold although Shaia was clearly the senior partner. The warmth of his reception may have been tempered with some of the unspoken reservations accorded to a rather prodigal son – in an interview years later he conceded that he was 'something of the family black sheep'. While working on the side as a freelance correspondent for overseas Russian-language newspapers, most likely those serving the émigré community on the Continent, he was put in charge of Sobranie's 'customer relations', which at that time meant writing letters to customers soliciting their orders, answering queries and fielding complaints. Working men were already heavily taken with the smoking habit – W. D. and H. O. Wills had introduced the Wild Woodbine, the world's best-selling cheap cigarette before the turn of the century – and Sobranie and other quality brands continued to make inroads among the chattering classes, even if society ladies were still considered 'fast' if they smoked and were careful to do so only in their own homes.

David and Manya lived at 10 Clarendon Gardens in London's 'Little Venice', so-called because it adjoins the Grand Canal in Maida Vale. It is an address which seems surprisingly *haute bourgeoise* for a newly arrived family of limited means. It is a rather elegant road in an estate first developed in the 1840s and 1850s, and even though some of the houses had been subdivided – two are shown in the 1908 Post Office Directory as 'apartments' – it must have had a certain presence. The cartoonist Osbert Lancaster, an Edwardian-era child living not far away in Notting Hill, captured from his infant memories a sense of how we might see Clarendon Gardens: 'The stucco, creamy and bright, gleamed softly in what in reminisce seems to have been a perpetually cloudless sky. Geraniums in urns flanked each brass-enriched front door, while over the area railings moustachioed policemen made love to buxom cooks'. The Redstones were probably in a set of furnished rooms like those rented by the crooked Mr Golspie in J. B. Priestley's *Angel Pavement*, who dismissed the area as 'stiff with Jews' – it was still far better than the sparsely fitted rooms in Pentonville where Lenin and his wife, Nadezhda Krupskaya, had made their home just a few years earlier, battling with a diet of 'oxtails, skate fried in fat and indigestible cakes not made for Russian stomachs'.

For David and Manya, unlike the cosmopolitan Lenins, it must have been like landing on another planet. London was a city of 4.5 million people, while Chita was still a provincial backwater, even though the Trans-Siberian Railway had boosted Chita's population from the 197,000 recorded in the 1897 census. Russia was a great power, with all the splendid trappings of church and state on display even in provincial cities, but here was majesty of a different scale: the pomp, circumstance, brass bands and bunting of the capital of an empire on which the sun never set, ruler of over 400 million people (little over 10 per cent of them white). They had come to a country that was sure of itself and believed the words of 'Rule, Britannia', for whom war was the memory of the distant victories in South Africa, with no idea of the horrors to come in the fields of Flanders. It was a country that prided itself on being civilised and vaguely Liberal, provided the privileges and incomes of the rich were undisturbed, but at the same time a country which had seen its last public hanging as recently as 1868, when the Fenian Michael Barrett died for his part in an attempt to blow up Clerkenwell Prison. Britain did not abolish flogging as a punishment in the army until 1881 and only got around to demolishing the grim bulk of Newgate Prison in 1902. Though noble families still owned mansions in Park Lane alongside 'statesmen and politicians' (a distinction impossible to draw today), a newspaper of the period deplored that 'of late a tendency has rather manifested itself among prominent financiers and South African multi-millionaires to take up residence in this exclusive quarter . . .'. More meaningful social movement included the first steps towards subsidised secondary education and the old age pension. Liberal attitudes only went so far, however. In an effort to reach out to the working classes, King Edward VII invited two Labour stalwarts to spend the weekend at his country mansion at Sandringham. One brought the wrong evening clothes and found himself dining alone in his bedroom.

Society, when it thought at all, would have been sure that London's centre of gravity was somewhere around Mayfair; financiers would have placed it in the City; and tourists Whitehall or Trafalgar Square. In fact, looking at London as a circle, drawn around the centre of maximum population density, the epicentre of my grandparents' London back then was Rotherhithe, not really surprising given its great docks, but not what one might have expected.

The Redstones' world was grey, gritty and hazy, fuelled by coal and mainly lit by gas; as they travelled about London, they could hardly have missed 'Jumbo', the 5 million ton telescopic iron gas storage tank known as a 'gasometer', built in Vauxhall in 1906. The climate was more extreme than today. In the winter, the city could be blanketed for days in heavy swirling fog, the 'London Particular', in which an innocent passer-by looming up shadow-like on a dim side street in a heavy greatcoat, with the shoulder cape flapping like wings, would bring spine-chilling thoughts of Jack the Ripper. The temperature regularly stayed below freezing for long enough that there were skating clubs on the Serpentine, Regent's Park Lake, Hampstead Heath and the various London reservoirs. In contrast, the image of those long, languorous Edwardian summers of straw-berries, cream, croquet and country-house copulation may not be just a fond delusion; looking back through social diaries, there certainly seem to have been far more outdoor events – picnics, regattas, croquet, steamer trips – than today's summers would encourage. Though the buses carried advertising for Nestlé, Bovril and Pears soap, all still around today, the riptide of the consumer age had still to roll across the Atlantic from the US, which was already revelling in Coca-Cola, Shredded Wheat, peanut butter and Campbell's Condensed Soups.

The humble horse was still to be seen everywhere, pulling the shiny carriages of the rich, the four-passenger 'growlers' and the hansom cabs, their drivers mounted high at the back behind the curved roof of their two-seater compartment. They charged two shillings to travel up to four miles from Charing Cross, and double rate beyond. There were 'knife board' omnibuses (or, as Thomas Carlyle insisted, 'omnibi'), with ladies travelling inside and men on the top deck. There were canvas-hooded wagons, making way with difficulty for the jangling horse-drawn fire engines with their brass pumps and seven-man team in equally bright brass helmets, or ebony-black horse-drawn hearses with black plumes on the roof; 'mutes' to walk stone-faced alongside dressed from top to toe in black drab and carrying black-draped staves were an optional extra. Horses left pungent droppings in their plodding wake, and 'street orderlies' darted nimbly through the traffic with shovel and bucket to keep the streets clean. Horses needed water so, before the filling-station era, each main London artery and many squares had stone water troughs installed at regular intervals. Horses made noise, and wealthier house-owners laid straw down in the street outside if someone inside was sick or dying. Robert Lewis kept a cask of shag tobacco just inside its front door for any hansom cab or carriage driver who brought a customer to take a free fill of his pipe.

Though the Central Underground Line from Bank to Shepherds Bush, nicknamed the 'Tu'penny Tube' since it charged a flat 2d fare, had been opened in 1900, London's age of urban sprawl still lay ahead. In 1902, the Lenins, in sharp contrast to the havoc they would soon let loose upon the wider world, would relax by cycling up the Archway Road into the countryside to eat their sandwiches on the grassy hillsides. A young boy growing up circa 1906 in a wealthy home on the edge of what was then the city's northern fringe wrote that he and a groom from the local livery stable would ride on horseback 'over Hampstead Heath to Barnet, Finchley, Edgware and Highgate. We would canter along soft unmetalled roads and bridle paths and sometimes do some jumping over hedges and ditches in lonely meadows.' On one outing they even went 'to a meet at Barnet and followed the hunt for a few miles'. Most buses were still horse-drawn and the first Rolls Royce 'Phantom' glided onto the streets in 1906, although Austin and several smaller car-makers were already in business. The private automobile still meant status and wealth. Goggled Mr Toads roared out of London and the major cities through narrow country lanes, raising clouds of dust, frightening animals, sending the locals scurrying for cover, and arguably sharpening the resentment felt by countrymen for 'townies'.

The first motor taxis were already nibbling at the monopoly of the hansom cabs, and the horses that had plodded through the streets pulling trams were giving way to electric power from overhead cables; George V as Prince of Wales had travelled in the first electric tram across Westminster Bridge in 1905, and by 1910 London had 120 miles of tram track and their overhead power cables. Though hot-air ballooning had been a fashionable sport for the rich and foolhardy, air travel for the Redstones was something out of H. G. Wells. It was not until 1909 that Bleriot's flimsy plane sputtered across the Channel in 37 minutes, bringing yet another dimension to travel as well as to warfare.

For Manya, London was foreign and overwhelming. It was exile – an exile which, in its own way, may have been even harder for her than David's Siberian experience, which had at least been warmed by the fire of idealism, and the loneliness and danger had been shared with a tightly knit group. She had never before been outside Siberia, or away from her family. She spoke no English. David was out all day, while she was at home trying to cope. It is impossible to know how much English David himself then spoke but, as he was a quick learner and had to handle the Sobranie office correspondence, he must have managed quite well. And it must have been far easier for him. He was with family and working in a part of London with some resemblances, weather apart, to the foreign bustle of Odessa. Manya had been a professional woman, respected in her community; now she was a moping Maida Vale mother.

On the streets there were organ grinders, bell-ringing muffin men, their trays balanced on their heads, seat caners and men carrying sandwich boards advertising household polish or 'The End of the World'. There were knife-sharpeners and umbrella-menders, known for some reason as 'mush-fakers'. There were flower girls, with their trademark hoop earrings and white shoes, and pavement artists who produced winsome images of children and cats in coloured chalk on the flagstones. There were even itinerant locksmiths, whose complex equipment as shown in an old photograph suggests again that this was not the correct translation of David's trade. Manya would have pushed Nina in her high-wheeled bassinette past Punch and Judy shows, with hook-nosed puppets jerking across the high shelf of a striped canvas booth, yelling and beating each other with clubs and strings of sausages, and ending on the gallows, in a not so parodic imitation of English working-class life. If they had seen any of the fur-hatted men who led huge brown 'dancing bears' around suburban streets, Nina would have gurgled in a mix of fright and delight but Manya might have thought of home, where bears roamed dangerously but free and were in mythical form objects of worship. Neither would have made much of the street reciter, a popular figure whose speciality was reeling off the works of Shakespeare backwards. Herself a demonstrator and a radical's wife, Manya may have had more than a sneaking sympathy for the Suffragettes (a term coined by the *Daily Mail*), who noisily chained themselves to railings for the sake of the women's vote and were force-fed with gruel by muscular wardresses when they went on hunger strike in Holloway Jail.

Instead of the snow-capped ridges of the Yablonovyi Mountains and the sunny meadows below, there was Hyde Park, with its swarming green stretches, nannies with high-wheeled prams grouped around the white-pillared bandstand while 'bassoon, flute and euphonium' produced their medley of middle-class melodies, and the boating lake crammed with cheerfully splashing Cockneys. At Speakers' Corner both Manya and David would have been surprised at the freedoms given to passionate tub-thumpers to rant about their political ideas and religious beliefs, some violent, some just plain odd, while the police looked on benignly. Instead of Siberia's extraordinary range of birds – over 300 in an ornithologist's 1900 count – and the cranes that migrated south in August 'steering with harsh screams towards the lonely Mongolian steppe', there were scruffy sparrows, preening pigeons and cawing crows. Men wore hats as a matter of course, and even the smallest boys had cloth caps; on the pavements Manya saw a sea of bobbing black bowlers and Homburgs instead of Evenk fur hoods and beaded Buryat skullcaps. The exotica from the East piled in her father's trading compound and kerchiefed old crones in the Nerchinsk market-place stalls selling spices and mushrooms were now replaced by shops called 'butchers' and 'greengrocers'. Shopping was an alien experience in an alien tongue. Even the weights were alien and the greengrocers' helpful prompt, 'Them's tuppence a pound, luv,' must have been incomprehensible, all the more since, though the Russians used *'funt'* as a measure, an untuned ear might well confuse it with *'pood'*, or 36 pounds. It was also a battle with money. Though Bank of England notes circulated in larger denominations, coins were the stuff of everyday life. There were gold sovereigns, silver crowns, half crowns, florins, shillings, and six- and three-penny pieces (which to confuse the foreigner even more were known respectively as a 'bob', a 'tanner' and a 'joey'). Today small change is a nuisance. In those halcyon times before inflation, bronze coins had value, and Manya would have had to sift through her purse for pennies, half-pennies and the humble farthing. To compound confusion, though it had gone out of circulation as a coin, the guinea, worth one pound and one shilling, was still used by doctors and lawyers as a genteel unit of currency to jack up their bills. Cigarettes were one thing Manya did not need to buy. Just as well, since in most little shops of the time, she would have had to ask for 'fags' – a word derived from the useless tail end of a piece of cloth clattering out of a weaving loom – to make herself understood.

For more important shopping there were the big stores. In the West End, Waring and Gillow had joined Marshall & Snellgrove and Swears & Wells in the transformation of Oxford Street into a shopping centre with the American Gordon Selfridge (who claimed to have invented the motto, 'The customer is always right') close on their heels. Like the Underground magnate Yerkes, Selfridge had started his career in Chicago. Did Manya dare venture to these new retail Meccas, with their glass-roofed balconied halls and hydraulic lifts, money hissing mysteriously from the counters to the cashiers and back again down pneumatic tubes or zipping across the heads of shoppers in brass containers propelled along an overhead wire by the salesgirls' sharp tug on a handle? Even getting to them must have been a trek, with streets laid out haphazardly and blank-faced men and women who usually did not understand her when she asked for directions, and, if they answered, did so in a 'nasal monotone', mentioned by more than one émigré, that was hard to follow. Closer to hand in Queensway, William Whiteley might have been a more comfortable store for her, a bustling emporium offering 'everything from a pin to an elephant'.

It was not just the shopping, the weather, and the language. Siberian homes were drum-tight against the cold and, if anything, overheated. English doors and windows never fitted, and draughts knifed through even the thickest curtains. Manya had grown up with huge log-fed tiled stoves sending out rolling waves of heat day and night, and homes where every chink between the timber balks was hermetically sealed with moss. Here, even though 'Blair's Pills' promised with glib sincerity swift relief for sufferers from rheumatism, she had to cope with sullen grates, chimneys which gusted thick smoke back into the rooms when the wind changed direction, and the new world of coal. The pavement of Clarendon Gardens and almost every other London street was punctuated by cast-iron covers, often embellished with fancy scrollwork, through which the Rickett & Cockerill coalman, an oilskin hat with a deep back flap hanging over his shoulders to stop chafing, sent bag after bag of Wallsend Derby Brights or Best Gas Coke rumbling down into the cellar in a cloud of dust.

At home there was no radio or television, just a wind-up gramophone and perhaps a piano. Not everything was old-fashioned, however. Impertinent lads from the Post Office, pillbox caps on their heads, delivered telegrams at all hours of the day and much of the night, and there were between six and twelve mail deliveries a day. David borrowed books weekly from the middle-class setting of Boots or Mudies Libraries. He had a choice of several serious newspapers – 'top people', in the words of a much later advertising campaign, took *The Times*, which was still able to command a premium 3d, three times the price of rivals such as the *Telegraph*, the *Daily News* and the *Morning Post*. Manya may have flicked through the effervescent *Daily Mail*, famously dismissed in its early days by Lord Salisbury as 'written by office boys for office boys', or one of the many illustrated journals targeted at women. Several reading rooms had a selection of European and Russian newspapers available for a modest entry fee.

In the outside world there were galleries, concerts and London's fifty theatres, which around that time seemed to be offering an extensive range of deservedly forgotten operettas. The raucous music halls, of which London had some five hundred, were not for the Redstones, nor the pubs, where a glass of beer cost 1½d. They might have allowed themselves the occasional meal at a local café, where a 'small plate of hot meat with bread and vegetables' could be had for around 6d, the same price as a pint of claret or hock. Sport – football, boxing, cricket, or horseracing, the pastime of costermongers as much as kings – would have left David cold, though it did not escape Baedeker's eagle eye that baseball, unlikely though it seems, was 'played extensively in the Midlands counties'. He also gives more page space to rugby than association football, merely noting that the best venues for the latter were Crystal Palace and the 'Essex County Ground at Leyton'. The cinema was only just beginning to be an alternative. In 1906, Gaumont opened The Daily Bioscope in a converted shop in Bishopsgate, offering 120 seats at 2d and 4d, and a special show for office workers between 1 and 2 p.m. It was intended less as a move into popular entertainment than as a showcase where music-hall operators and entrepreneurs from around the country could see the potential of the new idea, and be persuaded to buy their projectors and rent their newsreels from the Gaumont firm. It succeeded. During the Redstones' first spell in London, cinemas mushroomed, though it was a different experience; one early house had a violinist, the manager was the part-time pianist and the audience was shown to its seats by a 'page boy'.

On a different level, Manya may have found solace in the Greek Chapel (Russian) in Cavendish Square and could equally well have followed familiar rituals at the Greek Orthodox church, not far from Whiteley's store; its address was Moscow Road, while the closest synagogue was equally nostalgically located in St Petersburg Place.

Clarendon Gardens is the address David and Manya gave when registering the birth of my mother on 4 September 1909. They recorded her name as Sofia, the Greek for 'wisdom'. It is also the capital of Bulgaria, location of the original Sobranie building shown on that early logo. Whether she was just indulging a teenage whim, whether she was teased, I have no idea, but at some stage 'Sofia' began to grate, and my mother became first 'Sonya' and later 'Sonia'.

18

Back to the Future

David and Manya had separate versions of what triggered their next move. With Sonia just a few months old, David left Sobranie and took the family all the way back to Siberia. Clarendon Gardens had turned out to be just another *étape* on their exile journey.

In later years David would laugh off this risky about-turn as being prompted by no more than his aversion to the British weather. With all respect to him, from a man who claimed that he had left Siberia because the climate was too harsh, this strikes an unconvincing note. Surely even a London February, with the damp cold seeping through the soles of his shoes, and the leaden sky pressing down on the rooftops, must have seemed like Hawaii compared to a winter east of the Urals, though, to be fair, even Lenin, who also knew at first hand what Siberia was like, thought the British weather 'disgusting'. However, it may not have been wholly untrue. Both my grandparents had grown up with light – in David's case, sparkling off the sea; in Manya's, clear icy blue skies above the mountains. Living in light myself these past years I realise that, like plants, humans can become phototropic, drawn to the light, so that perpetual twilight, cloud and fog become a serious deprivation.

As related to her awe-struck grandchildren half a century later (though she muddled up the name of the hospital), Manya's story of what forced the move is more circumstantial. She told us that my mother's birth had been the final straw – literally. In those days most women gave birth at home; the risk of cross-infection meant that the infant mortality rate in hospitals was almost three times higher, and the 'lying in-hospitals', like Queen Charlotte's, then in Lisson Grove, where my mother first saw the grey light of a London day, took in the poor and the legion of 'fallen' women. Queen Charlotte's original charter spoke starkly of providing 'an asylum for indigent females during the awful period of childbirth'. In their later lives Nina was always early in everything, my mother more casual. But Sonia, my mother, started into the world well ahead of time, and though David had arranged for a doctor to attend, he had gone out of London on a Sobranie trip and Manya had no idea who to call or where to find him. It must have been her landlady or a neighbour who bundled her off to Queen Charlotte's. It was a dialogue of the deaf: her mix of pidgin English and Russian versus what she remembered as the impenetrable Irish brogue of the nurses, compounded by the hauteur of the ward sister convinced that another indigent foreigner was trying to pull a fast one by claiming special treatment. A carefully posed contemporary photograph of one of the small, gas-lit wards shows it to be tidy, the floor clean and sparkling, with a nurse in starched cowls and the patients neatly squared away under their blankets with not a baby in sight. Manya's recollection, still vivid forty years later for the grandchildren, was very different: Dickensian grime, screams and, above all, straw mattresses, with their painful memories of Irkutsk Jail.

When David finally turned up, so her story went, she had made up her mind. She would not stay in this awful country any more. If he wanted to stay in England, fine, but she was heading home. When later in life I learned Russian myself, it was a delight and a mild shock to know that her repertoire in her native tongue included words that silver-haired ladies were not generally believed to know, let alone to use, and I can imagine that the message was delivered with some pungency.

Perhaps there were factors beyond just keeping Manya happy and the family together. David may have been frustrated with his junior role in the Sobranie business. Maybe he thought he had a role to play in the next stage of the revolutionary struggle. It was a hard choice for a radical with two infant children. Back in Russia the tide was again running in the direction of repression and, though he had been amnestied, David's name was surely still inked in a police file as 'politically unreliable'. Nonetheless, many Russian émigrés did return around this time for whatever reason; a Friendly Society was formed to raise money for those who could not afford the fare.

In any event, early in 1910 the Redstones returned, not to Odessa but to Chita, to Manya's family rather than his, suggesting that homesickness really did lay heavy on her. Their most likely route would have been across the North Sea to Bremen or Hamburg (a stomach-heaving forty-hour voyage) and weeks in trains across Prussia, Poland and Russia. For David, the last leg into Siberia must have been an eerie retracing as a free man of his frightening voyage into exile.

It was the Kuznetsov Museum on the other side of the world which provided the clue as to why they went there. Having become used to David's name appearing in the Romanovka literature, I had vaguely hoped, though not expected, that some further trace of him would be found there. I was not disappointed. But I was elated when they unearthed yet another find, a single sheet of paper written years after his death about the life and work of Manya's brother Pavel. I had known nothing about him and had no idea of his prominence or his career, but suddenly there he was on the stage. When the Redstones went back, Manya armed with her nursing and midwifery skills, Pavel, then 23, was just about to graduate with honours from Siberia's leading medical school, and was thus well placed to help her find work and provide moral if not material support. Pavel, we find, was not just a medical man noted for his 'high level of education, humanitarianism and commitment to [his] medical duties', but like his two sisters had a liberal if not rebellious streak. He was one of those in his graduating class who signed a protest against the death penalty and declared that they would never participate as doctors in any executions. His first surgery was in a little railway town, but by 1912 he had transferred to the Chita City Hospital. (In the First World War, he served as medical officer in the local unit of the Eastern Siberian heavy artillery division, and he and David must have shared some strangely contrasting stories of life among the gunners.)

Manya worked in her brother's hospital, eventually becoming the Matron. We know from family anecdote and brief mentions in some of the literature, as well as by inference from the fact that he took shorthand notes at the Romanovka trials, that David was a journalist. That is another term that has become significantly debased in today's coinage. Back then it meant a serious contributor of commentary, reviews and the more light-hearted but still elegant and classically based pieces known in another French borrowing as *feuilletons*. I had not dreamed of being able to go much further than this in finding out what he actually did, but the Kuznetsov Museum came riding to the rescue again like a curatorial Seventh Calvary, revealing yet another doll, David the Man of Learning. In addition to his writing, he was secretary of the Transbaikal section of 'The Society for the Study of Siberia and Improvement of Its Way of Life'. Described in local archives as 'Economist and Man of Letters', he also worked for the Chita Export Chamber of Commerce and his writing covered a gamut of topics. 'Letters from England' and 'Letters from Germany' were probably synopses of news from abroad. Closer to home he wrote on the local economy, the Co-operative Movement and 'The Role of the Russian Union of Contributors to Periodicals'. 'The War and New Trade Ties' was a timely piece for 1914, as later was 'The Workers' Issue in Transbaikal'. It was the habit in Europe and Russia that contributors often used pen names, mainly to dodge the censor but sometimes also to give the impression that the paper had a larger stable of contributors. For David to sign a piece with the Russian letters spelling 'D. R-n' was thin cover, but 'D. Krasnov' ('David The Red') was a nice joke. How delightful, though, that his third pen name was one only the family would understand. 'Soninirksy' combines Son[ia] and Nin[a] and it is an odd feeling that all those years later, as the only one left in the family who reads Russian, it fell to me quite by chance to spot and record it, less as a fact of any historical value whatever, but in the vague hopes that some future grandchild or great-grandchild might think it cute!

He also wrote for local newspapers. It is extraordinary that, after all that Chita has been through, carefully bound volumes of the local liberal daily *Zabaikal'skii Nov'* ('Transbaikal News') going back to the turn of the last century should still exist. The top half of the front page of the edition for Sunday 11 August 1911, is a patchwork of theatre and variety advertisements. How strange to think that David and Manya might have gone to see *Saved on the Steps of the Scaffold*, or what translates almost exactly as *The Little House on the Prairie*, with its 'beautiful and touching scenes from American life'. But for no reason I can put my finger on, it was a distinctly curious feeling to read his article on one of the inside pages. It was not the content – a report on British dock strikes culled from Reuters' cables and written with restrained sympathy for the strikers. It was more the sense of hearing 'a voice from beyond the grave' – as if I had found some long-discarded wax cylinder with a scratchy recording of his voice. To give colour to his story he datelines it London and quotes an imagined conversation 'with a tram conductor I know' about the prospect for a successful General Strike, acceptable journalistic licence at one level and at another a twist which in this case rings true. David was always charming, ready for a chat and interested in people. I have no doubt at all that when he and Manya were living in Maida Vale, he did indeed take a tram to Soho at the same time every day – he was always a meticulous timekeeper – seeing the same conductor several times a week, and talking to him about everything under the sun. The bearded refugee with a prison past, and the Cockney conductor worrying about the future; I have no doubt it happened.

David then moved on to the *Zabaikal'skii Rabochii*, the newspaper whose creation as an illegal broadsheet we noted in the brief history of the Chita Republic, when its prime mover was 'The Marksman' of the Romanovka, Kurnatovsky. Was this the long arm of coincidence? Whatever the facts, I am sure my mother took childish pleasure in knowing that her father's newspaper office was on Sofia Street, with her own Christian name up there on the painted sign for all to see.

The family lived first in Chita itself and then in a country village. They were there through war and revolution, some of the most troubled years in Russia's history. And yet when we read Nina's memories of their life, apart from a few troubled days at the outbreak of war, it was not until the very end that the outside world pushed its snout into their placid lives. The family must have had 'abundant parnassah', since Manya had taken the children to Livadia on the Crimea, the summer home of the Tsars, for a holiday when David cabled them to come back urgently because the war had started. It was easier said than done, but, though nerve-racking, the journey must have been relatively easy compared to the perilous voyages they would undertake later. Portraits of my mother and Nina, sympathetically caught by a woman photographer, E. Konovalova, in Chita in 1916, show them as every inch the bourgeois, neatly dressed with lace collars, calm and serious. To make a leap of imagination from another anonymous Siberian street photograph taken that summer, with a classical background of two loitering black-robed priests, a carpenter with his saw and a gaggle of workmen, Nina might well have promenaded in a young girl's version of a sailor suit, with a little white pom-pom hat, a white blouse, a dark blue skirt with a band of white lace about two inches above the hem, itself demurely at mid-calf, her hair hanging loose over the deep 'sailors' collar. A girl of my mother's age can be seen in a high-waisted light linen frock, a straw hat and long gloves, while two mothers parade gravely, much as Manya would have done, in dresses that sweep the ground, their hats crowned with bursts of artificial flowers. A studio portrait of David around the same time gives the same impression – settled, a man if not of property then of gravitas and standing.

His first teenage dash to freedom had been on the iron rails out of Odessa; for him, the train had been both an instrument of banishment and a route to freedom. Now it was a subject for research: he was nominated by the Transbaikal Section of the Russian Geographical Society to produce a paper making the case for a new railway line from Chita, across the rocky Ulun plateau and through the mountain range to the gold-mining centre of Bodaibo, some 400 miles to the north-east on the Vitim River, with the aim of capturing an important new stream of traffic. Though the idea was widely discussed and supported at the time, St Petersburg claimed that it did not have the funds to pay for a survey party and the project remained a dream – a dream of which, like so much else, David never spoke.

It is even more ironic that David should find himself taking a dispassionate professional interest in yet another bloodstained location. Remote Bodaibo had been the setting in 1912 of a large-scale massacre of striking workers at the Lena River Gold Mines. Though listed on the Stock Exchange in London and with many British investors on its register, the company which owned the mine was controlled by the Russian de Gunzburg banking family and run by a local management whose exploitation and inhumanity were remarkable for their harshness even by the standards of the time. They urged the local gendarmes to open fire as the strikers milled around the plant, killing 170 and wounding close to 150 more. The Europe-wide outcry to which David may have contributed as a correspondent for foreign newspapers was not helped by the glacial mantra of tsarist Minister Makarov that, 'This is how it always was, and this is how it is always going to be.' He was more right than he knew.

Nina's notes of family life were later scribbled in shorthand form for a lecture but they are all the more vivid for it. She remembered:

Four Seasons. . .
Autumn . . . wild geese, all birds, sparrows and swallows fly away. Rain for one month in September. Preparation for winter – jams, preserves, pickles – all kinds of veg. and fowl put in cellars [which served in Siberia as year-round freezers, chilled by large blocks of ice cut from the rivers in winter]. Cattle taken into sheds. Very little fresh milk in winter – frozen, bought by the pound. Cattle and horses small but very fast and hardy. Double windows put in, doors padded with felt. Piles of wood prepared for the stoves.
Winter. Starts almost at once . . . middle of October. By the end of October the rivers freeze up solidly. Snow falls in December, January and February, nearly always 50 degrees below zero but very sunny and dry . . . all country cottages and many town houses built of wooden logs . . . for warmth. Life in villages very lonely – between 100–200 miles apart locked and isolated by snow.

Life in towns, interesting in those years – because of many political prisoners, who were the cream of the intelligentsia of

Russia – because of isolation – Many parties – all holidays & birthdays celebrated with a great deal of food, wine & innumerable glasses of tea – singing all sorts of folk songs – still remember quite a few, & always talk on politics. Almost the first words I learned were 'Social Democracy'. Because of the isolation – latest books ordered & discussed, travelling theatre groups were the greatest event & a small town like Chita had its own opera house & I heard my first opera 'Snow Maiden' there.

One of the nicest things I remember is riding in a sleigh in snow with bells jingling & coming into warm house.

Spring . . . Breaking up of the ice on the river. Swallows return – special 'Swallow Sunday' for children. Windows opened out, houses prepared for Spring. Snow melts. Masses of flowers – crocii all over the fields – very lush & beautiful.

Summer . . . June–August very hot. Marvellous flowers. Peonies, lilies & even wild orchids – no roses. Berries of all sorts, apples & pears but no apricots, peaches or oranges or bananas. [Had] never seen a banana until I came to Japan. Everyone gathers wild strawberries, red & black currants, blueberries, mushrooms. Long expeditions into the woods for 2–3 weeks . . . Catching fish – cooking fish over open fire. Sleep in the open on pine needles – lovely life. Lived in small village – very simple life – always eating outside & visits from many friends – lovely singing & balalaika in the moonlight in the garden.

Travel by horses – covered wagon – stop in inns – masses of food – never travel after Sept. as wolves come & in the Winter wolves come to the villages.

As Nina recalled, Siberia was not infected by the endemic anti-Semitism of Mother Russia, and that when she was first exposed to it – she does not tell us where – it was a 'great shock'.

It is sad to write of a new human life that we do not know when David and Manya's third child, Valentin, was born, but it was probably around 1912 or 1913. His life was sad: as a toddler he was knocked over by a carriage and contracted tuberculosis of the hip, which spread fast and meant that in the difficult times that lay ahead he was bedridden. Although his parents could never for an instant have thought of him that way, he was an extra worry and responsibility when the troubles started a few years later.

During his years in Chita, David would surely have spotted in the press names he had known in the past appearing in new contexts. Alexsandr Zarudny's career continued to flourish. He was one of Trotsky's defence lawyers at the trial of the Petrograd Soviet in 1906, and in 1913 was a leading member of the team that secured the acquittal of Mendel Beilis, the Jewish foreman of a Kiev brick kiln, who was falsely accused of the 'ritual murder' of a Christian child. It was a victory won against all odds from a Russian jury not predisposed, to put it mildly, to give Jews the benefit of the doubt, and in spite of the crude stacking of the deck of evidence by the authorities who in fact knew from the outset that the murder had been committed by local thugs. Indeed, the local police chief had over-confidently cabled his superiors that, although the case against Beilis was flimsy, the jury would still find him guilty because of 'their hostility towards his race'.

As the war rolled bitterly along, David would also have seen news of Chita's nemesis, General Rennekampf. His role in the Russo–Japanese War has been described by one historian as 'undistinguished' and, more critically, his failure to provide support at a key moment was blamed for the Russian defeat at Tannenberg in 1914. The Germans took 100,000 prisoners and Rennekampf's Commander-in-Chief, General Samsonov, took his life. The Germany victory, which was even more symbolic as a reversal of the defeat the Teutonic Knights suffered in the same spot at the hands of Slav armies in 1410, escalated into charges of incompetence and treason – Rennenkampf was a Baltic German by birth – and he was thrown out of office.

The Chita telegraph wires would have hummed with satisfaction in December 1916 with news of the murder of the dissolute monk Rasputin, whose mesmeric hold on the Tsarina Alexandra had the Court and Russia terrified. The news of his assassination by a group of aristocrats flashed around the world. It is doubtful that even the imaginative compilers of the Reuters codebook had come up with a phrase which quite covered the totality of the act, requiring as it did poison-filled cakes, pistol shots, clubbing and immersion of the still twitching prelate in the frozen Neva River before he finally died. (Many years later, the group's leader, Prince Yousupoff, commented sadly that, 'We killed the wrong man. We should have killed Lenin. And Trotsky.')

The news travelled wider than those in power had hoped, due, it seems, to the grief of the Tsarina. She had become widely unpopular not only because she had fallen under Rasputin's spell but also because as 'Nemka', or 'The German Woman' (Duchess of Hesse and a granddaughter of Queen Victoria), she was thought to have, at best, divided loyalties in the war. Now distraught, as The Times corre-spondent in St Petersburg, Robert Wilton, wrote privately to his editor in London, she had decided to flout the Court consensus that 'the matter should be hushed up as far as possible'. Wilton wondered 'whether it is perhaps time for us to speak out . . . the young Empress and her clique of women have evidently got the reins entirely in their own hands and the Emperor is being blindly driven into acts that will sooner or later precipitate grave disorders unless a palace revolution averts a general smother [sic]. Unless everybody is grievously mistaken we have only two or three months left in which to take decisive and energetic measures. After that anything can happen. What everybody hopes is that before that interval is over the people who are responsible for playing pranks [sic] with the destiny of the country will have been removed . . .'

Events rolled towards their climax like a Trans-Siberian express train careering full tilt towards the buffers, the frock-coated signal-room staff in St Petersburg tugging in panic at any brass-handled lever that came to hand, bereft of maps or new ideas. In the words of an earlier tsarist minister, 'The paralytics in the government are struggling feebly, indecisively, as if unwillingly with the epileptics of the revolution.'

A rising tide, eventually to become a tidal wave, of desertions from the demoralised army and a population growing hungrier because agricultural workers had been sent to the front – and what food supplies there were had become bogged down in a railway system collapsing under the weight of military traffic – led to strikes and demonstrations in St Petersburg, and on 11 March 1917 Wilton's predictions came true. The Tsar abdicated, writing in his diary the laconic epitaph: 'Good, long sleep. It is cold, and the sun is shining.' The sense this gives of the real man hopelessly trapped inside the gilded carapace is reinforced by the comments of Harry Burrough, whose first impressions of Odessa were quoted earlier and who had seen the Tsar at close range at a ceremony in Sevastopol. 'I could not believe my eyes,' he wrote some forty years later. Though the Tsarina was 'queenly', her husband, 'whose name meant terror and authority across Russia, was a small fearful man . . . his face was careworn, almost haggard. His step and bearing were nervous, apprehensive . . .'

Among the many wrong-footed by the Emperor's sudden abdication was Chita's other nemesis, General Meller-Zakomelsky, of the second armoured train. A few weeks earlier he had been dispatched to England with a leather steamer trunk loaded with decorations that his Imperial Master had awarded to British officers. When he reached London, he was given a lavish formal dinner of welcome, with the distribution of the enamelled and ribboned Orders in the names of various obscure Saints due two days later. Neither hosts nor the guest of honour were aware of the drama being played out in St Petersburg. In the light of events, the medals were not handed out but vanished without trace. Many probably found their way to Paris, where in the 1920s, Russian émigrés working as nightclub doormen and cab drivers were anxious to demonstrate a touch of nobility to reinforce their luxuriant white whiskers. The General died in exile. General Rennekampf, commander of the other armoured train, was less fortunate. The vengeful Reds caught him in 1918 and promptly shot him out of hand.

Meanwhile, the Redstones' life in Chita had daily been growing more difficult. As in the rest of Russia, food supplies were short. Between 1914 and 1918 the value of the rouble had depreciated by 80 per cent without any increase in incomes. Money was fast replaced by barter, which soon established its own 'exchange rates' – 1 kilo of soap, for instance, was worth 2½ kilos of fat. 'Food riots' and looting across Transbaikal broke out. The workday was increased to twelve hours or more, overtime became broadly compulsory, and trouble-making workers were fired and 'put at the disposal of the military authorities'. This did not prevent major industrial unrest.

Interviewed in the 1980s for BBC TV's *Timewatch* programme, Nina remembered how the news of the abdication struck a ten-year-old girl: 'We shouted revolutionary slogans, had parties, everyone congratulating each other that the revolution was here at last. At school we sang revolutionary songs . . . though I didn't know what all the words meant. Everything was absolutely marvellous . . . for about six months.' That short-lived rush of hope and joy was universal among the peasants still left in the villages and the hundreds of thousands squatting in muddy trenches waiting to go home: they all felt that the land they toiled on would soon be theirs. Those who owned the land, the factories, the banks, mines and department stores could be forgiven for feeling less euphoric. William Gerhardie, the British author born in Russia to an English mill-owning family and attached at the time to the Embassy in St Petersburg, observed with a clumsy double negative that: 'Not one Englishman in the Embassy was not enthusiastic. It is exhilarating to see something cumbersome at last overthrown and the long-suffering underdog yelping with delight . . . The Tsar fell like Humpty Dumpty – so quickly and painlessly that his best friends could not suppress a smile.'

On 3 April, Lenin returned to Russia from Switzerland in a sealed train 'like a plague bacillus', in Churchill's phrase, his safe conduct across Germany negotiated by the arch-fixer Parvus, who persuaded the Germans that Lenin could and would stop the war. To over-summarise a complex chain of events, there followed two provisional governments, the second run by the ineffectual wordsmith Kerensky (whose father had been Lenin's headmaster), an attempt to arrest Lenin, a failed coup by General Kornilov, and only then the Bolshevik coup d'état in the capital and Moscow. Even then there was no clean sweep by the Bolsheviks across the entire country and no wholesale replacement of pictures of the royal family by images of Lenin and Trotsky managing to look simultaneously intellectual and heroic. It was to take many years and much blood to cement the new regime in place. Russia was still at war, haemorrhaging horribly, with millions of young men dead or prisoners of war, and hundreds of thousands more starting to throw down their guns and desert. There were the powerful White Armies still to contend with and, after the unilateral armistice with Germany, the interventionist forces of Russia's erstwhile allies, desperate to keep her in the war and anxious to do what they could in support of the Whites to prevent the creation of a Communist state. Russia's need for army officers may be a more substantive reason than liberal conscience why one of Kerensky's first acts was to abolish the restrictions on Jews being granted commissions. Many Jewish teenagers came forward to join cadet schools, by Solzhenitsyn's account; and Captain Tsam must have smiled in his grave. In some cities the Bolsheviks joined forces with the Socialist Revolutionaries and the Mensheviks; in others they grabbed control for themselves and hung on for dear life, much of it other people's. Many of the borderlands, however, including much of Siberia – still overwhelmingly rural and without a working-class core – would take much force and time to fall into their hands. It is a nice topic for one of the new wave of 'What if . . .?' quasi-histories to speculate what might have happened in Siberia had Russia itself not been engulfed by revolution; quite probably not very much, and it might well have muddled on for decades, even ended up independent.

19

Maelstrom

When David and Manya first went to Chita after David's release, the town was roiled by struggle. At that time it was between the supposedly irresistible forces of revolution and the supposedly immovable forces of the Tsar. After their return and the remission of their placid family years, the cancer of strife metastasised into a battle with many sides, like some international tag-wrestling tourney at the old Wonderland Hall in Whitechapel.

The year 1917 saw the start of a fight to the death not only between Bolsheviks and Mensheviks, but also between many local and international factions. Despite the distortions of history, the supposed 'clean sweep' of righteous Red triumph was neither clean nor swift. We have a direct sense of that part of the battlefield from Soviet historians who were looking back at the Transbaikal region nearly fifty years later. Soviet-era judgements need to be treated with considerable scepticism, but these seem more objective than most if only because rather than the usual portrayal of gallant workers and peasants sweeping to victory on a riptide of popular acclaim, they make no attempt to hide the fragility of the situation, the see-sawing of control, the terrifying tornado of events whistling over the Redstones' heads and, above all, the conclusion that the local Bolsheviks were for much of the time misguided and outmanoeuvred by the resourceful and determined Mensheviks.

The railway workshops in Chita – Kostyushko's happy hunting ground eleven years previously – were shut by strikes on 4 February, and March brought the formation of the first local Soviet of Soldiers' and Workers' Deputies. As a counterweight, the Mensheviks promptly set up a Committee of Public Safety, including Bolshevik sympathisers, which, despite the French Revolutionary resonance of its name, was more a council of local worthies doing their desperate best to bring some semblance of order to the disintegrating structure of society. How were people to be fed, what would they use for money, where would they get fuel, where would hospitals and doctors get their medical supplies, who would usher babies into the menacing world and who would bury the dead? The increasingly tense balance of power in the Committee's structure, which again contrary to historical folklore was mirrored in many other parts of Russia, was castigated by the Communist Party's historians. How could 'real' Bolsheviks have such a lack of discipline? they asked. Again we need to take care in defining our image of the platforms of the two main political factions. In the Ukraine, for instance, the Mensheviks were pushing a far from 'liberal' programme: a government that was to be 'all-democratic' but which would exclude any participation by the propertied classes, forcibly transfer estates to 'land committees', and put production under state control.

When I first read about the Chita Committee, I had thought of it as no more than another group, another effort to stem the tide. Then, when I was trying to track down more about Manya's brother, the Kuznetsov Museum sent me a photograph of the Committee, pointing out that Pavel Flegontov had been one of the members, and highlighting him for me. Given the pecking order of such staged events, we can assume that he was quite a significant member since he was in the centre of the second row just behind the chairman, one of forty-five grave local dignitaries – doctors, lawyers, teachers, men in various uniforms, and a few women. It presents a solidly respectable image, confirming the historians' assertion that Chita did not fall at the first Bolshevik push but was, like other towns in the region, 'more petty bourgeois' in the Soviet vocabulary, essentially run by the merchant class with the support and connivance of local civil servants. Since the museum staff were not looking out for anyone else, they can be forgiven for not spotting, as I did with a jump, that standing next to Pavel was his brother-in-law David, captioned as 'from the *Zabaikal'skii Rabochii* newspaper'.

As if that were not enough for one day, when I looked at the women in the group, I noticed that one school-marmish figure in the second row was identified as 'M. A. Spiridonova, then living in Chita'. Appearances can be deceptive since Spiridonova was not a teacher but a terrorist 'heroine', a member of the Socialist Revolutionaries' Combat Organisation, the group of fanatics who had taken so many lives among the Court and State structure with bomb or bullet. How had she ended up alongside my gentle grandfather?

The story is a sequence of tragedies full of the desperate moral ambiguities of the period. A few months after her twenty-first birthday, Spiridonova had shot and mortally wounded the reviled Luzhenovksy, Vice-Governor of her home town of Tambov, 200 miles south-east of Moscow, pulling a revolver out of her fur muff as he scurried across a station platform to his train, surrounded by a bodyguard of police and Cossacks. It was clearly a crime. On the other hand, Luzhenovksy, an active member of one of the ultra- right and poisonously anti-Semitic groupings known as the Black Hundreds, had spearheaded the suppression of local peasant uprisings with a brutality remarkable even by the standards of the time. In one village ten peasants were shot out of hand, men and women were stripped and forced to stand in the snow for hours, a girl killed herself after being raped, and a young liberal who tried to calm the peasants down was seized by the police and his body handed back to his family after four days 'looking like a pile of mincemeat'.

Spiridonova made no attempt to escape and begged the court which tried her to have her shot, as a martyr to the cause. She was sentenced to hang, but the sentence was changed to hard labour for life. She paid an extra price by being beaten, burned, whipped and raped by her jailers. News of what was happening to her inevitably leaked out and aroused worldwide attention, so that to the chagrin of the authorities her painful journey, as always beginning with a spell in Butyrki Prison, to the hard labour jail at Akatui was paid a great deal of attention. She spent nearly eleven years there (yet again the poverty of the phrase masks the unimaginable severity of the experience), the regime varying with the Russian political climate and the temperament of a succession of governors. At one extreme there were walks in the woods on parole, debates and sing-songs; at the other, head-shaving, shackles and deprivation of almost every liberty. She also recalled that the 'politicals' were generally not sent out to work in the mines, but that those who did so found it greatly preferable to being cooped up in the monotonous and disease-enhancing atmosphere of the jail itself, where conditions, in her words, had 'not changed since the time of Peter the Great'.

Amnestied, along with thousands of other 'politicals', by the provisional government, Spiridonova was now in Chita, the nearest large town. Undaunted by her long ordeal, she set busily to work organising action committees, getting her fellow exiles back to Russia and seeing to it that the Nerchinsk hard-labour system was abolished. In the latter respect, anything she achieved was sadly temporary. One account claims that she was elected mayor of Chita and promptly ordered the city jail to be blown up, a story that fits the myth but which has no basis in fact. Though a German journalist dismissed her as 'a passionate hysteric with a pince-nez', in historian Richard Pipes' more measured judgement, she was a woman 'possessed of a courage that in earlier centuries characterised religious martyrs but nothing remotely resembling common sense'. She must have cut an extraordinary figure in debate with the phalanx of Mensheviks in the few months of the Committee's life. Did she and David cross swords? Did they chat in the intervals of what were certainly interminable meetings of the Committee? About what? The relative value of the bullet versus the ballot? Jail? Family? Like Manya, Spiridonova had trained as a nurse.

(When she returned from Chita to St Petersburg, Spiridonova went on to play a central role for the Socialist Revolutionaries in the internecine battle with the Bolsheviks, which was probably within their power to win, though in the event they were outmanoeuvred. She did not let politicking divert her from her commitment to the salutary effects of murder as a tool for the greater good, and she orchestrated the assassination of the German Ambassador to St Petersburg, Count Mirbach, in an attempt to damage relationships between the Germans and her Bolshevik opponents.)

Back in Chita, the Committee of Public Safety set up several working groups to tackle a range of issues, probably the most interesting of which was trawling through the police files. The exercise must have delighted the vindictive and suspicious, and terrified those whose names might have been recorded as witting or unwitting informants. The Committee also organised what was claimed to be the first entirely free one-man one-vote election for a new city council, with no property qualifications to debar either votes or candidates, and no less than nine parties vying for office. It was a fine effort, though again short-lived.

The workers to whom the Bolsheviks should have been able to look for support were, in the case of the miners, scattered in remote settlements and hard to get at, while even after several years the thousands of railway workers still had vivid memories of those earlier punitive expeditions and were uninterested in supporting anything that would bring wrath on that scale down on their heads again. Until the last days of the regime, the railways were a priority surveillance target for the tsarist secret police, and Captain Bulakhov of the Corps of Gendarmes was said to have had 'such an extensive network of official and unofficial secret agents that for several years (right up to 1917) he was able to deal a series of painful blows to the workers' collectives and remove the leadership of the workers' movement'. And though we now see the demarcation lines between 'hard' men and liberals as clear, in those more fluid times they were blurred by shared painful experiences. Expressed in the words of a Soviet-era commentator, 'a number of the leaders of the Transbaikal Bolsheviks proved incapable of revising swiftly and decisively enough their personal and political relationships with the Mensheviks with whom they had only yesterday been serving side by side in the hard labour camps but who were today on the opposite side of the barricades . . .'

Though the Chita Committee did not last long – any group of that size is by definition unworkable – the Mensheviks still dominated the first Chita Congress of the Russian Social Democratic Workers' Party under whose banner the Bolsheviks also marched at that time, although only one of the Party's local committee was a Bolshevik.

So there was David, momentarily at the centre of events, but quite what he contributed beyond his intrinsic common sense we do not know. He drops out of sight again, when the Menshevik A. A. Rubinshtein took over the reins at the *Zabaikal'skii Rabochii* and generated much Bolshevik fury by publishing what they ranted were articles of 'an openly opportunistic nature' while denying them space, so that the newspaper's views came across as the collective policy of the two sparring factions. It is easy to forget that newspapers were still the only means of broad communication, were avidly read by those who could, and widely believed by those to whom the news was read or spread. To get the Bolshevik message out nationwide, and to give a Bolshevik 'spin' to news from abroad, meant that the press had to be put under the Party thumb; to Lenin, counter-revolutionary publications were as dangerous as the bomb or machine-gun. The pendulum swung again and Rubinshtein was pushed out and replaced by a Bolshevik. The leftward swing continued; the one surviving issue of the *Zabaikal'skii Rabochii* in the archives of the Library of Congress celebrates the May Day Holiday in 1918 with decidedly Communist overtones. Zealous Bolshevik bureaucrats were seeking to control food and to 'municipalise' the timber and fur trades, and the local mines. A Union of Domestic Servants was about to hold its first meeting in 'The Hall of the People'. Not to be outdone, 'Jozef the European Hairdresser' took the opportunity to announce to his clientele that he had a new stock of hair dye and that, since all his stylists were now co-owners of the business, there would be no more tipping. There were shortages of everything. Food and flour were rationed and the price of a bucket of water from the municipal wells was steeply hiked. Some normal life continued. The House of the People Theatre was offering *Everyone Does His Own Thing* and *Will O' The Wisp*; maybe the selection was someone's subtle joke, except that in that environment jokers had a short life expectancy. The playhouse in Nerchinsk was looking for actors and actresses for its summer season.

By August, the Committee was in Bolshevik hands and in September the Party formally split. Though this may have brought momentary comfort to the men in charge in what in August 1914 had been re-named Petrograd, the problems did not go away. The Chita

Bolsheviks refused to accept the leadership of the Russian Party's Leninist Central Committee and the Mensheviks meanwhile had found another outlet for their views in the newspaper *Novaya Zhizn* (*New Life*). In December the Bolsheviks set up a Red Guard, recruiting hundreds of workers from factories in the area. While it suited Soviet history to portray those enlisted in their cause in those early days as brave idealists from the proletarian vanguard, the truth is that the Bolshevik 'storm troops', from whom no house was safe, were, in the words of the French writer Grennard, no more than a 'rabble of sadists . . . the sort of men who rise to the top when a society has been turned upside down, criminals, rogues, the mentally unbalanced, degenerates and psychopaths'. They kicked in doors, shot out of hand most of those on their 'wanted lists' and stole anything that took their fancy. The lists themselves were little more than crude compilations of hate, envy and suspicion: 'half the country was informing on the other'.

The 'storm troops' were backed by the 'revolutionary-minded' 2nd Chita Cossack Regiments, and units of the new Red Army arrived in Chita and 'proclaimed Soviet power'. This was rather premature, but it did not stop them making it crystal clear that they planned to use that power in 'an all-out merciless fight against attempts to encroach on our revolutionary gains whether . . . from others in the city or outside it . . .' High on the list of encroachers were non-Bolshevik journalists like David.

The Bolsheviks began to campaign against 'sabotage and attempts to disrupt the work of [the city's] institutions and organisations', newspapers among them. But far bigger problems than settling scores were looming.

The situation rapidly degenerated into chaos. The defeated, demoralised and confused Russian government threw in the sponge and signed a separate armistice with the Germans at Brest Litovsk, ceding huge swathes of territory and in the process giving the Bolsheviks breathing room to try to tighten their fragile grip on the rest of the country. The Western powers and the Japanese, seeing their allies crumble, sent interventionist military units to Russia and Siberia to secure their supply lines for the Western front and to put their weight behind the anti-Bolshevik White forces. Of all those involved in this abortive imperialist foray, Great Britain played the major role driven by her own strategic imperatives. Setting a pattern of behaviour for the twenty-first century, the French were 'vociferous in principle but parsimonious in practice.' In the words of the historian Richard Ullman, the United States was a reluctant participant from the outset and the Japanese were there not to try to overthrow the new Soviet regime but to seek to limit the territory over which it held sway. Adding to the confusion, the Czech Legion, a 70,000-strong force, mostly deserters from the Austro-Hungarian army who had fought alongside the Tsarist forces against the Germans in the Ukraine, now wanted nothing more than to go home. (Among them was Jaroslav Hašek, one-time dog-thief, mental patient, cabaret performer, and author of another of my grandfather's favourite books, *The Good Soldier Svejk*. Did David know the link with the Czech Legion, whose tough troops he would surely have seen in Siberia? There was also the link with Irkutsk, where instead of going straight home, Hašek became a Bolshevik Political Commissar and spent two years writing in a comfortable house in Irkutsk before going back to Prague.)

The Legion could not cross the Western front and so were fighting their way back round the world to reach Vladivostok in several trains strung out along the length of the Trans-Siberian Railway. Until then, the US presence had been largely confined to the unsung Russian Railway Service Corps, American railway specialists recruited mainly from the Dakotas and Montana because of their experience with a severe climate, whose Herculean task it was to help the Russian railway staff ('a comic opera South American army with fifty generals and ten soldiers', as one of the Americans later wrote) keep the Trans-Siberian supply route going. But the Bolshevik attempts to crush the Czechs prompted a more sizeable American military presence, despite the reluctance of Washington politicians. At the peak in September 1918, there were 8,000 US troops and support personnel on the ground. For a while, some were under Japanese command, a misshapen piece in the jigsaw puzzle of history that it suited both sides to forget in later years. The last American troops were pulled out in 1920. Laying the psychological foundations for the Cold War, US accounts of the period speak of the Bolsheviks as 'the enemy'.

If confusion reigned on the ground, how much more so did it rule in the faraway diplomatic chanceries of Europe and Japan? A 'secret' British War Office memorandum of 2 November 1918, intended to reassure the Canadian premier that Allied and Imperial intervention in Russia was still justified, summed up: 'The main object of the Allies is to prevent Siberia from lapsing into anarchy', but 'their conflicting interests render the attainment of this object difficult. The British and French are united in desiring to see a strong independent Russian administration and army at the earliest possible moment. The Americans probably desire the same thing. The Japanese on the other hand scarcely make any efforts to conceal their intention to prevent Russian unity and independence . . . Siberia is in the throes of giving birth to a stable government,' he concluded, demonstrating how wrong such distant assessments can be. A more facetious but probably even more accurate view is that of William Gerhardie, whom we last saw in St Petersburg. Now transferred to the British Military Mission in Siberia, he wrote of telling a baffled senior officer that, 'Irkutsk is now once again in the hands of the Whites . . .The Reds . . . had taken it over . . . from the Social Revolutionaries after these had captured the town from the Kolchakites and had later defeated Semyonov . . . Of course, sir, I have said nothing of the Poles, the Letts, Latvians, and Lithuanians, the Czechs, Yanks, Japs, Romanians, French, Italians, Serbians, Slovenes, the Jugoslavians, the German, Austrian, Hungarian and Magyar war prisoners, the Chinese, Canadians and ourselves . . . the position of the Czechs is probably the most difficult of all . . . two years ago they fought the Bolsheviks, now the Bolsheviks are fighting the Czechs . . . as their traditional enemy of two years' duration . . .' Gerhardie concluded, 'We both sighed.'

If he was puzzled, how much more so were the stolid yeomen in a battalion of the Hampshire Regiment who, instead of being shipped home after service in India to British Prime Minister Lloyd George's promised 'land fit for heroes to live in' found themselves in November 1918 marching behind their fife and drum band across the cobbled streets and tramlines of Vladivostok en route to a thankfully brief tour of duty in Omsk.

Gerhardie can be forgiven for failing to mention the Koreans, of whom there were some 300,000, mainly farmers who had settled there over the centuries. While many sided with the Bolsheviks, probably an equal number joined the Whites and Japanese, and in fighting around Vladivostok, which changed hands six times in the latter part of 1918, 'thousands' of Koreans were killed by both sides. Even the term 'both sides' is an oversimplification. There were armies, units cut off from their commands who seized their own initiative to kill and plunder, local factions pursuing vendettas, outlaw bands, men in stolen bloody uniforms, men in tattered civilian clothes and criminals on the run.

Gerhardie's 'Semyonov' was Grigory, a plump half-Cossack half-Buryat voluptuary with a gypsy mistress. Then only twenty-seven, but already a battle-hardened much-decorated officer who spoke Mongolian and Kalmuck as well as his two native languages, he was the ataman or 'warlord' of the Special Manchurian Detachment, a pitiless band of Cossacks, Buryats and ragtag deserters from foreign armies, nominally White-supporting but far more driven by their insatiable appetite for killing, raping and looting. Leading his own force of mercenaries in Mongolia was another ataman, once one of Semyonov's right-hand men, the 'Bloody Baron' Roman Fyodorovich Ungern-Sternberg. There was nothing remotely Byronic about Ungern-Sternberg, but like the poet he was clearly a man who was 'mad, bad and dangerous to know'. His ship-owner grandfather had been exiled to Siberia for murdering one of his sea captains and his father had ended his life in a lunatic asylum. The Baron himself made a jarring first impression: he had an unnaturally small head scarred by 'a terrible sword cut which pulsed with red veins', perched on broad shoulders surmounted by a mop of wild blond hair and bisected by an almost lipless mouth. Supported for a while by both the French and Japanese (the latter also backed Semyonov as part of their strategy to create a non-Soviet Mongolia as a buffer against Bolshevism), and surrounded by forty Japanese bodyguards, he ruled Mongolia in place of its 'blind, syphilitic' ruler

Boghd Khan for a terrifying twelve months. It is hard to separate myth from reality, but some of the stories told of him suggest his nickname was deserved. His entourage included another man with a possibly invented nickname, Colonel 'Dead Fish' Sepailoff, who suffered from Tourette's Syndrome, which gave him strange facial tics, and a habit of compulsive swearing and meaningless singing as he went about his job of killing people. Another of the Baron's constant companions was known as 'The Teapot' because he had forgotten his real name and spent his time brewing glass after glass of tea, when not called on to strangle Ungern-Sternberg's unwanted or impertinent guests. When Japanese support evaporated, the Baron was captured by the Reds and paraded station by station along the railway to Novosibirsk. When he was shot, the firing squad aimed at his naked chest decorated with shamanistic amulets and the cross of St George because his head was too small a target. Mongolia celebrated his demise with a procession in what is now Ulan Bator, Bogdh Khan leading the way in an automobile presented to him by the Soviet ambassador; as he had neglected to explain how it actually worked, it was towed by oxen.

Though Bolshevik forces beat his detachment back, Semyonov attacked again in April 1918. Seen from Chita, worlds were falling apart and the centre could not hold. The struggles, in one historian's words, 'drenched the land in blood, ruined its farms and fields, closed its mines and factories and brought an era of barbarism'. Death did not always come by gun or club or starvation. It came invisibly too, tendrils of typhus and cholera, much of it brought back from the front lines by returning soldiers, spreading from home to home.

Soviet forces suffered defeats at Semyonov's hands in heavy fighting around Lake Baikal and the Bolsheviks began to evacuate Chita, putting in place Communist underground 'stay behind' cells of young Party members who were unknown to the police. A contemporary report unearthed by the Chita Museum neatly illustrates the naivety of the locals and the brutal arrogance of Semyonov's men. A group from the Chita Soviet, 'supported by soldiers of the Red Guard', went out to meet the Cossack leader at a nearby railway barracks, suggesting that he and his men lay down their arms to avoid further bloodshed. They must have been crest-fallen to be received by 'guffaws of malevolent laughter' and the earthy but sincerely meant threat that the Cossacks were about to 'pull the Red Guard out of the soil by the roots like a head of cabbage and leave the town of Chita looking like a freshly ploughed field'. The delegation scuttled away.

Given everything else that was happening in 1918, the subsequent fate of General Rennekampf was hardly front-page news, but David and many others in Chita who remembered the armoured trains would have been gratified to learn of the death of their one-time nemesis at the hands of a Bolshevik firing squad after being 'frightfully tortured'. Probably unnoted even in Russia at the time was the death in April 1918 of Yevno Azef, who, as we have seen, had compounded Plehve's assassination with that of Grand Duke Sergei to prove his revolutionary credentials. Finally exposed by his comrades to be the agent provocateur he was, he escaped to Germany, where he escaped their vengeance and, unlike his illustrious targets, died peacefully in his sleep.

David would also have read, with worries about family and friends, the news cables from Odessa reporting another ill-judged intervention mounted in December 1918. In keeping with the city's multi-ethnic traditions, it was spearheaded by a force of some 65,000 French troops, many of them Senegalese and Algerian, despised by Russians as 'chernozhopye' ('the black-arsed ones'), an insult today applied mainly to swarthy Chechens, and backed by two Greek divisions and a posse of Poles. Instead of controlling the area down to the Romanian border, including Akkerman, the invaders found themselves, rather like the Siberian experience, infighting not only with Bolsheviks, but also with Ukrainian nationalists, ferocious anarchists and yet another group of rabid freebooters led by a Cossack Ataman named Grigoriyev. The folly lasted five months.

Back in Siberia, what on earth, or in hell, must it have been like for the Redstones – moving targets of merciless power struggles, which rolled arbitrarily in one direction, then another, in which it was never clear who were 'friends' and who 'foes', and which in the longer view of history achieved absolutely nothing other than misery, dislocation and death? There must have been many moments of blind panic and hopelessness, of having to ingratiate oneself with boors and killers to get through the next checkpoint, and of feeling guilty at carrying the responsibility not just for oneself but for three children. At times the temptation to give up and take whatever fate ordained must have been almost irresistible. However, unlike many others, the Redstones got away. Their travels were to begin again. A long road lay ahead, which was eventually to lead back to the aromatic little attic of the House of Sobranie.

20

On the Road Again

We cannot date precisely when David left Chita, nor how long it took for Manya to get herself and the children out, but it is hard to conceive that there would have been any story for us to tell if the Redstones had still been in the city on 26 August 1918 (a month or so after the Tsar and his family had been butchered in Yekaterinburg), when White units and the desperate Czechs took over the city; they were followed in September by Semyonov's bandits and Japanese interventionist forces. In the words of a Soviet-era historian, 'This marked a dark period . . . The White Guard carried through terror in the region . . .' At some point Semyonov set up a 'torture chamber' for his opponents outside Chita from which none of his captives ever emerged.

Back in Russia, the fires of even older hatreds were rekindled. It was said that the Jews were responsible for Russia's defeat and indeed the Revolution. Copies of *The Protocols of the Elders of Zion*, the purported secret Jewish master plan for world domination, began to pass from hand to hand in supposedly civilised circles and it was reprinted in the US by that paragon of capitalism Henry Ford. (One of history's more credible forgeries, since it told much of the world what it wanted to hear, it was in fact conceived by P. I. Rachkovsky, head of the Foreign Agency of the Tsar's Police Department, but was largely the work of Matvei Golivinsky, an Okhrana agent whose fervid imagination matched his prejudice.) In Germany too, making a chillingly early start on the road towards the Holocaust, the Pan

German League noted in April 1918 'a satisfactory growth in the anti-Semitic mood, which had already [developed] to an enormous extent. Our task will be to bring the movement out on to the national arena . . . for the Jews, the struggle for existence has begun.'

David passed some of his memories on to his son-in-law, Nina recorded hers in a television interview, and Manya related fragments to her grandchildren over the years. The story goes that David and Manya were at the theatre when someone tipped him off that he should get out of Chita immediately as he was high on the Bolsheviks' hit list.

It is hard to conceive what thoughts went through David and Manya's minds – what they said, what they hoped and what they promised. David stopped only long enough to change his appearance by shaving off his beard, leaving Manya with the three children to make their own way later. One consideration may well have been that if they left together and he was caught, they would all suffer, whereas the family would not be hurt if he were not there. This may have been sensible. It was not long before the heavy boot smashed open their door. In Manya's later retelling, she had put a bolster in David's bed, which the thugs riddled with bullets before realising that their target had flown. They clattered off in hot pursuit, without harming the family.

Her brother, Pavel was now at the military hospital, while a 'Comrade Flegontov' – identified as a member of the Bolshevik Party and 'Chief of Staff of the Amur Forces' – was photographed on horseback with a dashing fur hat. Infuriatingly the caption to the photograph dug out by the Chita Museum does not give his initials, so we cannot be sure whether he was another brother.

In the eye of the storm, Manya gathered up Nina, my mother and Valentin, strapped to a board to protect his infected spine. Had she been able to say goodbye to her family? She never saw any of them again. There was only one way out, the railway, and the square in front of it was jammed. When she eventually managed to squeeze through the crush and get inside, she had to shove her way in with the children and their belongings through a solid wall of terrified people on the platform. Every train that steamed slowly in was already suffocatingly full inside, and men, women and children hung off every rail and bracket outside. Eventually one stopped with the rusty ladder to a carriage roof right opposite the huddled Redstones. Manya shooed Nina and Sonia up, then passed Valentin to them. They scrambled their way along the slatted walkway that ran along the roof and clung on desperately. As Nina recalled, 'There were hundreds and thousands of deserting soldiers . . . the train moved off and we were on the roof for what seems for ever although it was probably only a few hours. I was so petrified I don't remember how long. We lay there with our mother sort of spread-eagled over us. Eventually some people in the carriages made room and began to haul us in through the windows.' Later in life she told her children that at one point Manya had shut her in a laundry basket to keep her out of sight of the soldiers on the train.

Manya herself told my sister Natalie years later about the elderly priest who asked if the two girls would like to confess any sins, turning to them with a leer to suggest with graphic gestures some of the transgressions the poor puzzled things might have committed. She also remembered men and women being dragged off the train to be shot, and others killed when random bullets smashed through the windows. They took out of Russia their memories, a few bits and pieces of jewellery, and some gold coins hidden in Valentin's underclothes that Manya rightly calculated even the most savage border guards would not have the heart to search. As the train jerked fitfully towards the illusion of safety, the passengers saw that many of the wooden churches alongside the stations had been demolished, not out of anti-religious fervour but simply as a source of cooking fuel and warmth for the flood of refugees.

This train story brings us back to David's books, since Nina's memories echo one of his bookcase milestones, *Dr Zhivago*. As the Doctor's train drew in, 'people rolled down the hills like marbles, scrambled up the embankment, and, pushing each other, jumped onto the steps and buffers or climbed in through the windows or onto the roof. The train filled in an instant, while it was still moving and by the time it stood on the platform not only was it crammed but people hung over it from top to bottom.' Since David's copy of the book was in Russian, Manya may have read it herself; or perhaps not, since she might not have been happy to be reminded of the past by Pasternak's evocation of 'those years of change, moves, uncertainties, upheavals, the war, the revolution, scenes of destruction, scenes of death, shelling. Blown-up bridges, fires, ruins . . .'

The episode also evokes images of a later time: the ruined Anhalter Station in Berlin in 1945, and the men, women and children crowded on a train roof in the photographs reproduced by the historian Dagmar Barnouw. Since they represent a defeated nation, we are not supposed to feel the same sympathy for them as we do for 'real' refugees, but we do. They have the same grey, bewildered look, the same desperation as those fleeing Chita. For Barnouw, as it must have been for my grandmother, the train 'was the treacherous symbol of escape, of coming unstuck but also of hope and change for the better'. At the same time, 'the depression of the people on [the roof] weighs palpably on the train, in fact obscures it. It seems improbable that this train will ever leave the station, that there will ever again be the cooking of food, washing of clothes, sleeping in a bed, being private and protected.'

In Russia, the demands of the Great War and the industrial and political unrest had reduced the trains to what one caustic American observer called 'strings of matchboxes, coupled by hairpins and drawn by samovars', but we know that Manya and the children reached Harbin safely. Yet again the phrase does not do justice to the nail-biting 750-mile journey through what is left of the ramparts put up by Genghis Khan, mountain ranges, arid plains, alien landscapes and alien people, stopping at little wooden stations identical to those the length and breadth of Russia but with tongue-twisting Chinese names like Manchouli, Pokotu and Tsitsihar. Finally there was David on the platform of Harbin's pistachio-green Secessionist-style station, more appropriate to Karlsplatz in Vienna (though with Chinese symbols on the roof to avert evil spirits) than a railway town in Manchuria; he must have been a welcome sight. Once just a tiny, but strategically placed village, Harbin exploded into the administrative and maintenance centre of the Chinese eastern leg of the Trans-Siberian Railway. De jure under joint Russian and Chinese administration, de facto it was the centre of an autonomous Russian enclave in Manchuria, whose 'Tsar' was General Horvat, head of the Railway Administration. The railhead spawned a large and pros-perous community known in its heyday as 'Happy Horvatia', underpinned by a thriving network of trading businesses, factories, distilleries, workshops and banks. It was also, the Chinese govern-ment complained, a magnet for 'foreign adventurers, opium smugglers and other bad characters', and a safe haven for 'Chinese bandits, anarchists and criminals' who were out of the reach of the Chinese police and to whom the Russians turned a blind eye; one of its many intriguing clandestine visitors not long before the Redstones got there had been the future Communist leader Zhou En Lai, busy with 'revolutionary propaganda and organisation'. With the Revolution, Horvatia became less happy as it was overwhelmed by hordes of refugees, the Redstones among them, fleeing the turmoil in Siberia; for many thousands it was to be their makeshift home for years to come.

Nina remembered: 'We arrived at this small, dirty town which had two million refugees, had to live in a railway train for three or four months till some prefabricated houses were ready . . . We loved it but it was hard on my mother. We lived there for about a year . . . Life in Harbin was quite dangerous, as there were different "generals", mostly criminals, who were in charge. Money changed monthly – all worthless. Terrible inflation – like in Germany – one went shopping with baskets of notes.' The economics were devastatingly simple. The railway was Russian, so its currency was the rouble with which it paid not just its own employees but its thousands of Chinese workers, contractors and suppliers. The Tsar's money had thus become over the years not only a widely used regional currency, but also a store of value, the savings of countless Russian and Chinese families, more often than not crammed into heavy metal boxes (my grandparents lugged one all the way to England), stuffed in mattresses or buried under the floor. When the Revolution dragged the currency's value down to that of toilet paper, everyone lost. For the Chinese, the financial damage did much to stoke the resentment at the 'unfair' railroad treaty that had brought aliens into their

19. David Redstone, every inch the editor, Chita, c. 1916.

20. Happy family: Manya, Nina, Sonia and Valentin, Chita, c. 1912.

21. 'Two little maids from school': my mother, Sonia, and her sister, Nina, Chita, 1916.

The Committee for Public Safety, Chita, 1917. David Redstone is fifth from the
[lef]t in the second row; the diminutive terrorist 'heroine' Maria Spiridonova is first
[on] the right. In an early example of Bolshevik revision of history, the clumsily
[bla]nked space near the right-hand corner of the second row from the back indicates
[som]eone the system chose to consign to oblivion.

23. The station in Harbin, the exile crossroads. The Redstone
family squatted in a train behind this station for several months.

24. 'But a good cigar is a smoke…' Fred Croley and José de Sola Pinto of Robert Lewis & Co.

25. The photograph Chaliapi inscribed to David Redstone as a sign of friendship.

26. A Sobranie trademark, taken from a porcelain cigarette box; and a packet of Sobranie Black Russian, bought in Yakutsk in 2004.

The Boys from Bessarabia: the ...dstone brothers sketched by Ghilchik ...Punch magazine, 1949.

David

Isaiah

28. 'We made it.' David and Manya, deservedly proud and happy at their golden wedding anniversary.

29. The Romanovka at the time of the siege.

30. The Romanovka, still standing 100 years on.

31. The Romanovka: once a bullet-ridden Cossack target, later a museum.

32. Geoffrey Elliott at the Romanovka, 2004

celestial kingdom and in the process 'pierced the helmet' of its defensive shield of mountains.

Harbin, overcrowded, impoverished and exposed, must have been a dreadful place to live in. Crime rose as the city spilled over any manageable boundaries and the social fabric began to come apart at the seams. Russia's troubles spilled into Harbin's streets, with demonstrations and counter-demonstrations, strikes and religious processions, which incited as much discontent as they brought solace. As in Chita, David and his family must have snuffed out their oil lamps when they heard the drumbeat of pounding feet and pursuing horses, even the crackle of gunfire, in the street outside. In a contemporary photograph, the shabby single-storey clapboard exterior of Danilov's Opera and Operetta Theatre has a dead and dispirited air. Normal life was already ebbing away and the over-the-hill touring players would never again bring back to the middle of Manchuria the all-too-fleeting glamour of the flickering candles in the footlights, the hoarse whispers of the prompter, the moth-eaten wigs, creased crinolines and the much loved words and melodies. We do not know how long the Redstones stayed nor what difficulties they had over money, papers and the things today's travellers take for granted, as General Horvat juggled ever more clumsily and eventually in vain to preserve Harbin's Russianness, and all the more its 'White Russianness'. This meant shifting alliances not just with the intervening allies but also into an uneasy cohabitation and then confrontation with the terrifying Semyonov.

In 1917 there were demonstrations by left-wingers and striking railway workers. In 1918 religious groups filled the Square to pray for the success of the Allied intervention. In June 1920 censer-swinging priests led the faithful in mass prayer to commemorate White officers and soldiers slaughtered by the Bolsheviks. When the congregation spotted the Jewish editor of Harbin's Socialist newspaper in their midst, they lynched him on the spot, a harsh and probably unnecessary reminder to the Jewish refugee community that the old Russian values had not been left behind. The train, too, continued to prove its versatility as an instrument of death: a group of Red partisans captured the previous month had been shoved alive into the fiery furnace of a handy locomotive.

It would have been impossible for the Redstones to know from one day to the next who really had power and where the next peril would emerge – all the more since we now know that David had a relationship with the British Consul, which might well have made him suspicious to one or more sets of hostile eyes. The consular files for that period have been thoroughly weeded, and all that remains of David is a tantalising reference to him in the British Public Records Office as 'propaganda agent, Harbin War Publicity Bureau', and a 1919 card index reference noting a 'tribute' to his work in that role.

So the family left on the 1,000-mile journey across China to Shanghai. Here again we are condensing into bland words a rattling ride across a barren hinterland, where warlords feuded and Semyonov's raiders and 'red beard' bandits robbed trains and mined the tracks, where natural ambush by flood and landslide could bring more delay and despair, and where every inspection of papers and bags meant petty bribery at least and always the risk of being hauled off because some stamp was missing, while the train steamed away into the distance.

Fortunately, the family spent only a few months in Shanghai. The city oozed vice, extreme poverty and extreme wealth. Extracted from the Chinese as a British 'concession' and a hub of the British mercantile empire in Asia, it was run like Hong Kong by British (often Scottish) *taipans* from the merchant houses and banks, in a barely concealed concatenation of mutual interest with the French, Americans and Japanese, and, more importantly for the smooth running of the city, Chinese gangsters, drug smugglers and revolutionaries. If Edwardian London was a study in extreme social contrasts, how much more so this moral cesspit, its faecal odours barely masked by the scent of cheap perfume. This was a place where, after a few leisurely hours in his panelled office looking down on the crowds teeming along the broad embankment road, a merchant prince could jog by rickshaw to swallow a gin sling at the Shanghai Club, which boasted the longest bar in the world. He could then move on in sweaty anticipation to the less formal delights of spots like the Black Cat Club, whose Korean hostesses all had effigies of the club's mascot tattooed on their pert ivory backsides, or the Casanova, which had gambling parlours upstairs and doubled as the centre of a spy ring run by the French and Japanese police. Many Russian girls were forced into, or more often actually sought, work in the mob-dominated dance halls, clubs and brothels; one of the earliest references to a 'massage parlour' is to be found in the literature about Shanghai in this strange period. Against this it is wholesome to note that there was also a flourishing '5th Shanghai (Jewish) Boy Scout Troop'.

China's first Jewish community dates back to the eleventh century but Shanghai itself was first and foremost a fiefdom of the rich Sephardi merchants, the Kadoories, Sassoons, Baruchs and Hardoons, who had moved from Baghdad, Bombay and Cairo when China opened its doors to foreign trade in the 1840s. They did what they could to help immigrants, but the perceived flood of Jews from Russia led both the community and the British authorities to seek to discourage what they saw as a potentially dangerous influx. The Russian Aid Society organised makeshift accommodation and provided two hot meals a day and extra milk for the children, but even so the newcomers, like refugees everywhere in every century, were seen as undesirable, to be moved on wherever and whenever possible lest Shanghai become a 'dumping ground'. The Jewish immigrants also came under withering attack from the White exiles, who had brought with them their prejudices and their well-thumbed copies of *The Protocols of the Elders of Zion*, and who assiduously spread the word among anyone who would listen – and there were many – that the Jews had started the Revolution; they had betrayed the Tsar at Port Arthur and Jewish bankers had financed Russia's enemy, Japan. Their miserable ranks, the Whites alleged, contained Bolshevik agents under cover, bent on fomenting trouble in China. In fact there were Bolsheviks, perhaps even some under refugee cover but more often masquerading as diplomats, journalists and traders (the Singer Sewing Machine agency in the city was a Red underground front for several years), spying on the exiles of all persuasions and building their own espionage and subversion networks for operations in the Far East. The Soviet intelligence outstations in

Harbin and Shanghai were staffed by some of the best and brightest men and women in the service, almost every last one of them later executed by Stalin in the 1930s purges.

Against this bizarre background it is all the more charming that Nina's abiding memory of the city known, unfairly to France, as 'the Paris of the East', was that it gave her her first sight of an escalator.

Nina recalls that 'we had two tutors who came with us', which suggests a lifestyle above the breadline, though the tutors may have been penniless students or even relatives. As the pressure in the city grew, David found work in Japan and the family followed, as Nina records, on 'our first trip by boat'. After six months in Tokyo – 'mostly wooden and paper buildings . . . great Emperor worship . . . cherry blossom a lovely sight' – they moved across Tokyo Bay to Yokohama. They must have been running on their reserve tanks of courage. What were they doing? Where were they going? Bertolt Brecht remarked that the 'exiles' trade is hoping', and they certainly hoped. They clearly also had enormous psychological resources. But as the Japanese twittered incomprehensibly and giggled behind their hands in baffled condescension, as the earth tremors rumbled under their floor, as money ran short and as the issue of citizenship loomed ever larger, there must have been bleak night-time moments.

When the Bostonian millionairess Isabella Stewart Gardner called at Yokohama on a world tour in 1883, it was already a place 'given over to many foreigners, who live here charmingly but without local atmosphere and are here for money getting'. Japan was then an even more closed society than today and treated its immigrants with 'a sort of kindly contempt'. They nevertheless remembered the help their country had received in raising finance under the aegis of the powerful New York banker Jacob Schiff, a compelling response on his part to Tsarist anti-Semitism, and with Schiff's encouragement, were reasonably welcoming to the Jewish exiles.

White Russian émigrés with money, or the ability to wheedle credit from its flinty-eyed manager, gravitated to the Imperial Hotel, where the displaced, disgraced but not discomfited Ataman Semyonov and his hangers-on had commandeered the top floor. They were said to be living off the proceeds of looting most of the tsarist gold reserves on one of their raids, in a style that 'shocked . . . the bellboys', who had presumably seen a party or two in their time. (When the city was razed in the 1923 earthquake, parties of rumour-stoked Russian émigrés took the train to Yokohama from Tokyo every day for weeks, scrabbling through the debris of the Imperial in search of the gold hoard; in vain, since in a complex barter involving free passage for the Czech Legion and the handover of the White leader Admiral Kolchak to the Red commissars, who tortured and killed him, the gold had been handed back to the Bolsheviks soon after it was first stolen.)

For those a notch or two down the ladder, the Miuraya Boarding House and the Maisonette Hotel were almost exclusively Russian, while the cramped floors above the dining room of a cheap lodging house served as a refuge of last resort for those with virtually no money. Edgar Nathan's notes tell us that the Redstones lived in 'a small village at the foot of the Holy Mountain of Fuji', which again suggests that they were not penniless. It is another touching example of the defence mechanisms of childhood that, faced yet again with the many mysteries and uncertainties of a new and very foreign world, one of the longer lasting memories of Japan for Nina and my mother was eating half-a-dozen bananas. They also lived through their first earthquake, a less pleasant but equally exciting memory.

The rich in Yokohama could buy, and the poor could ogle and salivate over, the Russian foods and pastries on display at the Fujiya patisserie. A restaurant called the Moscow Delicatessen soon opened and may have left its legacy as the Robovski, a Russian café which is today a feature of the main railway station. (It is also tempting to attribute Russian roots to the Yokohama Accordion Enthusiasts' Society, whose Tefekundo Orchestra still performs with panache.)

Harold Williams, a young Australian who had come out in 1919 to work for the Finlay Richardson trading house, remembered: 'There was as much Russian being spoken in the streets of Yokohama then as English . . . the streets were colourful with Russian officers in all manner of fine uniforms. Army, Navy and Cossack cavalry officers and thousands of people with hopes blighted and careers wrecked . . . the streets were thronged with people trampling about with no place to go . . . those Russian refugees were footsore and weary . . . buying and selling and gambling [in the bureaux de change] on news trickling in from Siberia.'

As in Tokyo, and mirroring the plight of the middle classes back home in Russia, some were reduced to sitting on the pavements, selling jewellery, clothing, icons and worthless tsarist rouble notes. Even more than that was on offer; as elsewhere in the Far East, 'Russian girl' was a euphemism for what one Westerner censoriously termed a 'Caucasian harlot', while 'taxi girls', many of them actually Japanese, tangoed and waltzed with gentlemen and players alike at Yokohama's Kagetsuen, Japan's first commercial dance hall. Many had been taught to dance by Elena Pavlova, an émigré graduate of the Imperial Ballet School in St Petersburg. In a wry mirror image of the 'Russia girl' stereotype, for most Siberians of Manya's generation 'Japanese women' meant the prostitutes who had been shipped out in droves by their organised crime pimps to comfort the workers building the Trans-Siberian Railway. The syphilis they brought with them was known as 'The Yellow Peril'.

We know that Nina and Sonia went to a convent school run by Irish and French nuns of the Sisters of Mercy, where they spoke Russian and French and where they also learned to speak English (William Gerhardie recalls that a Russian girl who was probably one of their fellow pupils acquired a distinctive Irish brogue in the process), but they wrote it in a script that for both remained idiosyncratic for the rest of their lives. We know from a letter written by David's brother that my grandfather was, to put it at its best, trying out various entrepreneurial ideas; a first cousin now in her late eighties remembers vague family gossip in London that he was 'smuggling things on the railway'. He was also, as Nina remembers, working for the news agency Reuters.

Reuters' bureau in Japan was a 'two-way street', sending news and commercial information such as commodity and currency prices back to Fleet Street and disseminating Reuter bulletins of world news to the local press. Its network was also used for substantial volumes of private 'business to business' traffic and money transfers. David's most likely role would have been as a reader and translator of Russian newspapers and periodicals, although he may also have worked as a 'stringer', handing in snippets of information picked up in the community. It is no surprise that Reuters today has no record of his diminutive cheerful presence, nor indeed of the myriad of other 'occasionals' whom it used. (He must have simply thought it of no consequence, but it is odd that he never mentioned this part of his life when I worked for Reuters myself in the 1960s as a rather good, if I dare say so, monitor of Russian radio broadcasts, and a rather bad sub-editor. The coincidence of finding that I was following his footsteps has a certain private appeal.)

Like so much else, it is not clear what happened to Count Kutaisov, whose harsh circulars sparked the Romanovka. He did not end hanging from a lamp post as the underground broadsheet had prophesied, but had been dismissed from office as soon as the Romanovka trial ended. One account says that the Count died in 1911. However, the family was extensive – the first Kutaisov had been ennobled by the 'capricious' Tsar Paul, who promoted him from his barber to an equerry – and the name proliferated. One studio photograph shows two spruce ten-year-olds both with the same title, so 'our' Count may not be the same man who was hacked to death by a group of marauding Reds in 1918. Remnants of the Kutaisov family estate *Snegiri* ('Bullfinches'), now a holiday village, seems from recent photographs to have retained some of the grand pines and spruces that he would have remembered. His Governor General's mansion in Irkutsk was relabelled the 'House of Freedom'; Grand Street was renamed after Karl Marx; and the other main thoroughfare, Amurskaya, became Lenin Street.

David would certainly have followed the next highlights of attorney Zarudny's career. As Minister of Justice in Kerensky's coalition government, he chaired the commission investigating the allegations that Lenin and the Bolsheviks had received massive financial aid and had even collaborated with the Kaiser's government to bring about Russia's surrender at Brest Litovsk. The commission assembled, according to Richard Pipes, '80 thick volumes of evidence', a fragment of which may have reminded Zarudny of Yakutsk since among many others named as having played a role in the money-go-round was one Vladimir Perasich, who by the name of *Solodukha* had been one of his Romanovka 'clients' and who after escaping via the tunnel had reached Switzerland and then Copenhagen, where he became part of the Parvus network.

In another of the role reversals characteristic of that troubled period, as the pendulum swung briefly back against the Bolsheviks, Zarudny, once Trotsky's defence counsel, found himself as Justice Minister ordering the revolutionary leader and seventeen other prominent Bolsheviks, Lenin not least among them, to be arrested and imprisoned in the Kresty Jail in St Petersburg. Trotsky told him pointedly that, 'The Dreyfus case and the Beilis case are nothing compared with this deliberate attempt at moral assassination.' Lenin escaped to Finland, and Trotsky was soon released, observing in one of the torrent of articles he wrote while locked up that the jail conditions, the investigators and the warders were just the same as they had been under the Tsars. More dangerously for Zarudny's long-term future, the arrest also included Lenin, who managed to escape to Finland.

David would have been well aware from the news cables that Russia was not the only victim of unrest. In 1918 and 1919 there had been police strikes in Britain, and the British intervention in Russia had sparked new labour militancy and threats of general strikes. In what may have struck him as an ominous echo of Russia, unrest amongst British troops due to delays in demobilisation had sparked mutinies and even the creation of 'Soviets' in British military depots in Kempton Park and Calais.

21

Slow Boat from China

A letter that Shaia wrote to David – in English – in June 1919, responding to one from him in April, is far more the letter of an elder brother than a younger. It is full of solicitude, reflection and good advice, but with a quasi-parental touch when it comes to money. 'I have received a wire from you from Tokio some two weeks ago and I have dispatched 1,000 yen which came with cable to Pounds 112/15 shillings and I shall be pleased if you would forward me this by the first opportunity.'

The sense is that the exchange followed a lengthy silence, not, as Shaia comments, 'because I never wanted to write or I do not have anything to write', but because with the burdens of family and business he had just not had time. David's letter had clearly upset him. 'Your uncertain position in life and much more do I feel the pain that we are far away from each other . . . not only do we lose the brotherhood of each other but there is something more, friendship. We forget each other's characters, ability, honesty and everything else that is good with a person.' David had reported plans to go into business with unidentified partners to manufacture cigarettes, an idea on which interestingly Shaia poured cold water, saying that without adequate capital to start with, it was a sure way to go bankrupt. He suggested instead that as the Far East was clearly a growth market, David would do far better to become a distributor and a wholesaler. He offered to start him off with a new line of Sobranie-made Virginia and cheaper Turkish cigarettes tailored for the popular market rather than the connoisseur. Ever the entrepreneur as well as a fond brother, he offered to package them 'with the representation of a Red Stone'. By that time Shaia had brought their mother Tsivia over from Akkerman to London, though she was already ailing, as indeed David seemed to be: 'I also note in your letter that something is wrong with your heart. Please let me know at once what Doctor you have consulted and what is their opinion as it worries me very much.'

Even from the other side of the world, Shaia had a good instinct for the market potential. Looking today at the local cigarette brands on offer at the time in the East, many seem from their names – 'Double Crown', 'The Castles' and 'Pirate' – to be emulating a British image, though quite what the consumer was supposed to make of 'Pinhead' or 'My Dear' is a puzzle. The Sa-Bei brand, on the other hand, made no secret of the message it wanted its cigarettes to convey, decorating its boxes with an engraving of 'two semi-naked girls massaging each other on a bed'. It was almost certainly the 'house brand' of one of the better class of Shanghai's thousands of bordellos, offered to waiting clients along with a bowl of green tea, a dish of pumpkin seeds and a towel.

How Manya felt and coped in Japan is hard to imagine. If she found London and its language alien, how much more so besieged in a Russian 'Fort Zindeneuf' in the middle of Asia? How much they must have agonised, keeping their voices low to try not to worry the children, but there is no way that my mother and Nina can have been unaware of the stress. No matter how much David might have hoped to strike out on his own, and no matter how much Manya detested London, Russia was over for them. Going back to London was the only way out of the trap. It was easier said than done, not just in terms of money but the physical struggle in clamouring crowds, the nervous bribes to arrogant officials, hopes rising one moment, dashed the next, involved in getting the travel documents so desperately sought by the newly minted stateless of the world.

The knockout punch for the post-Revolution Russian refugees came in 1921, when the Soviet government revoked their citizenship and invalidated their passports. A Russian passport was a fast-depreciating asset, but at least it was official recognition that its holder had a name, a life and a country. No more. They were literally stateless persons, a huge problem resolved by the distinguished Norwegian explorer Fridtjof Nansen, who chaired a League of Nations' Commission on the plight of Russian refugees and came up with the idea of the temporary 'passports' that bore his name. (As an example of the unfairness of history, though Nansen's name lives on, that of the Commission's representative in the deeply troubled Ukraine may be even better remembered; he was a then unknown Norwegian army captain, Vidkun Quisling.) The passports were little more than an identity card to help refugees find work. They carried no rights of abode, domicile or asylum, to use today's idiom, but were at least a laissez-passer that the world's suspicious immigration officers would recognise, albeit reluctantly.

The Redstones' Nansen passports carried them back round the world to London via Hong Kong, Singapore, Ceylon, Aden, the Suez Canal, Gibraltar and Southampton. With them came their Russian mementoes, the *paskha* mould, their tin box containing hard-earned, now worthless banknotes, Manya's midwifery manual and a few souvenirs of the Far East: a couple of japanned tea trays, an exquisite Japanese ivory carving of a peddler and, a favourite plaything for the grandchildren, a stereoptikon, a hand-held aluminium 3-D viewer through which we squinted at fading photographs of temples and rickshaws. It was also family lore that the wind-up HMV gramophone and a treadle sewing-machine in their little London house had been lugged by Manya all the way from Siberia, but this is improbable given the mad scramble to get out. Wherever the gramophone was bought, it came with a stack of original scratchy Russian vinyl records of nursery rhymes – 'There once was an old woman who had a little goat' (the original, *'Zhil byl u babushki malen'kii kozlyk'*, is more euphonious).

To judge from the UK shipping arrivals (the actual passenger lists for the period have been lost), they sailed on Canadian Pacific Lines *Scotian*. Sea travel from the Far East in that era conjures up Somerset Maugham images of P&O liners: the antics of the 'gully gully men' in Port Said, making eggs and chickens appear and disappear from their sleeves; bronzed planters and their pale, fluttering wives, army officers and mysterious businessmen, sipping mid-morning beef consommé in their teak deckchairs wrapped in plaid rugs; quoits, bridge, cocktails in Art Deco lounges, dressing for dinner, the Captain's table, starlit romance and dawn farewells on the boat deck as the Isle of Wight loomed through the drizzle. In fact there were 'no-frills' shipping lines much as there are budget airlines today, and it is hardly surprising that an émigré family with hardly a penny to its name would have no other option. The *Scotian*, its one yellow funnel singling it out as a maritime 'poor relation' by contrast with the majestic stacks of larger liners, had been built in Belfast in 1898 and was coming to the end of its useful life. It did not even have first class accommodation; its 10,332 gross ton hull had been refitted to take 304 cabin class and 542 third class passengers. Its twin screws pushed it across the world at a steady 14 knots. When the Redstones boarded, she may well have been out in the Far East on one of the four trips she made around that time taking British troops to India.

As they sailed across the Mediterranean, Russia was being ever more deeply ravaged by famine and disease; the Civil War had proved, in the words of Richard Pipes, 'the most devastating event in that country's history since the Mongol invasions of the thirteenth century'. Lenin launched what came to be known as the 'Red Terror', haranguing his henchmen that 'terror should be substantive and legalised . . . the more members of the reactionary bourgeoisie and the clergy we manage to shoot, the better'. From the Ukraine, Quisling reported to the League of Nations that three million people were starving; in a ghoulish reaffirmation of the adage that revolutions end by devouring their own children, many had been reduced to cannibalism in a desperate bid to stay alive. As Ted Friedgut has commented with notable understatement on the Bolsheviks' failure to tackle the problem in the Ukraine, 'whether ignorance, incompetence, sheer neglect, or malevolence was at the bottom of this behaviour, the ignoring of millions of starving peasants and workers cannot reflect any credit on the Soviet regime'.

On the other hand, quite a few more fortunate Russians were still able to enjoy the champagne, strawberries and indiscretions of the then fashionable winter season in Cannes. Villas and hotel suites were in short supply and the golf club opened a week earlier than usual to accommodate the influx. Its President had been the late Russian Grand Duke Michael, and its committee still included the Grand Duke Cyril, Prince Philippe de Bourbon, the improbably Proustian Duc Doudeauville and Lord Brougham and Vaux. The Duke of Westminster and Lord Rocksavage were working on their backhands at the Carlton Lawn Tennis Club. In Paris, émigré groups continued their irresistible and debilitating internecine battles, with two rival factions supporting different pretenders to the painfully vacated Russian throne. In Berlin the battle proved fatal for Vladimir Nabokov's father, once a leading politician and later editor of the city's leading Russian newspaper; he was shot dead by White assassins at an émigré meeting in the Berlin Philharmonic's concert hall.

(Some White Russians worked in the riviera casinos as *physionomistes*, using a photographic memory for faces and names to spot cheats and cheque-bouncers. Many of them found gainful employment during the Second World War with the Gestapo on the border between the occupied north and the unoccupied south of France. They applied a combination of their job skills and their anti-Semitism to 'spot' Jewish refugees attempting to cross to safety using false Aryan identities. 'It's the ear lobes,' one claimed proudly.)

Baedeker advised travellers of the time that the customs' examination in Southampton was generally 'lenient', the officers' attention being focused on nothing more serious than copies of English books published out of copyright in Europe. Even so, it must have been a nerve-racking experience for new arrivals with flimsy documentation. Passengers waited in the echoing hall for their bags to be stacked under the initials of their surnames painted along the wall, and shifted nervously until the inspector had scribbled his chalk hieroglyph of clearance on the cases. They then faced the immigration officer, professionally cynical and xenophobic.

Nina remembers arriving in London itself 'on a very foggy day on 11 November 1922', a day when Britain was remembering its First World War dead. Thirty million 'Flanders poppies' made by ex-servicemen had been on sale, and King George V and his two sons led the solemn crowd at the Cenotaph in singing 'Almighty, Invisible, God Only Wise . . .'. As a sign of the wave of marches by the unemployed that were a sad feature of British life in the 1920s and 1930s, 25,000 out-of-work Londoners attached themselves to the ceremony, carrying at the head of their procession a large wreath inscribed, 'From the living victims – the unemployed – to our dead comrades who died in vain.' Out of middle-class sight in Poplar and Lambeth, a smallpox epidemic was gaining momentum. That same week the British Broadcasting Company, which 60 years later (as the BBC) was to invite Nina to record her memories for television, used the Marconi call sign 2LO for the first time in a broadcast from the roof of Selfridges.

On 30 December, Lenin proclaimed the creation of the Union of Soviet Socialist Republics. (More accurately, it was proclaimed in Lenin's name; he had suffered a second stroke on 15 December and on the 24th the Politburo had ordered that he be kept in isolation.) David and Manya's wandering years, and whatever hopes went with them, were over. The country to which they returned was physically the same, but psychologically much had changed. They had left an Edwardian England, hub of the world's trade and heart of an empire. The England they came back to had lost over 600,000 men in the First World War (leaving out of account the losses of its colonies and dominions) and had nursed 1.66 million wounded, some so maimed that they would never work again. In historical terms the sun was setting fast. The country had been bled by a war that had solved nothing, but had sown and fertilised the seeds for the next, and was about to be further drained by the war's economic and social consequences: the slump, industrial and class strife, and the collapse of its cherished currency. The certainty of empire was crumbling and British rule would soon yield, not without more bloody struggle and rebellion, to self-determination and the more nebulous concept of the Commonwealth.

On the day the Redstones arrived in London, Robert Lewis's loyal customer Winston Churchill told his Dundee constituents, 'What a terrible disappointment the twentieth century has been. How terrible and how melancholy is the long series of disastrous events which have darkened the first twenty years. We have seen in every country a dissolution, a weakening of the bonds, a challenge to those principles, a decay of faith, an abridgment of hope on which the structure and ultimate existence of civilised society depends.' The sadness of those words is that they could have been repeated with even greater validity every twenty years thereafter.

In the words of the Annual Register, 1921 had been 'a more disappointing and depressing period in British commerce and finance than had been experienced for 100 years. 1922 was a little less depressing but the aggregate improvement was by no means negligible.' Much worse was to come. However, the Redstones had more basic concerns to worry about than the state of the world. Restarting a life cannot have been easy, all the more since we have to doubt whether Manya had overcome her aversion to all things English. On the other hand, they had run out of options and it had to be made to work.

They lived first in Shaia's home in Clapton, which was a 'way station' on the East European émigré trail of upward mobility to Hampstead, Golders Green and the leafy slopes of Mill Hill. It must have been almost totally Russian once the front door was shut on England. David, Manya and their three children crammed in alongside Shaia, his second wife Bella (extracted with difficulty with her four-year-old daughter Nadya from the chaos of post-Revolution Ukraine), Shaia's son Charles, and the family matriarch Tsivia, known as *Mamochka*.

They had left London as cinema was starting. Now, if David and Manya had the time and coins to spare, the children could stare goggle-eyed at the antics of Mickey Mouse's forerunner Felix the Cat. For adults, though sound had still to come, and the boom in cinema building was ten years off, London's West End already had five cinemas, showing at one end of the spectrum *The Four Horsemen of the Apocalypse*, which launched Rudolph Valentino's career, and at the other *Flames of Passion*, which a reviewer found 'distasteful . . . strangling babies is not a pleasant subject for entertainment'. Though not yet converted from theatre to cinema, the London Pavilion was festooned with the first large electric advertising hoardings and, showing how enduring some careers can be, Fred Astaire starred in *Stop Flirting* at the Shaftsbury Theatre and Noël Coward was one of the principal performers in *London Calling*, a revue that borrowed the first signature call-sign of the BBC. Football was firmly in place as the No. 1 spectator sport. Baseball had failed to win acceptance, despite an extraordinary game at London's Stamford Bridge ground on 4 July 1918, celebrating the Anglo-US alliance. Thirty-eight thousand spectators watched the US Navy beat the US Army, probably none more bemused than the guests of honour, King George V and Queen Mary, by both the alien rituals and the painful reminder of what George III had done to make the date memorable.

Even though the car quickly changed the look and tempo of the country, Britain's economy remained in many ways as old-fashioned as the King. The government's measurement of commodity prices that year still included only one quotation for 'Petroleum, American Refined, per barrel' compared to three benchmarks for different grades of coal, four for wool and no less than six for cotton. Hides came in two grades – 'English Ox First' and 'Cape Dry' – and even the price level of 'Livonian Flax Z.K.' went into the equation. Though there were some overseas foodstuffs in the index – rice from Burma and frozen mutton from New Zealand – others had a sturdy yeoman flavour: 'Cheese, English Cheddar' and 'Potatoes, English, Good.'

Then, as indeed later, there was something about large London stores that led their owners into complex personal lifestyles. Gordon Selfridge was by then famous for his success with the store and notorious for his dalliance with the Dolly Sisters, Hungarian 'cabaret artistes', for whom he bought the lease of Lord Shelburne's former mansion off Berkeley Square. Invitations to their parties at which they demonstrated the 'Black Bottom' and 'The Charleston' were much sought-after. The house has gone through as many structural alterations as the Sisters no doubt did and is now the genteel Lansdowne Club. William Whiteley was another man who partied; he had a string of mistresses and was shot dead in his store at the opening of a grand sale by a young man claiming to be his illegitimate son; bemused customers thought at first it was all part of the publicity. When the Redstones were first in London, Whiteley's and Harrods were in business and Selfridges was getting under way. Now there were stores galore, many of them a roll call of euphonious double-barrelled names – among them the now long-gone Marshall & Snelgrove, Swears & Wells, Bourne & Hollingsworth and Swan & Edgar. The real estate adventures of Mr Bourne and Mr Hollingsworth on Oxford Street show just how hard it was to assemble a large West End site from a warren of small buildings. It took them several years to buy out a brothel, a 'nest of Polish tailors' and a small cigarette factory.

It was the beginning of the age of commercial flight. Croydon Aerodrome, as it was first called, had been opened in 1921 using the site and buildings of a First World War Royal Flying Corps base. Converted wartime Vickers Vimy biplane bombers bounced down the grass runways carrying passengers, mail and freight to Paris, Amsterdam and Rotterdam. Travellers were ferried to the aerodrome from Central London by motor-coach, and were encouraged to 'carry gloves and a warm light coat in case extra height is necessary to avoid clouds'. They could buy lunch boxes at the airport, but, as *Baedeker* counselled, 'for an initial trip it is wiser to depend upon a few dry biscuits and a little fruit'. There was no radar or air-traffic control, just a compass and an Ordnance Survey map strapped on the navigator's knee. Pilots coming in to land could be sure they were in the right place only when they saw 'CROYDON' painted in large white letters on the runway.

The landscape over which those first passengers roared queasily through the clouds was also changing, but not yet that rapidly. When David and his family came back in 1922, Edgware and Hendon as seen in aerial photos were still largely green fields; just north of where Edgware Station now stands, Cannons, once the country mansion of the Duke of Chandos, stood in sad isolation waiting to be engulfed like a sandcastle by the incoming tide. But the photos also show that the Northern Line was just pushing its tendrils northwards from Golders Green, etched in the fields like the first trenches cutting across Flanders. By 1930, the two stations had spawned developments of side roads, shops and ribbons of houses that in Hendon's case obliterated almost every vestige of the countryside of which David Garrick had once been Lord of the Manor; one of the little houses in the Hendon photo became David and Manya's home. Measuring population-shift involves some of the same risks as comparing money values, but in the twenty-five years or so from the Redstones' first brief stay in London and the time they bought their house, the population of what was known as 'The County of London', the inner districts, remained static at around 4.5 million; that of the wider agglomeration known as 'Greater London' rose from 6.5 to around 8.1 million.

The Redstones' house was like thousands of others. Its layout was almost identical, for instance, to homes in a new development being marketed around that time a little further north, in Harrow, whose specifications even included – as did 33 The Drive, NW11 – a coke-fired 'Ideal' boiler and a gas-heated 'copper' for the laundry. It was offered at £825 – £45 down and repayments of £25 / 4d per week with no legal fees to pay and a twelve-month warranty (assuming that the builder was still in business a year later). A local agent estimates that No. 33 would today sell for between £350,000 and £400,000.

Not long after they moved in, a London art-house cinema, the Paris Pullman, was offering *October*, Eisenstein's sweeping, propagandistic version of the start of the Revolution, and I find it hard to believe that David and Manya did not take the Tube ride to see it themselves. Though they had not been in St Petersburg, they had seen enough of the Revolution for these black-and-white images and triumphant commentary to represent a disturbing blend of reality and world revolution and a propagandist's distortion of it. The depiction of Provisional Prime Minister Kerensky caught the sharp film critic's eye of Graham Greene in 'the gleam of gaiters, the Napoleonic gesture, the neurotic hands, the thin, frightened, defiant, egotistical face'. But Eisenstein shows us the true face of the Revolution when he closes in on the sweaty face of a supposed sailor from the battleship *Aurora* grinning lewdly as he lifts the wooden lid of the Tsarina's commode – 'supposed' because, although some of the original revolutionary soldiers and sailors were used as extras, the film was a re-enactment. That did not stop the Soviets showing this

Bolshevik-boosting barnstormer to their captive audiences for years under the guise of a documentary rather than the rewriting of history by the victors. And if David and Manya went to see Marlene Dietrich and Anna May Wong in the 1932 epic *Shanghai Express*, they would have remembered the dangerous train journey across bandit-infested China, since it was based on a true story of one of the train ambushes they had been so lucky to avoid.

I wonder, too, whether Manya would have noticed that, at about the time they bought their home, Queen Charlotte's Hospital, that nightmare scene etched in her memory, was moving into serious fundraising, leaving its roots far behind. Orchestrated by Society matrons, the Queen Charlotte's Ball soon became a highlight of the London season, when young debutantes, rich *jeunes filles en fleur*, in long white dresses, gloves and their grandmothers' jewels, were 'presented' in a ritual known rather quaintly to today's ears as 'coming out'. By the time the Redstones moved in, the BBC too had moved on from its 2LO days, although extracts from a programme for the Home Service on the 365-metre waveband would not do much for today's *Big Brother*-sated audiences: news at 10 a.m., an unspecified 'talk' at 3.15 p.m., Purcell's *Dido and Aeneas* at 8 p.m. and, to round off the evening at 10 p.m., 'extracts from the review "Bubbly"'. And so to bed.

Sadness lingered. David and Manya watched and prayed as poor Valentin, too young for any of their travails and efforts to save him to have made any sense, faded and died in the crisp linen sheets of a Stoke Mandeville hospital bed. Manya rarely spoke to us about him, but had photos of him in her album, wide eyes staring from the depths of one of those old-fashioned wickerwork invalid carriages in a row lined up neatly along a hospital veranda. His portrait in a wooden oval frame hung on her dining-room wall, where the light from the front window would catch it. Beneath it a delicate china vase was fixed to the wall, its tiny sprig of flowers regularly replaced to the accompaniment of a silent prayer. My sister Natalie once came across a scrap of blue notepaper in an unmarked envelope in David's desk – children are inveterate pryers – on which was written, in a painstaking script, 'To My Dear Daddy, from Valentin'. She put it back.

22

Nice Little Business

Thanks to courage and clever footwork by Shaia, the House of Sobranie that David was rejoining, although still tiny by tobacco industry standards, had made considerable financial and business progress. The outbreak of the First World War had presented Albert Weinberg with a painful choice. A later account says that feeling increasingly pulled towards Vienna by his wife and his own cultural interests, and realising that his son had no interest in taking over the business, he moved back to Austria and placed the company in the hands of a trustee until Shaia could take full responsibility. The official files suggest, however, that despite Albert's naturalisation, and most likely because he had moved back to Vienna, the business actually passed into the hands of a trustee under the Trading with the Enemy Act and that Shaia had to go to court to regain the trademarks. Getting the company back must have been no small victory; the 'enemy' owners of the Bechstein Piano Company, whose London showrooms were similarly put into trusteeship, saw them sold off to another of those ubiquitous department stores with the ampersands, Debenham & Freebody, happily to re-emerge later as the Wigmore Hall. (When the Bechstein family opened the doors of their gilded Munich drawing room to an ambitious politician named Hitler, and Madame Bechstein even pawned her jewels to help his fledgling party over an early financial crisis, those with long memories concluded that they deserved not to get their showrooms back.) Albert died along with the Austro-Hungarian empire in 1918. Albert's son, born

Karl but now known as Charles, listed himself in some of the London High Court legal papers in the case as 'a gentleman of no occupation' with an address in the leafy little spa of Baden half an hour outside Vienna; he later moved back to London and lived the life of a genteel but indigent bachelor in Swiss Cottage, whose coffee houses and nests of Central European émigrés must have been a rather sad substitute for the *gemütlich* ambience of the Hapsburg days.

In a couple of early interviews given to tobacco trade journals, the two brothers say that it was the firm of Robert Lewis that in effect re-launched Sobranie in 1919 – by lending Shaia the money to buy tobacco from the 1919 harvest direct from the Balkan growers, and also by introducing him to the Midland Bank, which provided working capital. Probably reflecting de Sola Pinto's roots, it was the bank's Whitechapel branch which granted the overdraft. Its manager, a Mr Bass, had successfully cornered a large share of the East End Jewish business market, knowing whom to back, whom to turn down, when to foreclose and when to extend a helping dose of extra liquidity. Some of his early customers, such as Tesco, stayed with the branch for many years, even though they had outgrown its capacity. However, the background suggests that it was not actually the Lewis firm, but de Sola Pinto's influence, that was the key, since while his wholesaling business continued to flourish in the capable hands of his partner Fred Croley, Lewis itself entered the 1920s in poor financial health and was turned around only when Croley moved across to take charge. However the financing was arranged, in the words of his younger son Isidore, Shaia was in fact taking 'the biggest business gamble of his life' by breaking the traditional pattern of small firms' financial dependence on the Greek and Syrian leaf merchants whose well-manicured hands on the hot and cold taps of credit meant that they could juggle prices to suit themselves. 'Indeed if they so desired, they simply put one maker out of business and replaced him with another more compliant with their wishes and prices.'

The help (the amount involved was said to be 'some £4000', a sizeable sum in those days) was not entirely string-free. The quid pro quo was an unwritten agreement by Sobranie to stick to manufacturing. The stores, such as Lewis, who commanded the top end of London's cigar and cigarette market were worried about a developing appetite on the part of manufacturers to move 'downstream' into the retail end of the trade. Philip Morris, which was established in 1847, had an elegant double-fronted store on Bond Street, as did Benson & Hedges; and Sullivan & Powell, whom we shall meet again later, ran three West End stores as outlets for their Egyptian and Turkish cigarettes. Another maker, Fribourg and Treyer, 'At the Sign of the Rasp and Crown', looked out on the world from bay windows in Haymarket (still there, though the business itself has vanished along with its curious sideline in 'Treyer's Portable Soup' and its customers, among them the Marquess of Queensbury, no doubt avoiding Messrs Robert Lewis for fear of bumping into his son's bumptious friend Oscar Wilde). Before the greater profit margins of popular catering became evident in 1894, the Salmon and Gluckstein families who built J. Lyons (now, alas, yet another once instantly recognisable name that has slipped into oblivion) had owned a chain of tobacconists in and around London.

(Philip Morris made cigarettes under various very British labels, notably its own name and 'Marlborough', after the West End street where the company had its workshop. The business had its ups and then rather more downs, and was eventually reincarnated in the United States, where the brand became 'Marlboro' and was re-launched in 1925 for the woman smoker. Proclaiming a smoke 'as mild as May', and tackling head-on the perception that women who smoked were 'fast', the copywriters asked: 'Has smoking got any more to do with morals than the colour of a woman's hair? Women quickly develop discerning taste. That's why Marlboros now ride in so many limousines, attend so many bridge parties, repose in so many handbags.' The power of marketing over the actual product was demonstrated with another change of target in 1964. 'Come to where the flavour is. Come to Marlboro Country', men in grey flannel suits were urged, and the grizzled Marlboro Man was born to bring fulfilment to their Walter Mitty side.)

By 1921, Sobranie had moved across Soho to 3 Carlisle Street, again a nest of small businesses including the Au Bebe Rose ice cream company, a goldsmith, a diamond merchant and, in a sign of changing times, a film agent. *Private Eye* is now the most recognisable tenant. By 1928 David and Shaia had moved to 33 Newman Street, once a street of sculptors but notable today only for a public house serving the finest steak and kidney pies in London, and its surrounding skein of Dickensian alleyways which have somehow survived the wrecking ball. For reasons known only to Albert and later the Redstone brothers, until well into the 1940s the name of 'Sobranie' itself does not appear in the London trades directories, which show only 'A. Weinberg' or 'I. Redstone, cigarette manufacturer' at the various addresses. Competition was if anything tougher, even though the cigarette habit was growing fast, boosted by the tensions, changing habits and the emergence of a new status for women in the First World War. Sobranie had its niche, untroubled by the major giants, but there was almost a page of small cigarette manufacturers listed in the business directory, many with Ruritanian brand names – de Reszke, Markovitch, Abdulla, Alexander Boguslavsky and the Imperial Ottoman Tobacco Company – clearly targeting the same market.

The two girls moved along the conveyor belt of education and assimilation at different speeds. Nina did well at the North London Collegiate School, which by her day had abolished the very British entry criterion that the daughters of tradesmen could be admitted only if their parents did not live above the shop. My mother by her anecdotes was a rather less disciplined child who was once locked in the toilet at La Sagesse Convent for the best part of a day for pulling off a nun's hood to settle an argument with other girls about whether the good sisters shaved their heads.

Like so many partnerships, David and Shaia must have had a chemical, telepathic relationship, but taking David back into the business again must have been tricky for both of them. Though as an instinctive businessman as well as a brother, Shaia may have seen the value of a gregarious 'Mr Outside' to complement his skills inside. Shaia was held in some awe in the wider family; so much so that it was only when I started this research that I realised that David was the elder of the two. Years later an interviewer commented that they had a 'complete understanding of thought and mood', to which Shaia remarked: 'If we have had differences, we have never had disagreements or we couldn't have done it.' He brought a clear head, years of experience – he knew how to shred, to blend and to roll – and flair. They had a quality product; as others have discovered before and since, when markets slump, some of the rich go bankrupt and many draw in their horns, but they do go on spending, making a small, low-overhead manufacturer of luxury goods with a solid overseas clientele less vulnerable than a business exposed to consumer markets.

Shaia had a fine business head and a deep knowledge of every aspect of the trade, but it took David's salesmanship and legwork as the main face of the firm (and in later years the hard work of Shaia's sons Charles and Isidore) to get the products into the market. Both brothers won ready acceptance from the very British, very upper-class leaders of the major tobacco companies. In part this stemmed from their expertise. When the Chairman of Imperial Tobacco proudly showed off to Shaia the package for a new brand of cigarettes about to be launched with great fanfare and expense, Shaia remarked succinctly, 'It won't work.' And it didn't. David won hearts and minds by his genuine friendliness. (If we hark back to the matryoshka doll analogy, the image of my grandfather in those Sobranie years might be called 'David the Gregarious', if that did not make him sound like an especially obscure saint.) Over and above that, I suspect that they were accepted because they were honest and did not pretend to be anything other than they were. They did not become upwardly mobile. They did not hanker after ever grander homes as a sign of success or put themselves about for the benefit of fashionable charities. They were quiet men, very much un-Anglicised, unreconstructed and unassimilated, with heavy accents. Foreignness was a plus for their product, although both brothers had been naturalised as British. Shaia's 'memorial', as the application was quaintly called back then, was approved in 1910, with an accompanying assurance from a CID sergeant who interviewed him that he spoke and wrote English 'quite well'. The certificate was granted by that essence of Britishness and early buyer of 'large Balkans', Winston Churchill, then Home Secretary.

Given his own history, it seems appropriate somehow that when David applied in 1930, his certificate was issued under the authority of a Labour Home Secretary, J. G. 'Jimmy' Clines, a veteran trades-unionist whose youthful skills as a professional clog-dancer no doubt boosted his advancement up politics' slippery slopes, and who the year before had refused the now rather better known Odessite, Leon Trotsky, permission to settle in Britain in case it would offend the Soviet government. Britain could at least claim to be even-handed in indirectly condemning men to death, since in 1917 King George V had encouraged his government in its decision to refuse refuge to his deposed cousin, the Tsar, on the grounds that his presence in Britain might give rise to working-class resentment and even mutiny in the armed forces.

Even when in the 1950s and 1960s I knew Sobranie as an international business and a public company, my own memory of it is as a remarkably frugal operation. There was no fancy lobby with decorative flower displays, no pert receptionist behind a rosewood credenza, no glossy annual reports laid out on low glass tables. When they were not travelling or David was not out courting the trade, who soon nicknamed him 'Uncle David', the brothers would eat at their desks, my grandfather's lunch box put together by Manya before she waved him off after breakfast, usually with black olives, maybe a piece of cold fried fish and a handful of lettuce leaves. Until quite late in life he would commute by Tube.

In the City Road factory to which they moved in the late 1930s (the first time the Sobranie name was recorded on a building), the entire administration seemed to the outsider to rest on the long-suffering and capable shoulders of the Company Secretary, Mr Rose – first name informality was unthinkable back then – with a handful of clerks scribbling away and cranking lever-operated accounting machines behind semi-glazed partitions. In a pattern typical then of the loyalty family-controlled firms commanded, Mr Rose worked for Sobranie for forty-eight years and retired at the age of 79. Upstairs, where bales of tobacco were stacked on the floors, cheery East End ladies in headscarves still hand-rolled some of the brands while others were ejected with great rapidity from a pair of Molins machines that my grandfather regarded with some suspicion. The ladies worked at blurring speed, still able to chat and keep half an ear on the radio. My sister remembers walking around the factory floor with David, who, like the cheerful patriarch he was, yelled about the din, 'Are you happy, girls?' Their jolly chorus that all was well seemed to her quite genuine. It would be interesting to know how they compared to one of Sobranie's male rollers in its earlier years in Newman Street, written up with some awe in the trade press as producing 3,500 cigarettes by hand in an eight-hour day. Since he had been rolling since the age of 8, his lifetime total must have been stupendous.

Two 'ingredients' were blended into the product with as much skill as the tobacco. One was Shaia's flair for packaging, which built on old Albert's porcelain containers to create boxes that always had strong visual appeal, especially 'Black Russians', whose gold-embossed boxes of heavyweight board with a slight texture to it had an almost tactile appeal. The other was to strike just the right note in an advertising campaign that positioned what had started in a Soho attic as a business of distinction with a three-generation tradition of manufacturing a product that was not only of high quality but that was also redolent with class, snob appeal even, and worldly style, but at the same time could fit acceptably into the fixtures, fittings and habits of the British upper-class way of life.

In its heyday, cigarette advertising was an art form. One classic (though non-Sobranie) advert is reproduced by Gregor Dallas in his history of 1918, when a brand named – rather mundanely – Kenilworth pitched its product directly into Siegfried Sassoon territory. The couple in the engraving are nestled decorously in the firelight on a chintzy sofa, he in what the French would call *'un Smoking'* with a bow tie, she in a demure dress, with a terrier curled loyally at their feet.

'You've seen it through,' Kenilworth declared reassuringly, implying that after struggling out of thigh-deep Flanders mud, the reek of mustard gas and rotting horse and human flesh choking the nostrils, and maybe a spell trembling shell-shocked in an Edwardian estate on the South Downs converted into a convalescent home, all the returning young officer needed to set him straight was the love of a good woman and a long pull on one of their Virginia cigarettes at 1/4d for twenty. 'You don't want to talk about it. You don't want to think about it. You just want to lean back and feel that the day you have been dreaming of since that first August of 1914 has come at long last. It's good to be alive. It's good to be with her . . .'

Sobranie used *Punch* (then a readable staple of Home Counties drawing rooms and private doctors' surgeries), the *Daily Telegraph*, *The Times* and *The Tatler* as the main outlets for a brand message that, while today sounding more than slightly Woosterish, clearly worked well. One series revolved around a character named Willougby, at least one of whose cheery thoughts would raise an eyebrow nowadays at the Advertising Standards Authority were cigarette advertising itself not effectively banned anyway. Under the Jesuitical heading 'The End Justifies the Means', Willoughby chortled, 'For example when I fill my case with the pater's cigarettes, I feel more like a Christian seeking Heaven than Satan robbing a Church. And with a smile he handed me a case of Balkan Sobranie . . .' Another of the home thoughts of this philosopher of the smoking room, ending with the same punch line, declared that, 'A man must keep a few pleasures to himself. And I'll confess to you that my greatest secret pleasure is the possession of a case full of cigarettes that make me feel that I'm entitled to an escort of Household Cavalry . . .'

It is not clear at what point two talented men at Vernons advertising agency took on the Sobranie account. Colin Fitton, later a member of the Royal Academy, dealt with the artwork while the text was the province of Harold Hutchinson, author of several serious works of history and also copywriter for an acclaimed series of London Transport posters in those distant days when the system had merits that it was bold enough to advertise. The advertising was the backdrop against which David pounded the pavements, first the length and breadth of the UK and then the Continent, with his cardboard case of samples – he claimed that once he arrived in a city, he never took a cab. If his sales technique followed that of de Sola Pinto and Fred Croley, he would have taken a room in a good hotel, laid out his samples neatly and invited in the local retailers for a smoke, a drink and hopefully an order. Reading his tales of calling on the crusty colonels of regiments of the Line, or being so liberally dosed with whiskey in a Portsmouth wardroom, how far in every sense he had come from the fiery revolutionary ready to risk all to the avuncular, neat, persistent but always jovial salesman, so foreign that it made the product seem more 'real'. The brand became synonymous, in one fan's words, with 'long cigarette holders, elegance, pink gin and Earl Grey tea'. An early victory – and, when one thinks about it, a rather remarkable one for a bearded raconteur from Akkerman without connections in high places – was getting Sobranie selected as the 'on-board' cigarette when the Duke and Duchess of York, later George VI and Queen Elizabeth, toured the Empire in the battleship *Renown*. That they were first cousins of the Tsar for whose downfall he had agitated would never have occurred to him.

Over the years, Shaia had registered a portfolio of exotic cigarette trademarks, some of which never made it on to the tobacconists' shelves. They included 'Navrati', 'Natalka', 'Salim' (whose box bore an image of a camel laden with bales prominently labelled with the brand name), 'Vanity Fair', 'Karsavina' (named after the prima ballerina of Diaghilev's Ballets Russes) and 'Boyar'; by some Victorian quirk of the patent laws, some were officially deemed to be valid 'so long as the product is available for sale in the House of Commons and the House of Lords'. But 'Sobranie' became the focus.

It would have been fun to have been present at the lunch when David persuaded the legendary Russian bass Fyodor Chaliapin to put his name on a Sobranie brand of cigarettes, with the traditional cardboard-tube tips which Russians believed cooled the smoke to soothing levels. When David got the endorsement, Chaliapin was at the height of his fame. How did he and my diminutive grandfather meet? Thirty years or so later, David told a journalist only that, 'My great friend Fyodor Chaliapin . . . was offered $30,000 for his endorsement for a mass produced cigarette. No, he said, I only smoke Sobranie. And his wife [the Italian ballerina Iola Tornaghi], I remember, was rather cross with him . . .'

Some tangible mementoes of this relationship have survived the years. The endorsement letters were handwritten in two English versions and, for some now long-forgotten marketing reasons, in

Spanish. In July that year, Chaliapin had appeared at Covent Garden as 'Boris Godunov' and one English version declares that 'Boris Godounov [*sic*] finds Chaliapin cigarettes well worthy [*sic*] their name; he has recommended them to the Volga Boatmen.' The second tells the world that 'I have not smoked cigarettes since 1913 until you offered me your Balkan Sobranie. I have smoked most brands of tobacco – once. But never have I found such flavour, such aroma, such exquisite smoking before. The Balkan Sobranie is a great discovery for me.'

There is also a photograph dated simply '1928' and dedicated 'To dear Mr David Redstone, with best wishes for your remarkable business.' Chaliapin had a penchant for dashing off little sketches and self-portraits and he also gave David a drawing of himself on Savoy Hotel notepaper. At a domestic level, the Redstones' stack of cardboard-wrapped 78 r.p.m. vinyl records included a scratchy version of Chaliapin singing '*Blokha*' ('The Flea'), a fine song in itself and also a reminder of the Russian obsession with bed and body invaders. However, as the critic Sir Neville Cardus warned, 'You can no more get an idea of Chaliapin from a gramophone record than you get of a pterodactyl by looking at a skeleton preserved in a museum, because he was such an enormous, abounding personality on the stage.'

Chaliapin was in every sense a commanding figure. He earned large sums of money, lived well and did not need to give endorsements. Chaliapin was intuitive, a man given to swift likes and dislikes, and I suspect his intuition quickly told him that he and the cheerful little cigarette salesman had much in common. His childhood in a poor peasant family had been far tougher than David's and had also included a considerable stretch of poverty-stricken adolescent wandering. He had seen the Revolution and met its makers, and it had greatly saddened him to see his beloved homeland taken over by what his son later called 'a monarchy of louts'. He had left Russia for good in 1922 and felt his exile deeply; I have little doubt that it was this common bond of being irrevocably so far from home, whatever the material rewards, that brought him and David together.

(How his name should be spelled in English is of interest only to pedants. In Russian it is spelled 'Shalyapin'. His biographer uses the now accepted English spelling 'Chaliapin'. The singer himself, Covent Garden and the Albert Hall all used the spelling 'Chaliapine', as indeed did Sobranie. It has not the slightest relevance to his magic.)

Chaliapine was not the only exotic Sobranie product. There was also the legendary Black Russian, its matt black box set off by the gold-embossed tsarist double eagle. Capitalising on that symbol of the old world to make money in the new must have given David and his brother a quiet chuckle. Suggested by an Oxford retailer who had an exiled grand duke as a customer, the gold tips on the black-paper cigarettes themselves were less a stroke of design genius than a practical way of preventing black stains on smokers' fingers. The legend lives on. The two brothers would have been mystified by the name and the music of Captain Beefheart, whose description of Black Russian and its strong tobacco as 'refreshing like watercress in a stream' is hard to reconcile with the memory of what I for one recall as its exceptionally rich taste; a fellow member of the Captain's 'Magic Band' was closer to the mark when he moaned about 'those evil-smelling Sobranie cigarettes'.

Showing off his prized Dennis Wheatley book, David told me how he got to know the raffish writer of thrillers and black-magic novels when he was making his sales calls and Wheatley was running – into the ground – his father's Mayfair wine merchants business. One day in 1927, he called into the panelled vintners at 26 South Audley Street, almost opposite Purdey the Gunsmiths. There he saw Wheatley standing unsteadily on the mahogany counter top, drinking champagne, surrounded by his louche hangers-on (in his memoirs Wheatley names some of them: 'Bino', Sternberg and Stambois – any of whom could have been in a cast list of one of his novels). David was taken aback, he told me, to learn that the noisy celebration was in honour of the death of Wheatley's father. I stored the anecdote away in my memory for nearly fifty years, probably with a mental note that if not *ben trovato*, it was perhaps an exaggeration. Then, whilst researching this book, I came across Wheatley's own version of that period of profligacy and pressure: 'I had earlier that year acquired a beautiful mistress. Somehow I managed to stave off my creditors through the last months of 1926 and the spring of 1927. Then I was unexpectedly saved. On 4th May my father died . . .' So we can even date almost to the day when David pushed open the door of Wheatley & Son ('Under the Sign of the Golden Flagon', telegraphic address, 'Bacchus'). Wheatley had a sideline in wholesaling cigars and cigarettes, some of them supplied by Sobranie, to regimental messes. Given the parlous state of business at the Golden Flagon, I suspect my grandfather was paying a 'dunning' call. If so, he cannot have been too offensive since he and Wheatley stayed in touch. Wheatley's paternal grandfather had once owned all the shops on the stretch on the eastern side of the street (now bracketed between Harry's Bar and George's, each with a glitterati clientele of which Wheatley would have thoroughly approved), and the author was convinced he was in line for quite a sizeable inheritance; hence the celebration. Sadly for Wheatley, the cork-popping proved premature since most of the money went to his mother, who remarried and took the fortune with her. Though he paid off his debts, it was only the fortunate acquisition of a rich second wife that enabled him to launch himself on his far more successful second career as an author.

The book of which David was so proud was the brainchild of one of Wheatley's oldest friends, J. G. Links. Links was also 'in trade' as the royal furrier (and as a member of one of the two founding families of the J. Lyons empire, fortified by the dividends from all those cups of coffee and slices of swiss roll), but is nowadays better known as the author of *Venice for Pleasure*. In 1936, Links and Wheatley joined forces to compile a crime story as the replica of a police dossier, with scene-of-crime photos, detectives' reports, witness statements, letters, telegrams, all printed on individual and apparently authentic forms, swatches of purportedly bloodstained fabric and a glassine envelope containing a cigarette butt. *Murder off Miami* sold 120,000 copies and must have been a production nightmare for its publishers, since each copy had to be put together by hand. The authors signed some of them, but only David Redstone's copy had another special feature: in the regular edition the cigarette butt was Senior Service; in his it was a Balkan Sobranie Turkish.

At David's urging – he was predominantly a pipe man – tobacco added a profitable new dimension to the cigarette business. The round tins, again with the Balkan logo, offered a range from Smoking Mixture, 'a unique blend of mature Virginia and rarest Yenidje leaf', to Flake, 'eleven selected leaves combine to give rich aroma and coolness'. Glossing over the fact that the tobacco was actually processed to Sobranie's specifications by Messrs George Dobie in the distinctly un-Balkan setting of Edinburgh, the copywriters sought with great success to woo smokers away from lesser brands: 'You may have been smoking a pipe for years and settled on your choice of blend. You may believe no other tobacco could give you so much satisfaction. You may be right. But many satisfied pipemen have borrowed a fill of Sobranie from a friend and found otherwise. They have said very little as the fragrant smoke has gently, richly, surprised their senses. But already they've joined the Sobranie circle. For three generations this has been happening as three generations of one gifted family have done their artful blending. Have you got a generous friend who smokes Sobranie?'

It is hard and usually misleading to calculate that, because of inflation, £10,000 in the 1930s is 'equivalent' to £500,000, or whatever, today. The equation has too many variables and assumptions. Purchasing and earning power have changed, as have lifestyles and relative incomes; even the relationship between capital and income. But it is clear that while Sobranie was successful, and was providing its directors with a decent living, it was still small in profit terms. In 1938, the first figures on the record, it made a net profit of £6,298, of which the directors shared about half.

It was still enough for David to have bought the three-bedroom semi-detached house in Brent, every nook and cranny of which I can walk through in my mind today, just as I can see and feel the sharp fronds of the monkey-puzzle tree in the paved front garden. It was also enough to send his daughters to good schools and to knock down the wall between the two downstairs rooms so that the girls could invite their friends, roll back the carpets and dance to the scratchy music record on black vinyl discs revolving at 78 r.p.m., then known as 'gramophone records' and now, like Sobranie boxes and treadle sewing machines, collectors' items. The ever prudish BBC felt that the British people should not be indulged, and played only about an hour of dance music a day, around lunch or teatime, neither likely to attract an adolescent audience.

The late 1920s and 1930s were grim times in Britain. There were hunger marches, the 1926 General Strike, the Slump, the Wall Street Crash, the Great Depression and the rise of the 'Great Dictators' and, closer to home, the aristocratic British fascist Oswald Mosley. All must have given refugees such as David and Manya even deeper anxiety than their British neighbours. They had made their home in this tiny grey country. Would it now be engulfed in a revolution of its own? Would the business survive? Would their savings once more go up, like the Sobranie products, in a puff of smoke?

Though history books capture the rolling inevitability of it all, it is curious that an isolated snapshot gives a mixed picture of just how real the danger was thought to be. Looking selfishly at *The Times* for the day I was born, 22 April 1939, just a few months before war came, advertisements for bomb shelters for air-raid wardens and for boarding schools 'in a safe, remote area' suggested that the public had the message. The City of London certainly did: gold shipments to the safety of the Unites States were at record levels. Perhaps the most poignant reminders of the real world were the many advertisements placed by Jews in Germany and Austria, even at the eleventh hour and fifty-ninth minute, desperately seeking any kind of domestic work in Britain. The news pages and editorials, however, preferred not to write about impending disaster, but about arcane developments in the politics of Romania, of a stately round of international conferences, and referred politely to 'Herr Hitler'.

23

Gulag and Gasmasks

If things looked bleak in 1930s London, they were unimaginably more awful under the dictatorship of the proletariat in the Soviet Union. It was a time of purges, deportations and forced labour in pursuit of ever more grandiose and unachievable Five Year Plans for economic development, paranoia, terror, informers (even among family members), forced confessions, show trials and human misery on a scale that made the tsarist era seem benign. It is an extraordinary tribute to the gullibility of liberals and intellectuals and the power of propaganda and spin that it took so long for the truth to come out. That is another story. Of the millions of man-made deaths in Russia in the 1930s and 1940s, a handful will serve to put our family story into that evil context.

Take Maria Spiridonova, the terrorist heroine and David's colleague for the short spring months of the Chita Public Safety Committee's existence. As an early and persistent opponent of the Bolsheviks, she must have been waiting stoically when the midnight knock came one day in 1937 and she was dragged away to be sentenced to twenty-five years' imprisonment for 'counter-revolutionary activities'. In 1941 she was in jail in Orel, some 200 miles south of Moscow, as the Germans approached. Even as all his efforts were concentrated on defending the Soviet Union, Stalin could still find time to indulge his paranoia about any of his supposed enemies falling into Nazi hands and being used against him in a propaganda war. Spiridonova was gagged 'by specially selected personnel', hauled from her cell, taken to a nearby room and told that she had been condemned to be shot. One wonders what went through the mind of the NKVD officer in charge of this grisly farce when he went on to tell his mute victim that the sentence 'does not include confiscation of the accused's assets, since she has none'. That evening, canvas-shrouded lorries rumbled out of the city to the Bear Woods, where Spiridonova and 156 other 'politicals' were shot like stray dogs. The NKVD had uprooted several large trees beforehand, dumped the bodies in the holes, and then put the earth and vegetation back; the bodies have never been found.

Then there was Eva Broido, who, heavily pregnant, supported her husband Mark and the Romanovka protestors from outside. After some time in Europe, the Broidos had returned to Russia, where in 1917 Mark ran the Secretariat of the Petrograd Soviet. Eva became secretary of the Central Committee of the Menshevik Party, a role which made her a natural target for arrest around 1927. She spent three years in solitary confinement in the grim prison that for centuries had been an integral part of the monastery at Suzdal' – another part of the system the Bolsheviks simply inherited rather than created. (In tsarist days it had housed mainly those reported to the Holy Synod for 'religious' offences; one priest discovered there almost by chance in 1904 had served twenty-five years for 'while drunk, speaking about the Emperor . . . without due reverence', and countless others vanished for up to fifty years for their 'blasphemous convictions', even 'laughing at the Holy icons'). Eva was then exiled first to Tashkent and later to a remote mountain village. She was shipped back to Moscow in 1931, where the NKVD hoped that intimidation and torture would shape her into one of those glazed, word-perfect witnesses at a show trial of the remaining Mensheviks. But when the trial took place in 1931, neither she nor three other leading members of the Party appeared in court. Only when some of the archives became accessible after the fall of the Soviet regime did her family learn that Eva had been sentenced to death by a military tribunal in 1940. Her sentence was commuted to fifteen years' imprisonment, but doubtless for the same motives that led him to exterminate Spiridonova, Stalin saw to it that she was retried, sentenced to death a second time and shot on 14 September 1941. Mark had died in 1934.

The previous year, at 1.30 a.m. on 27 January 1940, Isaac Babel, chronicler of the Odessa life that David remembered, had been shot as a 'French and Austrian spy', most likely in the Butyrki prison cellars, his corpse thrown into the back of a truck and bounced through the dark streets to the NKVD's crematorium at another requisitioned monastery, the Donskoi. Meantime, 'Uncle Joe' Stalin, Britain's beaming wartime ally, 'the great and wise leader', jovial recipient of bouquets of flowers from blushing Young Communist girls on his birthday, was pacing his Kremlin office, a pockmarked servant of Moloch, blue-pencilling the next day's list of sacrifices. (In 1939 he had told regional Party bosses to stop complaining about the NKVD's use of torture. 'Humanitarian methods of interrogation' got nowhere, he warned them, and 'the use of physical pressure against . . . evident enemies of the people who refuse to yield is . . . totally appropriate and expedient. Echoes of those sentiments are sadly heard again today even in supposedly far more enlightened countries.)

George Kennan would have been shocked but not surprised to see how the system whose depravities he had chronicled had burgeoned over the next half-century or so. In 1944, Lavrentii Beria, the pince-nezed paedophile who ran the NKVD, wrote a brisk and boastful report on the Gulag's contribution to the Soviet war effort. The camps now had a staff – excluding military guards – of 85,000 serving as slave-masters for over two million prisoners, near half of them jailed 'for counter-revolutionary and other dangerous crimes'. The Gulag was a mainstay of the Soviet war economy, producing ammunition, uniforms, timber and food – everything a reeling economy needed. Given the image of the Gulag, two things stand out in the chilling catalogue: first that its camps were spread across Russia, not just in Siberia; and second that, no doubt because of the demands of war, many more of the prisoners were being driven to build railways and roads than were working in the mines. This was despite the fact, as Beria's report notes blandly, that by 1942 only 19 per cent of the prisoners were fit for heavy work, compared to 35 per cent two years earlier, and a full 25 per cent were 'invalids or enfeebled'. Since Gulag doctors were not known for their sympathy or bedside manner, these statistics must have concealed a terrible roster of the sick and dying.

We saw what happened in the Lena Gold Fields in 1912 when striking workers died in a hail of gendarmerie bullets. By the standards of the later Soviet Union, the former management seems positively mild. In 1937, at the height of the purges, an NKVD detachment arrived at the Gold Field centre of Bodaibo (the subject of David's railway study), determined to wipe out 'enemies of the people' and 'Chinese' – it is not clear why the distinction was made between these two unfortunate targets. Since they had not a single dossier from which to begin to find candidates, let alone invent accusations and beat confessions out of their victims, 'we just had to sniff them out,' the local NKVD commanding officer complained in a mix of annoyance and pride. Over nine hundred people were killed or shipped off to the Gulag.

The year 1945 saw the end of the portly voluptuary Ataman Semyonov, who had survived in Port Arthur under the protection of his Japanese friends. When the Soviets caught up with him, five of his officers, treated as military men, were 'privileged' to be shot by firing squad. Semyonov's behaviour in Siberia was not forgotten and he departed jerking helplessly to a slow death at the end of a rope.

Most poignant was the fate of Manya's brother Pavel. After military service, he had moved steadily up the professional ladder. He had been given the job of organising and then running the largest hospital in Chita (named after Lenin, a man whose contribution to suffering was second to none), with 120 beds, and treating some 3,500 patients a year. When in 1935 and again in 1936 he was among those honoured by the regime for their 'outstandingly conscientious work', did he think perhaps about the warning of what the Gods did to those they were about to destroy? On 15 November 1937, two sheets of paper were pinned on the hospital notice board. The first announced that Pavel had been ordered to take two months' holiday. The next, a little later in the day, said baldly that, 'Dr Flegontov P. K. is hereby removed from the staff of the hospital.' A 1992 appreciation in a letter in the Kuznetsov Museum records flatly that 'His fate remains unknown.' I doubt if Manya ever heard about this.

Pavel is not listed in the valiant attempts made by the 'memorial' group in Russia in recent years to record the names and burial places of the millions who died. The first part of the task is tremendously diffcult, the latter probably impossible. After Stalin set the purge machinery into grim motion in the autumn of 1937, each region of the Soviet Union had its designated burial zone, run by the NKVD, into which bodies were tipped by the lorry load. One identified in Odessa was cynically hidden in the grounds of the 'Second Christian Cemetery'.

One of the few main characters in our story to die in his bed was attorney Zarudny, who retired from politics after the Revolution and seems to have pottered in relative obscurity until he passed on in November 1934. Had he lived just a few more months, his end would have been less tranquil; he would in all likelihood have been swept up along with several former members of the 'Junior Bar' and their families in the bloodbath unleashed by Stalin in the wake of the 'assassination' of his old Bolshevik henchman Sergei Kirov. That Kirov's death was more probably murder orchestrated at the behest of the 'wise leader' himself added a piquant note to the subsequent vengeance.

The cruelties listed above are just more fragments of evidence – if any more were needed – that the Soviet leaders and their pyramid of helpers, informers and killers bear a heavy burden of guilt for crimes of genocide and inhumanity: crimes for which none of them were tried. It is futile to calculate some moral relativity between the evils of Stalin and Hitler. Both were vile men. Hitler was a psychopath, Stalin a murderous throwback to medieval Russia. But we cannot leave this part of the Redstone story without citing the crushing scale of the Holocaust in their Bessarabian birthplace. It was beyond most imagining. We do not have numbers for Akkerman itself, but the town and those who were left of the Redstone family must have borne their share of the blows. The Romanians, Germany's allies, who occupied Bessarabia for most of the Second World War, played a central role in the carnage.

In 1939, there were about 250,000 Jews in Bessarabia. The Romanian dictator, Ion Antonescu, signed a secret order *'Curatirea Terului'* ('The Cleansing of the Ground') calling for on-the-spot extermination of Jews living in country villages, the concentration of city Jews into ghettoes, and the detention of all Communists and those who had served the Soviet regime. Those found guilty of collaboration would be shot. Between July and August 1941, just one frenzied bloodstained month, the Romanian Esalon Special ('Special Echelon') of the Iron Guard, as well as local police and soldiers, working enthusiastically alongside the SS Einsatz Gruppen and the Wehrmacht, killed some 150–160,000 Jews. Others were shipped to camps in Transnistria. The Akkerman Jews were shot in the sunny courtyards of the fort in which my grandfather and his brother would have played as children. According to the Simon Wiesenthal Center, when the next tally was taken on 4 September 1941, there were still 64,176 Jews left in Bessarabia. So much more to do, so little time, the killers fretted as they knocked back their schnapps and shuttered their memories of another working day. By 25 September, boosted by a wave of deportations which in themselves were a camouflage for murder, the total had been culled to 43,397. The extermination and deportation continued remorselessly until by May 1942 there were just 227 left, many of whom survived because they were classed as Jews only by virtue (or vice) of the Germanic pedantry of the race law definitions. After the war, some 7–10,000 of the Bessarabian Jews who had been deported to Siberia or fled into the Soviet interior returned. Another 50,000 were liberated from the camps in Transnistria, but how many actually returned is unknown.

(Not content with exterminating the people, someone – we do not know whether it was the Romanians, the Germans or even the Soviets – was determined to eradicate the traces of the victims. A recent research query in Odessa produced the answer that while, like Chita, many local archives have survived the successive ravages surprisingly well, pre-1945 records of 'citizens of Jewish nationality', in itself an interesting turn of phrase, have almost all disappeared, including the cemetery registers.)

Thankfully Shaia had brought his mother and two sisters over to

London before the Second World War. A third brother, Kal'man, also came but returned at some point to vanish into the night and fog. After such a massive effort to sandblast a people, their names and their memories off the face of the earth, it was astonishing to find still living in Odessa a frail old lady named Mariya Antonovna Roitenshtern, whose husband Georgy Mordukhovich Roitenshtern, who had died many years ago, had moved from Akkerman to Odessa with his parents in the 1930s. Sadly she has no knowledge or recollections of her parents-in-law, but it is hard not to believe that there is some connection and that someone else in the family shared David's luck, courage and instinct for self-preservation. Luck did not favour another likely family member (though his father had a different given name) born in Akkerman in 1900 and shot in the purge. Like the SS, the NKVD blended brutality with bureaucracy. Their records show he died on 27 August 1938.

Back in London and I hope unaware of most of this, David and Manya saw their girls married, Nina to one of the world's nicest and steadiest men, Edgar Nathan, for whom she had first worked as a secretary (they may then have still been known as 'lady typewriters') in Golden Square just round the corner from the various Sobranie habitats. Sadly my mother Sonia was less perceptive in her choice. One of the oddest aspects of her marriage was not that she chose my father, or he her. She was attractive; he was extremely handsome. He was an adventurer giving off the tantalising pheromones of the secret world; she had an exotic background that appealed to him. Though the speculation is uncharitable, the fact that her father was a partner in a well-known and apparently prosperous business may have added to her charm. No, the odd thing was rather that my father and David detested and distrusted each other and yet neither knew that they had so much in common in terms of courage and hardship.

David's adventures and bravery were of a different era, and motivated by a different ideology, but they stand up well in comparison to my father's own derring-do and spells in German and Hungarian jails. They had both had adolescent itchy feet. My father's took him at an early stage of his spy career to Sofia, home of Sobranie's trademark. He had even married a girl christened Sofia.

How sad that the two of them never sat down and shared life stories. Personal chemistry had much to do with it, since, though they had much in common, they were a study in contrasts. David was uxorious and abstemious, and never owned a car. My father was a hard drinker, given to fast cars and even faster ladies, both usually maintained on credit stretched to bungee-jumping elasticity. Perhaps because he had seen men of all types under pressure and felt that he could sort out the good from the bad, David was always suspicious of my father. This, of course, my father sensed, which did not help. At the same time he was convinced that David was rich, and thus well able to support my mother and her children and relieve him of any responsibility for such bourgeois baggage as school fees and mortgages. That David found this hard to do, and my mother was reluctant to ask, my father took as evidence of typical woman's weakness on her part and equally typical Jewish meanness on David's, rather than accepting the truth that David's shareholding in Sobranie was tiny and his means were limited. Though a self-made man of the world, international and polyglot, my father had by twenty-first century standards wildly incorrect social attitudes, detesting foreigners, Jews, intellectuals, liberals and men nowadays classified officially as having an 'orientation towards persons of the same sex'. He looked like a 1930s film star but thought like a Victorian colonel.

All that apart, both had good reason not to talk. As we know, David kept quiet about his background. My father too; even the facts of his parentage were a mystery. In later life his own wanderlust took him at an early age into the world of secrets and he was not about to share with anyone, even my mother, the background to his clandestine life. Had he and David been able to talk about such things, they might have found much to chat about in analysing the mental torment of a revolutionary, quoted by Richard Pipes in his elegant account of the Degaev Affair. If we substitute 'undercover agent' for 'terrorist', I believe the quote, even in my abbreviated form, mirrors exactly the strains that eventually undid my father and his mistress in post-war Hungary: 'The life of a terrorist,' Pipes quotes Lev Tikhomirov as saying, 'has a stupefying effect. It is the life of a hunted wolf. The dominant awareness is that he must be prepared to perish not just today or tomorrow but any second . . . [an] attachment of any seriousness and any kind is a genuine misfortune . . . Apart from five or ten like-minded persons, one must deceive from morn to night literally everyone . . . One needs extraordinary fortitude but even those who possess it, unless they extricate themselves from the quagmire of their situation, quickly go under . . .'

As the Second World War advanced, cigarette consumption rose, in part as more and more women became 'liberated' and joined the Services and the work force. Though theirs was not a mass-market product, Sobranie's profits also began to climb, the main cap on growth being the supply of tobacco; European sources were cut off and US tobacco was not yet available on any scale. Like other manufacturers, they bought up smaller, often dormant firms for their official tobacco allocations. But the war also showed just how small the core of the business still was. When the Blitz threatened London, the extended Redstone families and the business moved for two years to the relative calm of a large village house named St Peter's in Eynsham, on the road from Oxford to Whitney. David and Manya lived in the gatehouse, which must have been bulging at the seams, since it was also home not only to my mother and myself, but also over the next two years to my sisters, both born just up the road in the Dettol-scented floral gentility (it may be one of my earliest memories) of the Buddleia Nursing Home. Shaia and his family had the main house, and the barn-like building in the walled grounds served as the factory. Many of the rollers and packers were recruited from the local refugee community, and Shaia would commute weekly, taking the finished product to London for distribution and bringing back boxes of tobacco leaf.

Also housed on the property – which still stands today, though shorn of much of its grounds and outbuildings – was another Russian émigré family, friends of the Redstones. Mr Newman was in the garment trade and his wife was always supremely elegant. What the village folk made of this Slav enclave in their rural midst we can only wonder at. Before the war (and strutting poseurs like Oswald Mosley apart), British anti-Semitism has been described as 'casual', which seems to mean that it was taken for granted as part of the national mindset, rather than rabid. Certainly some of the popular writers of the more 'testosterone-loaded' adventures such as John Buchan, 'Sapper', Dornford Yates, or even more mainstream authors like J. B. Priestley himself, consistently couched their references to Jews in terms which are at best snide, when not overtly hostile. One observer who trawled through the list of the Higher Civil Service in 1939 could find only one official who was clearly Jewish, though two others, married to Christians, had names that might have indicated Jewish roots. A girl at St Paul's in the 1930s suggested that Jewishness in itself was not an issue among her fellow pupils; where resentment did arise was with Jewish girls who were 'pushy' or, as in one case – her parents ought to have known better – arrived at school in a chauffeured limousine with a footman in attendance.

Down in Eynsham, embedded British attitudes were compounded by ugly muttering about Jewish evacuees using their wealth to escape the dangers of the Blitz. Jews had profited from the First World War and were up to their tricks again, spluttered the blimps in the saloon bars of the Jolly Sportsman, the Red Lion and the village's half-dozen pubs. They were buying up empty London properties on the cheap and depriving Anglo-Saxon townsfolk of shelter by paying over the odds for houses and estates out of harm's way. There was even a bizarre rumour that gained wide if brief currency that the Luftwaffe had a list of properties owned by Jews in central London and had been paid to exclude them from their bombing targets.

Meanwhile, St Peter's – its tenants oblivious to most of this as they were not in the habit of meandering down to the local pub – was selling everything its little team could get the suppliers to manufacture. British Forces overseas were a good export market. Boxes of Virginia No. 40 even reached my father while he was locked up by the Germans in the prisoner-of-war camp, Spangenberg Castle. (In a couple of brief encounters I had with him in much later life, which formed the pitiful sum total of our acquaintanceship, and on which I have written elsewhere, my father's comments on anything Redstone-related, including my sad mother, were bitter to the point of paranoia. So the story that he was billed after the war for these supplies may well be distorted, if not a figment of his unhappy imagination.)

I cannot place Eynsham in my memory, though a faded photograph of me, aged about three, looking appallingly well fed and winsome, brings back a dream-like fragment of a high wall, a blue door and gravel paths. I have clearer, though still jumbled, memories of a later time, a sky studded with silver-grey barrage balloons like cartoon elephants, air-raid sirens, the dull crump of bombs and nights on a mattress in the allegedly safe triangular space under the Redstones' stairs. If things got really bad, we would gather up teddy bears and dolls and scuttle through the kitchen in our winceyette pyjamas to the incongruously large concrete-roofed air-raid shelter that dominated the tiny garden. Its builder must have come fresh from construction of the Maginot Line. It had wooden bunks, a clever emergency exit and a pervasive smell of damp, which reinforced the sense of claustrophobia and made the 'under the stairs' option a risk usually worth taking.

Then came the buzz of 'evacuation', a train journey north with my mother that to us seemed like a trip to the North Pole but which to her must have seemed like a weekend excursion compared to the many thousands of fear-filled miles she had travelled on so many railways. We were lugging our gas masks in their cardboard boxes, mine a grey-green rubber contraption with the filter cylinder jutting out at the front like a pig's snout, which looked as though it had been recycled from Ypres, my sisters with the body-wrapping baby models in red rubber with a huge celluloid face plate, forerunners of the helmets of the first moon-walkers. In Kendal there was the frosty reception automatically given to 'townies', who were – usually rightly – seen to have brought with them snot-slimed slum habits and, even worse, the scaly purple scabs of ringworm or the tell-tale red punctures of lice. Even that far away we saw on a wet hillside the charred rubber pipes and twisted aluminium in the wreckage of a German fighter plane. When we got back to London, the few cars around seemed all to be black. Some were fuelled by canvas balloons of gas filled at the Blue Star Garage, behind the flat which was our temporary home, at the Hampstead end of Hendon Way up which we walked to a government-run 'British Restaurant' in Platts Lane. There a stodgy Bisto-swamped meal could be had for a shilling, eaten at long tables with other pallid grateful families, all of us still wearing our worn coats, the men in hats and boys in caps, in the chilly hall. NW11 and the croaking cordon of my mother's relatives disapproving of his every move did not suit my father at all, and in one of his last initiatives before his circus left town he moved us south across the 'blood-brain barrier' from North London to Purley, on the leafy fringes of Surrey. Here, though the snuff mill on the River Wandle was long gone, the water was still clean enough to allow beds of watercress to thrive, as did good Christian values and men with black Homburg and bowler hats and tobacco-yellowed toothbrush moustaches who commuted to the City, voted Conservative and were deeply repressed.

Going to Golders Green as the Tube clattered into the daylight out of the tunnel under Hampstead Heath was truly a trip to foreign parts; the MacFisheries shop between the station and Brent still sold herrings and pickled cucumbers from brine-filled barrels, and the bakeries of Appenrodt and Grodzinsky would have brought a nostalgic tear to a Hapsburg eye. God knows what David and Manya made of us changelings, Church of England kids, kitted out by Daniel Neal, the school outfitters to Middle England, whose school mornings began with choruses bellowed from the Public Schools Hymn Book and whose musical tastes were shaped by Gilbert and Sullivan rather than Glazunov. We were Midwich Cuckoos in a Russian nest. But we spent many very happy times with our grandparents, listening on our own to 'Dick Barton, Special Agent', or with Manya and my mother to the story of a pre-NHS doctor's household as his wife shared with the audience the travails of her middle-class day – 'I'm worried about Jim' – in *Mrs Dale's Diary* and with my grandfather to Tommy Handley in 'ITMA'. The day's highpoint was the nine o'clock news delivered by John Snagge, or some other sonorous Establishment spokesman. It came as no surprise to learn years later that, to reinforce the gravitas, the unseen newsreaders were required to wear dinner jackets. I doubt we tuned in to the Midlands Service, which in 1948 broadcast the first regional programme about a farming family

known as 'The Archers'. As accompaniment to all this we had twice-
and thrice-told tales of Russia, and overheard whispered talk as my
mother tried to hide her worries from us – my father had by then left
her penniless and decamped to a new life of sweaty frolics under the
Caribbean sun.

Many basic foods and clothing were still rationed and many more
were in short supply. Alternatives were available, such as the chewy
pungency of whale meat, ox heart, horsemeat (did David remember
it with a slight shudder as a staple of the Yakutsk diet?) and a South
African fish marketed for some reason under its local but
unappetising name of 'Snoek'. (Nowadays it has been re-branded as
something like 'Cape Monkfish' and is much in demand.) These
unappetising culinary alternatives made us even more grateful for
Manya's skills in the kitchen, and for a distant relative who had made
it to Los Angeles and who would send food parcels bulging with all
sorts of unheard-of candies, glacé fruits, drinking chocolate and,
improbably, many large packs of dehydrated onion soup mix.

I am awkwardly, though not guiltily, conscious that mine was an
'easy' war. We were not refugees, we were not bombed out of house
and home, we did not have to spend endless nights coughing and
tossing fitfully on the platforms of Hampstead Tube Station, nor did
we go hungry. Nor did we lose anyone except, arguably, my father.
It is not a condemnation of him to say that had he actually been a
casualty of war, other lives and our memories of him would have
been better for it.

The Festival of Britain in 1951 did little to lift the horse blanket of
post-martial tristesse smothering a chilblained country, troubled by
the feeling that in preserving our freedom we had lost heavily in
terms of material wealth and empire.

24

'Whom the Gods Wish to Destroy . . .'

When Sobranie converted from a private family business and offered its shares to the public in 1948, the prospectus showed profits on a capital of a little over £100,000, rising from £6,700 in 1941 to £83,000 in 1947 (subject very much to the earlier caveat that, as with religion, monetary conversion is an art not a science, we can hazard that in today's terms the latter would be around £2 million), though National Defence Contribution, Profits Tax and Excess Profits Tax took over 50 per cent. All the talk of 'prospectus', the 'Accountant's Report', the legal flummery and the port-fumed patter of the stockbrokers must have been a heady mix of excitement and risk, since the London market was still trying to find its post-war feet, sterling was under heavy pressure and the country was roiled by a combination of freezing weather and fuel shortages. But the operation must have been very satisfying, not just in financial terms but as a measure of the light years Shaia and his brother had travelled from the Soho attic.

They had travelled physically, too, as they were now based on the western side of the City Road, between Old Street and the City itself. A boring stretch of heavily trafficked road, with none of the cosmopolitan history of Soho, City Road was supposed to have been named after its 'projector', the entrepreneur who drove it through towards Moorgate and the Bank of England from New Road. He wisely declined, on the grounds that Dingley Road did not have quite the same ring. He was right. The Victorian music-hall song about hatters pawning their tools – 'Pop Goes the Weasel' – would not have sounded quite as catchy had they been going 'Up and down the Dingley Road, In and out the Eagle . . .'. Nevertheless, as so often in unexpected London pockets, the road displays rich signposts to the past, from John Wesley's eighteenth-century chapel, cradle of the Methodist Church, to the Bunhill Fields Burial Ground, earthly terminus for a cross-section of British notables from John Bunyan and Daniel Defoe to William Blake.

My sister claimed that with the wind blowing from the south, she could pick up the smell of tobacco the moment she walked out of Old Street Underground Station. While given the distance that may have needed almost gale-force gusts, it was certainly the case that every time the swing doors of the factory opened, the spicy honey-tinged aromas of leaf tobacco eddied over the pavements before they were swallowed up by the diesel fumes from the crawling buses. Relating tobacco to honey may seem far-fetched, but when Fred Croley's son John was asked after many years at Robert Lewis how he chose a good cigar, he replied, 'I look at it, I smell it and if then I feel as though I could eat it, that's the cigar I want to smoke.'

Some of Sobranie's best tobacco was supplied by a blind Greek merchant from Smyrna, who, as David Redstone once told me, first agreed to give Sobranie credit 'because he liked the sound of our voices'. The first deal evolved into an annual ritual in which the merchant, guided by his daughter, would arrive in London, base himself in a comfortable hotel and set aside three days for leisurely haggling over next year's contract. Both sides were well aware that this was something of a ballet. A deal would always be done because Sobranie was the only UK customer for Yenidje leaf of this quality and the blind man from Smyrna the only supplier, but custom was custom and the three days were spent bargaining and sipping coffee as figures, offers and counter-offers were tossed to and fro with much waving and wringing of hands and a mutual obbligato of 'You're ruining me' and 'Next year, I'll be bankrupt.' The visit in 1948 found Shaia distracted by the share offering and, when the merchant named his opening price, Shaia simply said, 'OK,' and the deal was done, leaving the merchant with the rest of the three days to fill, and tormented by wondering whether he should have quoted a higher price.

Sobranie had planted itself firmly in smokers' minds. And on the printed page, too, used by writers from Dorothy L. Sayers to Cyril Connolly. Voracious reader that he was, David might well have seen Connolly's 1945 volume of essays *The Condemned Playground*. But what would he possibly have made of the author's camp pastiche of his old school: '. . . Eton, Henry's holy shade. An impression above all of arches, my dears, each with its handsome couple and study fireplaces always full of stubs of Balkan Sobranie'. Come to that, could either Redstone brother have related to John Betjeman's Oxford memories:

> Balkan Sobranie in a wooden box,
> The College arms upon the lid, Tokay
> And sherry in the cupboard.

Although we can regret that Ian Fleming resorted to the fictional Morland of Grosvenor Street to satisfy 007's heavy nicotine habit, it is some consolation to know that his real life, and larger-than-life, model for James Bond, the splendidly nicknamed Commander 'Biffy' Dunderdale, a legendary British Secret Intelligence Service officer, chain-smoked Balkan Sobranie Turkish through a long ivory holder. By coincidence, 'Biffy', also a child of the late nineteenth century, was born in Nikolayev, north of Odessa, where his English father ran a fleet of steamers which tramped up and down the Black Sea coast as far as Constantinople. Dunderdale was one example that smoking was not always a killer; he lived to ninety-one and was married three times.

Alan Furst's *Blood of Victory*, in his fine series of evocative novels about the clandestine world of Russia, Europe and the Balkans in the 1930s and 40s, unconsciously tied together more strands of our story than he realised when he portrayed his Russian hero chain-smoking Sobranie cigarettes as he ploughed through the night on a Bulgarian tramp-steamer from Odessa via Romania to Istanbul. His fictional ship would have passed within foghorn's range of Akkerman. Furst's book actually runs this one a close second in the number of references to Sobranie. When I asked him about it, he told me he simply felt it would have been the smoke of choice for a Russian-born spy.

John Mortimer, creator of 'Rumpole of the Bailey', the bibulous barrister who does well defending the underdog, but who is far too politically incorrect to be described as 'prominent civil rights lawyer' in the Zarudny league, was a user at university but later admitted to having outgrown his undergraduate fondness for such things as Brahms 4th Symphony, 'bow ties, Balkan Sobranie, and sherry and Bols boiled up in an electric kettle'. It was not just a 1930s fad. *Observer* writer Lynn Barber used to stock up on Black Russians in a hotel on Sark while on weekend jaunts with her shady boyfriend and the critic John Walsh remembers his 'Sobranie and Baudelaire' phase at Oxford in the 1970s. However, if it existed we should award the 'Redstone Prize' for the most imaginative use of a Balkan Sobranie tin to John Banville: in his *The Book Of Evidence*, it serves as the container for 'a curiously whorled, pale, gristly piece of meat, crusted with dried blood', in fact a severed ear delivered to the narrator as a grim warning.

Looking back at the industry's own figures, we can now see that in fact the end of the Second World War marked the high point of cigarette consumption in Britain, women having by then become a significant part of the market; they do not even figure on the graph until 1920. It fell off quite steeply in the period to 1950, then plateaued until the real downturn began in the 1970s. In 2000–01, 31,938 million cigarettes were 'released in the UK for consumption', HM Customs' rather heavy way of describing the aggregate of home production and imports, a healthy 50 per cent drop from the previous year's 74,829 million. Even so, George Orwell's complaint in 1946 that the British spend far more on drink and tobacco than on books is most likely even truer today, though with most of the money now going on drink.

Sobranie moved its factory a few hundred yards from City Road just north of the City of London boundary to Worship Street, which sounded far more attractive than its original sixteenth-century name, Hog Lane. The material rewards were satisfactory, but not immense.

Nonetheless, like those earlier generations in Akkerman, they had sufficient 'parnossah'. Neither David nor his brother went in for villas in the South of France, or winters in Barbados; David and Manya did travel together at least once to the French spa in Royat, a trip memorialised by Jacqueline Roginsky in an attractive plaster bust she made of David and which stood proudly in their dining room, but they were fondest of Harrogate, its healing waters good for their joints and digestion (the latter a staple topic of uninhibited conversation over many years of my childhood). Its cream teas, its string quartets scraping away at Strauss in the chintzy hotel lounge, the gas fires in the bedrooms and the hot water bottle tucked between the sheets were all so English that I suspect even the Anglophobic Manya actually derived some comfort from being cosseted in this Mrs Miniver time warp.

The business kept pushing forward and David travelled Europe, dispensing bonhomie and taking orders. There was even the professional thrill of yet more new brands, notably the Cocktail range, each box offering gold-tipped cigarettes in five different colours, giving modern women the chance to match their evening smoke to their evening dress. Not just women. They were soon taken up by undergraduates keen to flash their sophistication; John Walsh recalls how he 'sparked up expensive Cocktail cigarettes in garish pastel colours. I was especially fond of the pink, purple and apple green ones.' It is hardly surprising that the brand also found a ready market among some of the more flamboyant men of the theatrical community. To mark the Coronation in 1953, Sobranie nimbly produced small blue-purple boxes, each with three Virginia cigarettes, the company's name in gold on the lid and a rose, thistle, leek and shamrock embossed at the corner. Here again we may see a trace of Robert Lewis, whose St James's shop lay on the route of most major royal processions of the day. De Sola Pinto's partner, Fred Croley, never one to miss an opportunity, would have a stand erected outside for these state occasions, offering tickets for sale as well as inviting friends, and it is quite likely the mini-boxes were a memento. As so often in a good partnership, Croley was everything de Sola Pinto was not. He was a South Londoner, shrewd, meticulous and 'a man of simple beliefs. He believed in the essential goodness and decency of people, in the Masonic ideal and in English cricket.' Vivian de Sola Pinto remembered Croley in a poem in the *Times Literary Supplement* as 'the man I loved; the quiet man'.

David and Manya had earned the tributes they received at a dinner in 1954 to mark both David's 75th birthday and the firm's 75th anniversary. It was fitting that Croley should offer the toast to the House of Sobranie. It was equally appropriate that 'Uncle David' should be eulogised by the fast-rising, soon to become ultra-fashionable, London solicitor Mr (later Lord) Arnold Goodman. He was a friend from childhood of Shaia's elder son Charles, and the long-standing advisor to the firm and much of the extended Redstone family. Even when he became what a journalist called 'The British establishment's chief mediator and fixer' and, the ultimate accolade, was painted in his yellow pyjamas by Lucian Freud, he always found time to give even the errant and impoverished members of the family as much of his canny care and attention as he did his far more important clients.

After the guests had savoured their smoked salmon, turtle soup, sole and grilled chicken, helped down by sips of Zeltlinger Schlossberg Moselle and Chambolle Musigny 1945, they sat back comfortably with their brandies, and Goodman rolled into stately and mellifluous action. Goodman's style seems a touch florid today, though befitting a classically educated man of his generation whose initial passion had been for the arcana of Roman-Dutch law. We can have no doubt that his words were genuinely felt and reflected the sentiments of all those who knew David as a man with 'the genius for friendship. Such genius and the power to cultivate the friendships he has cultivated can only be achieved by a man who genuinely loves his fellow men.' There were few, Goodman declared, 'who lend as sympathetic an ear to the troubles and anxieties and misgivings of their fellow men . . .'. Goodman knew more than many about David's Siberian past and allowed himself as an old friend to touch on David's 'respect and fight for his principles. Many of you may not know that in defence of these principles and for their vindication he endured exceptional dangers and suffered incarceration . . . I am convinced that the serenity and tranquillity he has achieved are attributable to the fact that his life and ways have been tempered in the fires of adversity.'

After paying appropriate tribute to the two brothers as 'so perfect a team', teasing David for trying to defraud the insurance companies by claiming he was 75 when it was plain to all that this 'sprightly gentleman . . . young in mind and spirit' was nowhere near that age, Goodman went on to praise Manya and her marriage to David: 'A union of mind and spirit which is as perfect as any marriage relationship I have ever encountered. How much of his happiness and peace, how much of his success and kindliness is attributable to her, no mathematical calculation can assess.'

It is not uncharitable to say that while she would certainly have caught the sense of the tribute Goodman was deservedly paying her, she may not have understood more than one word in ten. Manya had emerged unbowed from a bare-knuckle fight with the English language, deciding to get by with a vocabulary that was fine for dealing with housekeeping, family and everyday conversation. Depending on the sensitivity of the topic (e.g. my errant father), she and David and their daughters veered seamlessly between Russian and a unique 'lingua Anglo-Slavica', in which Russian and English words tumbled over one another. 'Dai mne esche a tiny kusochek Christmas cake' ('Pass me another little slice of . . .').

What mattered, I am sure, is that she knew that all the risks – the scrambling across the world and back – and all the hard knocks had been worthwhile. Her husband, with her support, had earned a store of genuine affection and respect to sustain them on the last lap. But having made them happy, the Gods did their best to destroy them.

25

Death Comes Back

Their messenger was a drunken bookmaker, who smashed their younger daughter, my mother, to her death as he jumped the lights one evening on the Brighton Road in the centre of Purley, where the Tesco store now dominates. She was crossing the road to take the bus home. She was forty-six and rather jolly.

David and Manya were in their late seventies. It is impossible for me to imagine how the blow struck them, all the more since the aftermath was a self-centred blur of shock and denial, a period of days, weeks even, of which I remember little. My aunt Nina, always a tower of strength, and her husband Edgar took on the thankless burden of tidying up a finished life. I recall that she took me with her on a two-bus journey to Croydon Hospital, where I waited outside the mortuary while she went in to identify the body, emerging what seemed an eternity later and not saying a word as the No. 12 and No. 234A – the one my mother had been crossing the road to catch – took us back to a home that I learned now had to be sold, adding another load of disorientation to life. I had been hoping she would say, 'It's not her.' There was a perfunctory inquest, at which for some bizarre reason at the age of sixteen I had to give evidence about my mother's health and state of mind. There were no witnesses. Back then there were no breathalysers either. The local police, fresh from securing the hanging of the mentally incompetent Derek Bentley by the use of confected 'verbals', were always willing to help make ends meet by assisting those who could afford it to avoid embarrassment. No charges were brought. Sensitivity was not a strong point. When they came to the house to break the news, only my sisters were home; I was, God forgive me, out with a schoolfriend, hanging around in a coffee bar to show off my new duffle coat. 'Hmm,' the sergeant said to thirteen-year-old Natalie, 'in that case, you'd better come with us to identify the body.' Luckily the next door neighbour's intervention and telephone call to Nina saved her at least that part of a grim and ineradicable memory.

Did David and Manya pray to their respective Gods, and for what? His God allowed vengeance; her prayers would have been for a soul to rest in peace. Mixed with whatever prayers they offered up must have been, 'Why us?', 'If only . . .'. As I am now far closer to their age then than mine at the time, I could claim that old age does provide a sort of carapace and makes one more familiar with death as an experience and an inevitability. Even so, it must have been grim. But try as they might, the Gods did not destroy them. Certainly they must have shared private grief on a scale I cannot comprehend. But the stubborn pair of moving targets had come too far to be more than wounded. So many other forces had tried and failed to bring them down. What were a few Greek Fates?

Manya would surely have gone then and later to the Russian Orthodox Church in Buckingham Palace Road (the one in Ennismore Gardens was felt by her generation of exiles to be under the sway of Moscow) to light a candle and find reassurance in the Church's Slavonic promise of the second Beatitude: '*Blazheni plachushchii, yako tii uteshatsya*' – 'Blessed are They that Mourn, for They Shall be Comforted'?

My sisters and I had been there with her, in happier days when she and look-alike older ladies in black would cross themselves three times before they even entered the church, and then stand for what to us, used to the relative comfort of Anglican pews and hassocks, seemed hours. All bar us (now momentarily émigrés ourselves) knew just when to cross themselves, when and how deep to bow as the choir echoed the priest's deep basso call, '*Gospodi Pomilui*' ('Lord have mercy on us'), and at which key points to sink awkwardly to their knees in arthritic discomfort and touch their foreheads to the stone-flagged floor. There was no organist and none of the sturdily incorrect Church of England hymns with which we had grown up, such as 'Onward, Christian Soldiers, Marching as to War'. Candle-light fractured off the silver *oklads* that shrouded the icons. Scraps of paper were passed from hand to hand to the front to be given to the priest, seeking his intercession for loved ones whose names were scribbled on them. It was not just the liturgy and the ritual that were a new experience. The Church calendar itself hewed to the Greek Orthodox timetable. While technically we were entitled to a double Christmas, we did not get one – though, since Easter was a far more important highlight of her spiritual year, Manya went to great lengths to give us an authentic ethnic re-run a few weeks after the more prosaic English holiday, which had already begun to lose its religious significance to become a holiday rite of passage involving trips to the seaside and then candy floss and roundabouts at the fair on Hampstead Heath.

At my mother's funeral in a wet graveyard in Waddon, one of the few images of those weeks that I can download mentally, Manya I think showed her true colours, the steel that got her and her children out of Chita. Bereaved, but dignified, never letting go, she stood silent, upright, with a handkerchief crumpled in a gloved hand. By contrast, David, who had stoically endured so much cruelty and danger, wept bitterly and would have thrown himself into the muddy grave had the black-suited undertakers from Messrs Ebbutts not gently held him back.

Manya had brought three children out of danger spread-eagled on a train roof. Two were now dead. She had left behind Siberia and her family and was an exile in a very foreign land. Now she had to sustain herself with her memories and by metaphorically spread-eagling herself over her grandchildren. I know all too well that it was not easy. But she and David coped valiantly, and lived to see and love great-grandchildren from both daughters.

After our house was sold, living arrangements became a little confused for all three of us, far more for my younger and more vulnerable sisters than myself, since I was of an age when military service loomed and it was convenient to answer the call. I spent two years training to become a Russian interpreter. Though the accent and speech patterns had been in my ears from the cradle, until I picked up my first set of army issue textbooks, I knew only three words, which I had actually thought were one, so fast were they elided by Manya and her daughters. The mild imprecation *'Gospod I Bozhe Moi!'* (literally, 'My Lord and God!', but close to 'For Heaven's sake!') was always flying about even for small surprise like a spilled saucer of tea. I am not sure why, but as over the next two years the language became second nature through total immersion, I never dared try my Russian out on my grandparents until the time when I had become fluent. They knew what I was studying (when David heard that I had followed my father's suede footsteps into the Intelligence Corps, he was slightly apprehensive, wondering if history was repeating itself) but never pressed me. When finally I slipped smoothly into one of their conversations like a car easing down the ramp into freeway traffic, their reaction was splendid, pride being far outweighed by the sense that it was perfectly natural, and what had taken me so long?

That I had also become a consumer of the family product also went unremarked, even though I was in the habit of generously helping myself from David's large cases of cigarette samples, which he kept upstairs under the spare bed. I was thus able at far too early an age to posture about, waving the gamut of Sobranie products. There was something about the way the oval Turkish shaped the lips into a superior curl. Black Russian were really only good for arrant showing off, and for me at least any 'Gosh, what are those?' impact they may have made on an impressionable girl in a Soho coffee bar was far outweighed by a laxative side effect which tended to bring the evening to an abrupt, muscle-clenching close. Chaliapine were meant to be smoked with the cardboard holder bent at an angle, creating the effect of Franklin Roosevelt with his jaunty cigarette-holder, again a pose that did not work for anyone under forty. Pipe-smoking was something I tried just once; I had not realised that you were not meant to inhale.

David and Shaia inevitably moved back more and more from the business front line, leaving Shaia's sons Charles and Isidore to battle with an environment growing almost daily more hostile. But David could not resist at least one last flash of the old magic, when in 1958, just before his eightieth birthday, he agreed to be interviewed by the journalist Nancy Spain at the Savoy Grill. Over grilled salmon, strawberries and cream and a half-bottle of Pouilly Fuisse, he gave a virtuoso display. 'He looked,' she wrote, 'like a small, twinkling statesman . . . five foot tall, white imperial beard neatly clipped, bright eyes gleaming behind pebbled glasses, grey flannel suit.' Spain was a girls' girl not easily impressed by men, and she had not smoked since 1942. Such were his powers of persuasion that she was induced to try in quick succession a Sobranie Turkish and a Virginia No. 40 while David regaled her with tales of Old Russia and Rasputin. 'They really did taste rather good,' she admitted.

'Do you think I look like [the Boer War veteran and later South African President] Field Marshal Smuts?' David asked. 'It happens rather often when I come into a restaurant – people stand on their chairs because I look so like him . . .' (She was not to know that he was fond of telling another version of the same story involving the same confusion of identity on a train in rural Ireland.) He also told her one of his favourite stories, how one snowy day in Siberia he had been lined up in front of a firing squad but, as he was so short, the bullets had whistled over his head and the officer in charge had relented and released him. Though this sounds far-fetched and was also told in several versions over the years, it is likely to have had a basis in harsh fact. We know that in several of those riverside settlement incidents, when the guards tried to stop the exiles mingling, they used fists, rifle butts and then a volley of warning shots to keep order. In the retelling he made it sound amusing, but in reality, in the bellowing and near-hysteria on the riverbank, it must have been terrifying.

Having told her how he had won over to the Sobranie cause 'one great friend, the Colonel of a Highland regiment', he spoke with feigned regret about a less satisfactory experience with the navy. 'Oh, dear, this was the one time I failed. They gave me whiskies and soda like I have never seen . . . such big ones . . . triple, quadruple. And nothing happens to my head, you understand, but my feet they fail me and I have to go back to the hotel. So there are very many battleships that do not get a call that day from Uncle David.'

Though he tried his best to explain that he was not rich, since he only had a small shareholding in the business, she would not give in on the point and called him later because she had forgotten to ask her 'trademark' question about how he spent his money. He replied: 'I am working so hard all my life for the firm that I have not collected one single hobby. I live very simply and my wife is an excellent cook . . . I could say I have spent all my money on books yet when I go (which God forbid), I dare say my library will be sold for one pound. What can I say? I say I am not rich. You say I am. Perhaps I am rich in philosophy, hard work, in happiness?' Clearly his books meant much to him; just how much, I hope, these pages have brought out.

Manya had no hobbies, no bridge coterie, no ladies who lunched, though there was a tiny lady who, in the recesses of a very infant memory, can be seen perched birdlike on the sofa sipping tea and chatting in Russian. I could almost swear that she wore one of those varnished black straw hats and buttoned boots. I can remember her name with great clarity because it was one of those morsels of Slav exotica which stuck in a child's mind. She was Mrs Misyukevich. I had forgotten all about her for 50 years, but then I read the list of names of the Romanovka protestors. There, halfway down page 9, was 'Misyukevich, Anton', a 31-year-old carpenter from Vilensk, who had been exiled for five years for distributing 'revolutionary proclamations' in the streets of Krasnoyarsk. Was he her husband? Her brother? I shall never know. (Looking back, it is interesting that, although they kept the Russian fabric alive inside their home, and Manya had her Church, unlike the émigrés of their era in Paris and Berlin, they did not seek to keep alive the sacred flame of 'the motherland' by joining associations and clubs, whether counter-revolutionary, theatrical, poetic or social, or even mixing much with others. It was over.)

The Redstone house had a tiny garden, made even tinier by the air-raid shelter which had proved so solidly built that, when after the Second World War David sought quotations from contractors for its removal, they either went away muttering, never to be heard from again, or demanded sums for which a new house could have been built with change to spare. It had a Morello cherry tree from which

Manya would confect a mix of fruit and sour cream, but its beds were otherwise left to the lethargic proddings and pullings of a weekly handyman.

In a very Russian way, Manya's religion came inextricably bundled with an equally firm commitment to a droshky-load of traditional Russian superstitions, and a serious view on the meaning of dreams, most of which I have now forgotten or hopelessly muddled. Dreams on some days (I seem to recall Thursday) were more significant than others. Whether looking out of an uncurtained window when you wake up and before you tell anyone your dream is good or bad, I cannot remember, but it had some weight, as did whether you did the telling before or after noon. Dreams about anything from fish to fire each had an arcane symbolism dating back centuries before the innuendo-laden confessions of Freud's Viennese patients prompted him to study the subject seriously. Deep down she may have been a touch more sceptical about her claim that mermaids existed and that they were the souls of unbaptised children, but it came back to me when I read another account of the legend in a book of travellers' tales. Whistling indoors and cutting a loaf of bread with the crust underneath were anathema, as were opening an umbrella in the house and shaking hands across a doorstep; it was advisable to make a small sign of the Cross with your thumb over your open mouth when you yawned to stop the devil flying in. Dropping a knife meant the next visitor would be a man; and a fork, a woman. Even though she was medically expert, she still hankered after the old herbs and plants; the *bologolov* – literally, 'the headache plant' – was, she swore, far more effective than aspirin. As a child she would have joined her sisters and the village girls in fortune-telling – even now, taken extremely seriously: melting candle wax into a glass of water to see what patterns emerged, and counting how many grains of corn a chicken would peck at. Whether she made David sit on his packed suitcase for luck before he left on a trip, I have no idea, but since many modern Russians do so, she probably did. But she would probably not have gone as far as the peasant women she remembered from her Siberian childhood, who insisted that they switched their thick stockings from one leg to another before they went berry-picking in the dark woods, as otherwise they might be seized by bears and never return.

It was in her declining years, when she developed a senile hostility towards their Irish housekeeper, that I heard Manya use Russian words she must have learned on hospital wards, or in her father's compound, and whose meaning I had to dig out of specialist slang dictionaries. Luckily her target could not understand a word and chose in her almost saintly way to ignore the tone behind them: 'Sure, and don't they all get a bit cranky at that age.'

26

Cigarette Ends

In the 1960s, the two brothers made it all the way from Bessarabia to the Burlington Arcade. When they bought out the high-class tobacconist and small-scale manufacturer Sullivan & Powell, now down to one store in the arcade and shorn of its former chain of agents in 'Valparaiso, Tientsin and Bombay', they acquired a bow-fronted shop with a basket of geraniums hanging over the front door, an urbane staff and a roster of loyal customers, both real and at least one fictional – E. W. Hornung's 'Raffles' with his striped blazer indicating membership of the exclusive *I Zingari* cricket team and his ambiguous relationship with 'Bunny'. The arcade, patrolled by an imposing beadle who ensures that visitors do not run, sing, or carry open umbrellas and large parcels, had been created as the 1819 equivalent of a moat by Lord George Cavendish to stop passers-by from tossing the discarded shells of oysters – then a working-class staple – and other plebeian detritus into the grounds of Burlington House, then his London home and now the Royal Academy.

The Sobranie business itself was still growing nicely, opening new markets and developing new brands. But it was hard, uphill work and, like the illusion created by a mountain range, no sooner was one peak scaled, than another, still higher, reared up ahead. Being a 'niche player' was all well and good but of declining value against the multinational giants, who had immense marketing resources and equally large legal departments to counter the increasingly loud drumbeat of health issues. Profits were further squeezed as governments

266

convinced themselves that 'sin tax' revenues were a public benefit and ratcheted up tobacco duty with nearly every budget.

My sisters and I knew Shaia only as an amiable but distant relative whom we saw once or twice a year and with whom we were instinctively on our best behaviour. We had nothing to do with the business, other than to absorb its aromas passively and massively whenever we visited our relatives, nearly all of them smokers on a scale that today would bring out the banner-wavers and the fire brigade.

To admit today that one's family was 'in tobacco' is on a par with revealing that they got their start making land mines or publishing the sort of magazines sold in sealed wrappers from newsagents' top shelves. But in those pre-cancer-scare days, we were vicariously proud to see the cigarettes and tobaccos advertised in the newspapers and displayed on tobacconists' shelves, or even, as an adolescent out to impress, to offer them around insouciantly at parties as 'our own cigarettes'.

I even managed to do my little bit for the firm, again through the agency of the ubiquitous Lord Goodman, then just plain 'Mr'. I was navigating a troubled period between flouncing defiantly out of school and beginning military service. When my mother sought his counsel as to what she might do with me, he gave her a legal textbook, *Anson on Contract*, for me to read to see if I had any feeling for the law. I went to see him a week or so later, up two or three flights of Dickensian stairs in the Middle Temple. When he quizzed me gently about the book, I had luckily and truthfully found enough in it to be able to tell him why I thought it interesting; I had the sense not to say how puzzled I was by the similarity of many of the initials of the High Court judges whose decisions were cited. Knowing no better I had read the names much as one might those of contemporary cricketers – Bedser E., Bedser A., Compton D., Statham B. Why then so many 'J's? Was being christened John, James, Jack or Joseph a key to advancement to the Bench? Only a while later did I fathom that by venerable law-reporting protocol, irrespective of his given names, Mr Justice Smith, say, was referred to as 'Smith, J.' (The run of 'J's was broken by the occasional 'LCJ' for 'Lord Chief

Justice') and 'MR', for 'Master of the Rolls'. The latter took a lot of working out. As a final trap for the uninitiated, in cases heard by two judges, their names would appear in the report as 'McAndrew and Smithers, JJ'. Goodman offered me a temporary place in his firm. It was much more an act of kindness to my mother than a sign that he had spotted a budding jurist lurking under the lapels of the Montague Burton birds-eye weave suit David had generously bought for me as part of my passage to adulthood – an act I did shamefully little to repay. I sat first at a table in a corner of Goodman's room, face to the panelled wall, but adolescent ears swivelled through 180 degrees like radar dishes, pretending to draw up wills and property conveyances using the *Encyclopaedia of Forms and Precedents*, while he received his remarkable diapason of clients. Had I been entrepreneurial or indiscreet enough to write a diary, it would not have been believed. Even weaving the stories into a novel would have brought criticism of an overstretched imagination: a society lady seeking a divorce after just a few weeks of marriage because her husband had proved painfully unable to shed the sexual preferences acquired in the chilly changing rooms of Eton; a brace of temperamental orchestral conductors, actors and a famous American singer, who, office rumour claimed, had rewarded one of the junior solicitors in the office in a very personal way after he had helped her with a problem; impresarios, publishers, Labour politicians, smooth men planning the new world of independent television, property tycoons (one of whom gave me a valuable lecture on how to bribe planning officials; he ended badly) and authors. I once accompanied Goodman all the way to Walthamstow to see a Jewish tailor who was an old client. It is a mark of my callowness that instead of wondering what this contrast with the general flow of his practice was all about, my abiding interest was the PreSelector gear change in Goodman's Armstrong Siddeley Sapphire. There was the distraught and impoverished wife of a notorious vexatious 'litigant', who dragged their divorce proceedings as far as the House of Lords. And a taxi ride to the former Berkeley Hotel, then in the street of the same name, where I sat mute while Goodman conferred with 'Winky' Portman. The landowner had good reason to be grateful to the nimble-minded, if not nimble-bodied solicitor, who had 'broken the entail' on the family estates, giving the now deceased viscount access to cash at levels that enabled him to run the bottle-green Bentley Continental with its now classic tail line, a smooth 60-degree slope from roof to rear bumper, into which he climbed insouciantly when the meeting broke up.

One day, Goodman handed me a piece of paper, which turned out to be a County Court summons. It was a Sobranie task. I had to serve it by handing it personally to their laggard customer, who I was profoundly unhappy to see was the landlord of a pub in Covent Garden, then still a thriving and rambunctious market whose porters were unlikely to have much appetite for the pastel Cocktails. I had alarming visions of being set upon by beefy men in aprons and flung out on the cobblestones. Though I tried to get there around 8 a.m. when there would be no beer-flushed porters around, I had forgotten that by market practice, the pubs opened in the early morning and the customers were well stuck in to their liquid breakfast. Thankfully when I sidled apprehensively through the crowded bar and muttered that I wanted 'a word with the boss', the landlord proved to be even more nervous than I was and paid up in cash on the spot.

While I did my debt-collecting best, a bigger battle was being fought. The anti-tobacco lobby has been around almost as long as tobacco and its by-products have been inhaled. Although in 1621 Robert Burton praised tobacco as 'a sovereign remedy to all diseases' in his analysis of melancholy and other human failings, three years later we find Pope Urban threatening to excommunicate snuff takers, arguing (unkind critics wondered how he could judge) that snuff-induced sneezing was too close to sexual ecstasy. In 1634, Tsar Alexis threatened Russians with dire penalties for smoking, ranging from whipping to exile and execution. At about the same time, the Greek Orthodox Church also clamped down, claiming that tobacco had intoxicated Noah. King James I inveighed against it as 'a custom loathsome to the eye, hateful to the nose, harmful to the brain, dangerous to the lungs, and a later tub-thumper preached against tobacco's 'impairment of body and mind, its enslavement of the will, its disgusting encroachment of the pure air and other rights of those not addicted to it'. Putting up a stout defence, Victorian author Charles Kingsley thought smoking 'a lone man's companion, a bachelor's friend, a sad man's cordial, a wakeful man's sleep, a chilly man's fire'. He would have been interested to see his first idea taken up over half a century later by the copywriter of the slogan 'You're never alone with a Strand'. Russian dramatist Chekhov also addressed the subject, but with tongue (or pen) in cheek: his short monologue 'On the Harmful Effects of Tobacco' is not a polemic but a wry twist on a man's relationship with his overbearing wife. Not content with the misleading title, Chekhov has another little joke: his narrator's name is Nyukhin, roughly 'Sniffer' or 'Snuff-taker'.

As the evidence of tobacco's dangers mounted, the industry fought back. Hard. For example, in 1943 tobacco giant Philip Morris told doctors via an advertisement in the US *National Medical Journal*, '"Don't smoke" is hard advice for patients to swallow. May we suggest instead, "Smoke Philip Morris". Tests show that three out of every four cases of smoker's cough cleared on changing to Philip Morris.' Another manufacturer claimed that its menthol Kools would keep the head clear and give extra protection against colds. And in 1948 the *Journal of the American Medical Association* argued that 'more can be said as a form of escape from tension than against it'.

However, by the 1960s, the evidence was all too clear. It fell to Shaia's son Charles as chairman, and his brother Isidore, to take up cudgels for Sobranie in the industry's resolute rearguard action. (Despite that, even when in 1963 I joined what was fast becoming probably the best of London's merchant banks, cut-glass ashtrays glittered on the patinated mahogany tables in the meeting rooms, alongside a packet of expensive cigarettes. A gold Dunhill lighter, shaped like a small oblong briquette, and a leather-backed Asprey or Cartier 'jotter' were as much part of the uniform of every upwardly mobile executive as a Hermes ties and black shoes. All bar one of the merchant banks have now gone up in smoke, much like the habit itself.)

Charles Redstone was the epitome of wry humour and sound advice. He and his family were generous in extending a hand of welcome to my sisters when they were somewhat adrift after our mother died, and he took the helm at Sobranie in tricky times. He had to be a cheerleader for the company and its products, and he wrote to his shareholders in a style that comes as a refreshing reminder that annual reports were not always written in 'corporate speak'. He stated his position clearly: 'The older I get, the more convinced I am that moderate smoking is unlikely to do serious health damage and brings – if a good, well-seasoned and well-flavoured tobacco is used – such an accession of serenity and tranquillity as to make it a joy and a delight to those capable of exercising restraint and moderation. The man who gives up addictive smoking is wise. The man who gives up controlled and recreational smoking may well be unnecessarily depriving himself of an innocent pleasure.'

In 1974, after turnover had increased fractionally during the year to just over £4.5 million, he reported that 'each pound of that turnover is procured by laboriously pushing a stone up a hill inch by inch, until puffing and blowing – but triumphant – we attain the summit.' That in another context some of the 'puffing and blowing' might be attributable to the smoking habit itself was best left unsaid.

The next year he was more upbeat, declaring that, 'we British have a remarkable capacity for recovering from our governments and our doctors. We are confident therefore that we shall recover from the immense impost of Excise duty as well as a rather misplaced paternalism which constantly picks on cigarette smoking as the one area of human activity for strident guidance and warning yet leaves over-eating, over-drinking, over-wenching and every other form of uncontrolled self-indulgence free from restraint or admonition. I have said before and say again that I believe smoking in moderation soothes the energies, quietens many dangerous sensations and restores to civilised composure the raging cauldron that is, alas, so often the human psyche.' By then, however, the reports of the causal link with cancer were too numerous and too well researched to rebut, but as Charles was not slow to point out, 'The government deplores smoking and warns the nation against the practice but is never deterred from cashing in, in a fashion that would be regarded as positively immoral by lesser mortals.'

I recently stumbled on a copy of a memorandum circulated in 1976 within a trade group known as the Tobacco Advisory Council, whose members included Imperial Tobacco, Gallaher, Carreras, Rothman, British American Tobacco, Philip Morris and Sobranie (representing the dwindling group of independent manufacturers). They had been fretting about how to phrase a letter to the Minister of Health. We do not know what final form of words emerged, but the Council's Chairman recorded that 'the proposal that we should say flatly that "the manufacturers have never recognised that cigarettes constitute a health hazard or that smoking kills anyone" is not unanimously acceptable . . . It seems to me also to be a statement that if quoted in future by the Minister could precipitate just the kind of controversy the [Council] has been at pains to avoid . . .' (One corporate history tells us that the principal manufacturers introduced filter tips in 1949 'both to conserve leaf and to offer an economy to smokers'; health arguments such as the 'cooler smoke' are not mentioned. In what sounds like a rather cosy arrangement, the manufacturers had up till then agreed not to use filters 'until they all possessed specialised tipping machinery so that 5 per cent of their total output could be tipped'.)

The financial pressure would not abate. Charles summed it up neatly after one bad spell with the comment, 'It is unsurprising that in the past year we have done badly. It may be considered a miracle that we have done at all, and indeed not been completely done for,' though, 'we have a considerable amount of staying power'.

The company tried to spread its risk by diversifying into engineering, dry cleaning and the splendidly named 'Johanna Dearlove's Laundry'. Charles could even be lyrical about laundries. 'We believe,' he told shareholders, 'that a civilised life giving proper opportunities of recreation and repose calls for access to a good but moderately priced laundry. Many people do not have the time, the facilities or the inclination to carry out the tiresome task of washing, drying, ironing, folding and generally titivating their own clothes, outer and inner. To throw them into a basket or laundry bag and let them come back ready for immediate wear is far from being a social luxury. It is something that should be available to the generality of mankind,' he wrote, in words of which Anthony Trollope would have been proud.

Sobranie also set up a subsidiary to make herbal cigarettes, at first sight a slightly odd move but which is explained by Dr Isidore Redstone, another beneficiary of the shrewd and good-humoured Redstone genes. It was an initiative taken by several manufacturers, who, after a move in California to legalise cannabis, followed by a working party report in London suggesting the same outcome, began to prepare for the day that it would be allowed in the UK. He remembers serious meetings in Whitehall when the industry (no doubt again via the Tobacco Advisory Council) and officials talked at length about how the legal 'reefer' might be taxed. Nicotine cigarettes were taxed on the assumption that a smoker would get through perhaps twenty or thirty a day. If cannabis cigarettes were made legal, even the most passionate aficionado would, it was reckoned, not be able to cope with more than three or four a day without subsiding into catatonia, so some new scale would need to be thought up to balance demand and revenues. The Californian initiative died away and this fascinating topic seems not to have been pursued.

Exports to over a hundred countries (including a brand flavoured with, and called, Jasmine, billed as something 'feminine and different' which sold well in the Far East) made up two thirds of the company's sales. But despite all that effort and diversification, profits were at best sluggish, as cigarette consumption fell, and in real terms were not on a par with the halcyon days of 1948. They hit a high of £207,000 in 1974 and dropped to a loss of £186,000 in 1979, the latter dragged down by a disappointing investment in engineering. Along the way, in 1967 the company sold its main trademarks to the tobacco behemoth Gallaher, but leased them back, a neat way of raising capital while allowing Sobranie to continue on its way. The question was, for how long?

The firm's centenary occurred in 1979, an occasion gracefully noted by Charles Redstone in his Chairman's Statement: 'In a world where sentiment is at a discount, we may require a little forgiveness for choosing as the first and most important comment of the year that it is our firm's 100th year of business. Over the 100 years the same family have [worked] industriously away to maintain our reputation for honest and conscientious dealing. We have never had occasion except to be proud of our products and our transactions. Moreover we are, we believe, the last or almost the last of the independent cigarette companies. We are by the standards of the giants a midget of surprising repute. Our most prized possession is the friends we have made over the years. It is true to say that throughout the vicissitudes of the 100 years, throughout the economic convulsions and the wars and the social changes, the help and support of our friends has been crucial. We hope we have acknowledged it and in our own small way reciprocated it.'

However, just one year later, the day of the midgets was over. Charles rose to tell his shareholders that the unremitting 'economic constraints' had led Sobranie to terminate its leaseback, effectively transferring the brands and business directly to Gallaher. Given the tough times they had been through and the even more wrenching decisions they had had to make, he was certainly understating his feelings when he remarked that the past year had been 'undeniably a melancholy one, as witnessing the termination of a family association which has become in trading terms almost historic'.

Albert Weinberg, Shaia and David would have been equally sad but equally pragmatic; in a phrase that none of them would have uttered and most would not have understood, they had 'had a good innings'. But investors, creditors and bank managers do not have 'history' as a line item in their Excel spreadsheets. Cash flow, not family values, is king. The company changed its name and looked for new directions in the harshest business climate in Britain for many years. That in the end it did not succeed in rebuilding itself is outside the scope of our story and does nothing to diminish the value and reputation of what had been so painstakingly built over the previous 100 years.

After all this, who were David and Manya? My sister Natalie remembers a nursery verse that Manya liked to recite to her:

> *Chto khotitye,*
> *To beritye*
> *Ni Da ni Nyet ni govoritye*
> *I Vy poyedite na bal . . .*

This is a folk rhyme, far from Pushkin, but almost as difficult to capture in English. The sense is:

> Take what you want,
> Don't give up at all
> And, like Cinderella,
> You'll get to the ball. . .

This sums up as well as anything Manya's sense of determination that if you hang on, everything will come right in the end. I have no doubt that her determination, her commitment to keep things together, was the glue that preserved the family in one piece, even though not always in one place. Indeed, so strong was the glue that I think one – but only one – of the reasons my father headed for the palm-fringed hills of Jamaica was that he could not crack the shell and always felt an outsider.

Manya died three years before David. Her much maligned housekeeper found her body and offered up Roman Catholic prayers, which must surely have been just as welcome in heaven before Manya moved on to Golders Green Crematorium, its conveyor-belt, swish-of-the-curtain efficiency sympathetically softened by the rhythmic Slavonic blessings of the head of her church in London, the gentle, metropolitan Anthony Bloom.

There is an inscription on a tomb in the Church of St Bartholomew in Smithfield, which captures in seventeenth-century spelling how David must have felt:

> Shee first deceased,
> Hee for a little tryd,
> To live without her,
> Liked it not, and dy'd.

At the end of his own long journey, Russia called him back – it always does – with memories of schoolrooms, fig trees, donkeys, men in fez and baggy linen pants or yarmulkes and dusty black jackets, the streets of Odessa where he had walked in the footsteps of

Pushkin, Babel and Trotsky, the red glow of the firebox on the engine footplate, the White Fort in the sunlight, the happy moments with his children in the Siberian woods and his shared dangers with comrades fighting the good fight in the snow.

David died at his home, looking out on the monkey-puzzle tree, on 16 February 1967, aged eighty-seven or eighty-eight, depending on which calendar we apply. The *Financial Times* echoed Arnold Goodman in remembering his 'charm, persuasiveness and great capacity for making friends'. The tobacco trade – manufacturers, leaf merchants, wholesalers and retailers – turned out in force to say goodbye at his funeral and its journal regretted the passing of 'a unique personality whose charm and friendliness will give him a space in the affections of all who knew him at home and abroad'. That would have pleased David; Manya too. And both would have taken much pride in knowing that a recent Chita exhibition marking the 300th anniversary of the Russian press, orchestrated by his old and now reinvigorated newspaper the *Zabaikal'skii Rabochii*, displayed photographs of earlier generations of Siberian journalists 'including those who were forgotten in the Soviet era, such as Malyshyev, Vasil'yevskyi and Rotenshtern [sic]'. Turning for the last time to those matryoshka dolls, the last one in the set, the tiny kernel of the whole structure, is actually of solid wood. What could I call it in David's case? What was the essence of the man? Like a fine tobacco he was a blend: courageous, liberal, friendly, principled, obstinate, and somewhere between brave and foolhardy come to mind. He was a thinker too.

Biography seems to demand that we do our best to dig out the negatives along with the positives, the little peccadilloes and weaknesses. I suppose David must have had a darker side, a temper, though I never saw it. He would hardly have been human if he had not been prone to bouts of depression – though, again, if he did he shielded us from them. He was rueful but resigned about Russia and never showed a hint of what W. E . Aytoun once called 'the deep, unutterable woe that none save exiles feel'. In her last years Manya grew obsessively convinced that other women were out to snare him: the magazine in which the Nancy Spain interview appeared had to be intercepted by Nina in case Manya threw a tantrum at the idea of her husband lunching at the Savoy with another woman. However, though he liked to sparkle in front of an audience, there is not a shred of memory or evidence for David having a roving eye. In the end, the caption I would write for that that solid last little doll is 'David the Human Being'.

Looking back on her life, Nina Nathan, who shared many of her father's strengths, concluded that 'it is not important to children where they live as long as their parents are there.' Maybe, though, where David lived did in the end matter to him. His last words to Nina were: 'Find my passport. I have to go home.'

Afterword

But before we finally let him go, let us return to Yakutsk, where the main drama of David and Manya's life was played out. This time it is a morning in the second week of June 2004. It started out marginally above freezing but by noon had magically become the first day of the short Siberian spring, ushered in by a chorus of cuckoos. I had thought that air-dried salted horsemeat for lunch would be pushing my digestive luck, but it turned out to be rather good; less so, the glass of fermented mare's milk, *kumys*, with its ambiguous aftertaste. I had the sense of being very far away from the familiar world.

Just a few miles outside the city, hawks circle over birch trees turning greener by the minute, herds of wild horses toss their heads to greet the sun, and peasant families squat by the roadside selling plastic jugs of milk and berry juice. In Yakutsk itself, Lenin Square, the city's epicentre, is dominated by the great man's statue, his right hand offering a stiff Bolshevik 'high five' to the polyglot Asian-featured passers by, the streams of battered cars and dusty olive-green army surplus trucks. Between them weave ramshackle buses, unsafe at any speed, their windows curtained with what look to be strips cut from the loose covers of discarded 1950s sofas. On the roofs of the main government buildings around the square, Orwellian slogans indistinguishable from those of the Soviet era exhort the masses to 'Do Our Good Deeds For The Republic', and offer the citizens of a region which contains much of Russia's mineral wealth the grand if rather bland reassurance that 'The

Earth's Resources Are For The People'. 'Unity Is Our Strength' proclaims a third, echoing the slogan of the Russia's Putin-boosting ruling party.

And I wonder what David Redstone would have made of it.

Suppose by some miracle of gerontology, cryogenics or even shamanism, he and his comrades in arms could have joined my indomitable wife and myself on our tour, whose highlight was to be a visit to the Romanovka. Had they been returning to the city down the Lena, the breathtaking sprawl and size of the river, and the thousands of miles of emptiness which begin at its distant banks, would certainly have brought back to them that devastating sense of being utterly removed from the known world, the final spirit-numbing realisation of what exile really meant. As their barge drifted towards the city under the splendid Lena Pillars, just as amazing a sight as when attorney Berenshtam was awed by them in 1904, it would not take much to block out of their minds the decrepit gravel plant, a grim jail now used for the hopeless task of drying out local alcoholics, the haphazardly tilting telegraph poles and the rusting skeletons of abandoned cars. Pokrovsk, Berestyakh and the other villages along the banks look much the same as they did a hundred years ago: wooden houses; muddy fenced yards; cowsheds plastered against the winter with dried dung and clay; cows, painfully thin after the months of winter, snuffling along the shoreline, still intermit-tently ice-encrusted in mid June, for the first shoots of grass.

In 1904 the quay where the exile barges dropped their cargoes of despair was a timber building with fretwork verandahs running round each of its two storeys. Had it not been for the painted sign announcing, rather superfluously, 'Yakutsk', it would have served equally well as the Leander Club stand at some Edwardian-era Henley regatta. Now the site is the city's war memorial.

In 2004, shuffling around to get their bearings like Second World War veterans revisiting the Normandy beaches, our revenant revolutionaries would have to do some more blanking out before they got to the essence of the city they knew a hundred years back.

But not that much. Just one 'right click' on the airbrush button wipes away the signs that Yakutsk is very much 'on the move' – the latest glass-wrapped office buildings, the new four-star hotel, the National Theatre and the outcrops of luxury flats. (When we asked who could possibly afford to buy them, our friend Yevgenii shrugged: 'The civil servants who handle the Republic's gold, diamonds and oil – they all pocket hefty bribes.') One more click and we can erase from the landscape the peeling, crumbling apartment buildings, mud-moated legacies of the bankrupt Soviet regime, randomly connected by a spaghetti junction of sagging lengths of heating pipe, the insulation torn and windblown. To Western eyes these blocks with their small, boot-battered doorways seem the last refuges of the dispossessed and down and out, cold-country crack houses. But they are homes, and many of the flats inside are, against all odds, comfortable and well equipped, if painfully cramped. Up and down their cracked steps come proud mothers with almond-eyed babies, dumpy babushkas and twittering flocks of pretty, immaculately dressed girls who click their way insouciantly in the highest of heels between the shards of metal and stumps of wood which jut haphazardly from the uneven pavements.

But we are left with a surprisingly large swathe of the timber-built Yakutsk that David and Manya would remember. It was not until about 1940 that a bright engineer thought of setting buildings on concrete piles sunk into the soil, to prevent heat spreading downwards into the thick prehistoric crust of permanently frozen ground lurking like a Tolkien fantasy just a few feet below under the surface. Lacking that insulating space, most of the older, unpainted houses have long since thawed ground underneath them, split, lost their shutters and drainpipes, and sunk (sometimes a few inches, in some cases a few feet) into the soil. Some are keeling over at the gravity-defying angles of sinking ships. The impression of Russia's sempiternal squalor is reinforced by the muddy maze which is the Yakutsk version of a network of side streets, and the realisation that these houses have no running water; the blue columns standing at every few corners are water pumps.

But it is far from hopeless. Our visitors from the past with any hearing left would catch the carillon of bells jingling cheerfully from the brightly gilded onion-shaped domes of a church that was obviously new but at the same time curiously familiar. On the site of the old wooden Church of the Transfiguration, gutted on Stalin's orders, stands a replica built of a sandy-pink painted stone building with white trim and an altarpiece that is a blinding golden master-piece; in a nice example of the local dynamics, the reconstruction project was largely financed by the new republic's diamond monopoly. Nearby, the old Merchants Row, remembered by the lawyer Berenshtam, has been replaced by an almost identical timber building, now a small upmarket shopping centre, though business there is slow. (Often there are more security guards than customers.) The mud and stone in the Row's old forecourt has been carefully relaid with the wooden discs, a few inches in diameter, sliced like salami from tree branches, with which the streets of the old city were paved. The inn, where the traders drank, drank and drank some more, is also being rebuilt, as is the former girls' high school. Harder to find, because people seem reluctant to talk about it, is the site of the building noted by Berenshtam in 1904 as the city's only sub-stantial brick structure. It housed the offices, distillery and cellars of the old tsarist-era liquor monopoly. It has been pulled down and may well never rise again, as it was in its soundproof vaulted cellars that Stalin's secret police killers did most of their murderous work in the local 'repressions' of the 1930s.

That sad note apart, a new and confident Yakutsk rises on the ashes of the old – often literally, since the crumbling, tumbling shacks of yesterday are a classic fire hazard. And not just a new Yakutsk. In what would come as a great shock to those intellectually arrogant firebrands from European Russia who a hundred years ago dismissed the Yakuts as wild men, a new Yakutiya too, the Republic of Sakha. Yakut faces are everywhere, Yakuts in top jobs, switching seamlessly between Russian and their own Turkic-related language. Their own beliefs have been preserved as well: the old nature based rituals and rhythms, the significance, even worship, of horses and storks, the nomad cycles of the reindeer breeders, the significance of dreams, the value of horoscopes, the many faces and roles of the shaman, and the joyful celebration of the summer solstice, all so scorned by the exiles and earlier travellers, have turned out to be indelibly stamped into the fabric of Yakut life. Especially important are the solstice ceremonies, which in the words of the republic's leaders in 2004 'have been handed down to us across the ages as the time when the harmony of man and nature is reborn, when in the rays of the rising sun men and women are cleansed of the accumulations of the past year and charged with a new life force'. In the newly built Yakut spiritual centre the Dom Archy, which overlooks the Lena, the carved woodwork, prayer ribbons tied on long strands of horsehair, the chieftain's chair and the warm ashes of the ritual fire are freighted with potent symbolism. It is as symbolic and impressive in its context as the Church of the Transfiguration. And the Sakha native language theatre far outguns in sleek modernity and size the old Russian playhouse which proudly bears the name of Pushkin.

Russians and Yakuts have intermarried for generations and the two communities and cultures coexist in a frictionless unity, notably free of recrimination about past 'exploitation' of the indigenous people by 'colonialists', an object lesson to many other multi-ethnic societies. Part of the reason may be that despite the great wealth underground, the reality on the surface is so daunting – 25 per cent of people living below the poverty line, the incidence of disease 40 per cent above the average Russian level, and a life expectancy 10 per cent lower – that people don't have time for division.

Up to a point. Even in Siberia some Russian attitudes are hard to change. A newspaper picture of one of the more prominent 'oligarchs', a man with Jewish roots now prudently spending much of his time abroad, brought a sneer from our otherwise jovial driver: 'The surname tells you all you need to know.' When I asked Grigory, a sensible local businessman, about the size of the Jewish community in Yakutsk, he said gravely: 'There are a lot of them but you don't see them much. They operate behind the scenes. They have a huge influence on government and the diamond trade.' While he might well have been right, there was more than an echo of those age-old myths.

And now we come to the Romanovka itself. There the house still stands, the street outside now (by Yakutsk standards) a main road, but otherwise as David and Manya would remember it. Except for the bust on a pavement plinth commemorating Kurnatovsky, 'The Marksman'. Many of the group might resent that; it was after all a *collective* act of bravery. But the bust was put up at a time when history was seen through a Soviet prism, which required what happened at the Romanovka to be reflected as a daring coup by a handful of Bolshevik heroes, everyone else involved having little more than a walk-on role. Thus to the Yakutsk writer Modest Krotov in 1957, David Redstone and the others were an anonymous bunch of 'Socialist Revolutionaries, Mensheviks and other forever shilly-shallying and unreliable revolutionaries'.

But through the yard gates are the steps on which Chaplin stood, the attic where Matlakhov was shot, the window from which Kurnatovsky fired, the storage sheds rented by the Yakuts. Whenever we go back to houses in which we once lived, the schools of early childhood, or other places that that loomed large in our lives many years ago, the usual reaction is they must have shrunk; how small the reality is compared to the memory. If David Redstone had been able to see the Romanovka again, the same odd thought would have struck him, even from the outside: how small the yard was. To think of rifle volleys crashing across that small enclosed space, not much bigger than his London garden! No wonder Olga Viker used that vivid simile about being 'shot like fish in a barrel'.

From outside, the building cries out for repair. Inside, the exiles' fading photographs and the memorabilia of their time of terror are lovingly tended and their story enthusiastically recited by the curator Zoya Grigoryevna. Again, we wonder that over fifty people could have fitted in here even for a tea party, let alone for endless days and nights of ratcheting terror, stink, grime and deadly gunfire. The bullets embedded in the carefully preserved sections of their 'armour plate' are real enough, though, as are the twisted gun barrels of the weapons the protestors destroyed before their surrender, and even the tin water-holder (the Thonet bentwood chairs and the samovar are later additions). If David had really been there instead of just hovering close in my imagination, my bet is that true to form he would have twinkled and made a joke of it all. We know now that it was no joke. There was not much I could say. All I could do was offer a silent prayer.

And buy a small souvenir that rounded off the story rather neatly. Without help from our local friend Nikita I would not have tracked down one of the few places in the city selling 'international' cigarettes. It is a far cry in every sense from the urbane counters of James J. Fox & Robert Lewis, in one of yesterday's ramshackle wooden buildings, with creaking stairs, unlit and uneven corridors, solid doors on springs which crash shut behind you. Each room is home to its own small business, among them a second-floor greengrocer, an old woman overshadowed by a stack of cellophane-wrapped Y-fronts, and a man in a leather cap selling oily spare parts for the old Soviet Moskvich cars. The House of Cigarettes is actually an upstairs room, the counter protected by a lattice of steel bars with a few cartons of cigarettes on the shelves beyond. Overwhelmed by the feeling that I was engaged in something rather furtive, I murmured my order to a blank-faced bottle-blonde of Moskvich vintage. She handed the box out through a small hole in the side wall. I had closed the loop. After all those miles, all those years, I had in my hand, in Yakutsk, a packet of Balkan Sobranie Black Russian, made under license in a Moscow factory.

What a fine dinner-table story David would have made of it all.

Bibliography

I have wrestled over the listing that follows. This is not an academic work and I have not cross-referred to notes on the page along the way. Many of the books are obscure and long out of print. More to the point, presenting such a long list also risks being accused of showing off. I could have limited it to books of singular value but again, while a seminal study like that of George Kennan would clearly qualify, other sources that have suggested just a line or two, or sparked a thought that I pursued in greater detail, might have been unfairly left out. So I have opted to face the brickbats and stay with the longer version. I had originally intended also to list all the websites I had looked at but, while many proved valuable, some are not reliable on detail, some prove irritatingly inaccessible on a second visit, and in any event they often do not represent primary sources. I would thus only pay an (unsolicited) tribute to the *yandex.ru* search engine, which provides direct access to many otherwise hard-to-find Russian sites, with the bonus of a 'virtual keyboard' allowing those with English machines to make their enquiries in the Cyrillic alphabet.

Russian

Aleksyceva, A. N., *Romanovka – Vooruzhcnnyi Protest Yakutskikh Politicheskikh Ssyl'nykh*, Yakutsk, Goskomizdat, 1990.

Andreyev, V. M., and Sosina, I. A., in *Osvodboditel'noye Dvizhenie Rossii i Yakutskaya Politicheskaya Ssylka*, Yakutsk, 1990.

Andreyev, V. M., *Iskra – TsO RSDRP (Menshevikov) O Yakutskom Proteste 1904 goda*, ibid.

Anon., *Bolsheviki v Yakutskoi Ssylke*, Yakutsk, Yakutsk Book Publishers, 1988.

Anon., *Odesskii Spravochnik*, Odessa, 1914.

Baikalov, A.V., *Turukhanskyi 'Bunt' Politicheskikh Ssyl'nykh*, Prague, Sibirskii Arkhiv, Izdanie Obshchestva Sibiryakov v ChSR, 1929.

Berenshtam, V., *Okolo Politicheskikh*, Izdanie SV Bubin, St Petersburg, 1908.

Gogolyev, Z. V., *Yakutiya Na Rubezhe X1X i XX Vekov*, Novosibirsk, Akademiya Nauk SSSR, Sibirskoye Otdeleniye, 1970.

Ivantsova, E. (Ed.-in-Chief), *Odessa-Almanakh*, Odessa, 2002.

Krysin, L. P., *Tolkovyi Slovar' Inoyazychnykh Slov*, Moscow, 'Russkyi Yazyk', 2000.

Kurnatovsky, V. K., *Pis'mo V.K. Kurnatovskogo o Yakutskom Proteste Ssyl'nikh*, Moscow, Istorcheskii Arkhiv, No. 4, 1955.

Kurnatovsky, V. K., and A. A. Kostyushko Valyuzhanich, in *Sssyl'nie Bol'sheviki o Yakutii*, n.p., Yakutsk, 1982.

Lavrov, V. M., *Mariya Spiridonova, Terroristka i Zhertva Terrora*, Moscow, Arkheograficheskii Tsentr, 1998.

Lebanov, V., *Staraya Chita*, Chita, 2001.

Okhlopkov, V. E., *Istoriya Politicheskoi Ssylki v Yakutii*, Yakutsk, Yakutskoye Knizhnoye Izdatel'stvo, 1990.

Okladnikov, A. P. (ed.), *50 Let Osvobozhdeniya Zabaikail'ya Ot Belogvardeetsev i Innostrannykh Interventov*, Chita, 1972.

Rozental, P., *Romanovka (Yakutskii Protest 1904 goda), Iz Vospominaniii Uchastnika*, Leningrad and Moscow, Izdatel'stvo Tovarishchestvo 'Kniga', 1924.

Ministerstvo Putei Soobshcheniiya Rossii, *Dorozhnik Sobesednik-Putevoditel' po Transsibirskoi Magistrali*, Irkutsk, Izdatel'stvo Papirus, 1994.

Savinkov, B., *Vospominaniya Terrorista*, Khar'kov, Izadtel'stvo Proletarii, 1928.

Teplov, P., *Istoriya Yakutsogo Protesta (Delo Romanovtsev)*, Glagolev, St Petersburg, [n.d., 1906].

Troitskii, N. A., 'Sud'by Rossiiskikh Advokatov', Arkheograficheskii Ezhegodnik, n.p. 1998.

Troitskii, N. A., Advokatura v Rossii i Politicheskiye Protsessy 1866-1904, Avtograf, Tula, 2000.

Vilenskii, V. (ed.), Katorga i Ssylka, Vol. 12, Moscow, 1924.

Vilenskii, V., and Various, Biograficheskiye Ocherki 'Romanovtsy o Romanovtsakh', ibid., Issues Nos 3 and 4, 1929.

Odesskie Novosti, Odessa, 22 April–31 Dec 1894, 1 Jan–15 Oct 1895, 20, 22, 23 April 1901.

Sibirskoye Obozreniye, Irkutsk, 4 May–18 June 1906.

Sizikov, A. I., in Zapiski Zabaikal'skogo Otdela Geograficheskogo Obshchestva SSSR, No. 14, Chita, 1964.

Solzhenitsyn, A. I., Dvesti Let Vmeste, Vols 1 and 2, Moscow, Ruskii Put', 2002.

Irkutskii Vestnik, Irkutsk, 15 April–20 August 1906.

'Yakutiya-Yezhednyevnaya Respublikanskaya Gazeta', various dates, Yakutsk, 2002.

Zabaikal'skii Rabochii, Chita, 18 April 1918.

Other

Alden, D., Charles Boxer, An Uncommon Life, Lisbon, Fundacao Oriente, 2001.

[Anon] The Sino-Russian Crisis, Nanking, The International Relations Committee, n.d. [1929].

Ascherson, N., The Black Sea, London, Cape, 1995.

Atkinson, T. W., Oriental & Western Siberia & Chinese Tartary, London, Hurst & Blackett, 1858.

Babel, Natalie (ed.), Constantine, P. (trans.), The Complete Works of Isaac Babel, New York, W. W. Norton, 2002.

Baedeker, K., London and its Environs, 1900, reprinted by Old House Books, Moretonhampstead, 2001.

Baedeker, K., La Russie, Leipzig, 1902.

Bagehot, Walter, Lombard Street, reprinted New York, John Wiley, 1999.

Banville, John, The Book of Evidence, London, Secker & Warburg, 1989.

Barnouw, D., *Germany 1945 – Views of War and Violence*, Bloomington, Indiana University Press, 1996.

Betjeman, J., *Summoned by Bells*, London, John Murray, 1960.

Betjeman, J. (Intro.), *Victorian and Edwardian London from Old Photographs*, London, Batsford, 1970.

Binyon, T. J., *Pushkin*, London, HarperCollins, 2002.

Borovsky, V., *Chaliapin*, London, Hamish Hamilton, 1988.

Broido, V., *Daughter of Revolution*, London, Constable, 1998.

Brown, A., Kaser, M., and Smith, G. (eds), *The Cambridge Encyclopaedia of Russia and the Former Soviet Union*, Cambridge, CUP, 1999.

Burr, A., *In Bolshevik Siberia*, London, H., F. and G. Witherby, 1921.

Burroughs, Harry, *Tale of a Vanished Land*, London, George Allen & Unwin, 1930.

Campbell, J., *F. E. Smith*, London, Cape, 1983.

Carey, J. (ed.), *The Faber Book of Reportage*, London, Faber and Faber, 1987.

Carr, E. H., *The Bolshevik Revolution 1917–23*, London, Macmillan, 1923.

Clapham, Sir J., *The Bank of England – A History*, Cambridge, CUP, 2 Vols, 1944.

Cochrane, J. D., *Narrative of a Pedestrian Journey Through Russia and Siberian Tartary . . .*, London, Knight, 1825.

Cohen, T., *Philosophical Thoughts on Laughing Matters*, Chicago, Chicago University Press, 1999.

Connolly, Cyril, *The Condemned Playground*, London, Routledge, 1945.

Cook, A., *Sydney Reilly*, London, Tempus, 2002.

Cottrell, Charles, *Recollections of Siberia in the Years 1840–41*, London, John W. Parker, 1844.

Crankshaw, E., *The Shadow of the Winter Palace*, New York, Viking, 1976.

Daney, C., *Le Transiberien*, Paris, Herscher, 1980.

de la Planche, M. H., *Pilote de la Mer Noir*, Paris, Adolph Laine, 1869–80.

Deutscher, I., *Trotsky, The Prophet Armed*, Oxford, OUP, 1954.

Deutscher, I., *Stalin – A Political Biography*, revised edition, London, Penguin, 1966.

Dimitriyev-Mamonov, A. I., and Zdziarski, A. F. (eds), *Guide to the Great Siberian Railway*, St Petersburg, Artistic Printing Society, 1900.

Dowling, C. J., *Queen Charlotte's – The Story of a Hospital*, London, 1989.

Dubnov, Simon, *History of the Jews from the Congress of Vienna to the Emergence of Hitler*, Vol. V, South Brunswick, USA, A. S. Barnes & Co. Inc., 1973.

Dvornichenko, N., *Chita, Information Guide*, Chita, Chitinskoe Knizhnoe Izdatel'stvo, 1959.

Edmonds, Robin, *Pushkin, The Man and His Age*, London, Macmillan, 1994.

Ensor, Sir R., *England 1870–1914*, Oxford, Clarendon Press, 1968.

Evans, F. (ed.), *Rebecca West: Family Memories*, London, Virago, 1987.

Eyles, E., *Gaumont British Cinemas*, Burgess Hill, Cinema Theatre Association, 1996.

Fielding, D., *The Duchess of Jermyn Street*, with an Introduction by Evelyn Waugh, London, Eyre & Spottiswoode, 1964.

Figes, Orlando, and Kolonitskii, Boris, *Interpreting the Russian Revolution*, New Haven and London, Yale University Press, 1999.

Figes, Orlando, *Natasha's Dance*, London, Allen Lane, 2002.

Forsyth, James, *A History of the Peoples of Siberia*, Cambridge, CUP, 1992.

Fraser, John Foster, *The Real Siberia*, London, Cassell, 1902.

Friedgut, T. H., *Yuzovka and Revolution*, Vols 1 & 2, New Jersey, Princeton University Press, 1989 and 1994.

Fulop-Miller, R. (ed.), *The Ochrana – The Russian Secret Police*, by A. F. Vassilyev, London, Harrap, 1930.

Furst, Alan, *Blood of Victory*, New York, Random House, 2002.

Futrell, Michael, *Northern Underground, Episodes of Russian Revolutionary Transport and Communications through Scandinavia and Finland, 1863–1917*, London, Faber and Faber, 1963.

Galler, M., *Soviet Prison Camp Speech*, Hayward, California, Soviet Studies, 1977.

Gateley, Iain, *Tobacco, The Story of How Tobacco Seduced the World*, New York, Grove Press, 2001.

Gerhardie, William, *The Polyglots*, [and] *Memoirs of a Polyglot*, the 'revised and definitive edition', London, Macdonald & Co., 1947.

Gilbert, Sir Martin, *A History of the 20th Century*, Vol. 1, London, HarperCollins, 1997.

Gill, G. J., *Peasants and Government in the Russian Revolution*, London, Macmillan/London School of Economics, n.d.

Gilmour Rev. James, *Among the Mongols*, London, The Religious Tract Society, n.d. [?1886].

Grennard, F., *La Révolution Russe*, Paris, Armand Colin, 1933.

Hargrave, S., *The Russian Revolution of 1905*, London, Collier Books, 1964.

Hawes, C. H., *In the Uttermost East*, London, Harper & Brothers, 1903.

Henriot, C. (Castellino, N., trans.), *Prostitution and Sexuality in Shanghai: A Social History 1849-1949*, Cambridge, CUP, 2001.

Herlihy, P., *Odessa – A History*, Harvard, University Press, 1986.

Holman, J., *Voyages and Travels*, London, Smith & Elder, 1855.

Hoppen, K .T., *The Mid-Victorian Generation*, Oxford, Clarendon Press, 1998.

Hoskins, Geoffrey, *The Russians*, London, Alan Lane, 2000.

Howgego, J., *Victorian and Edwardian City of London from Old Photographs*, London, Batsford, 1977.

Jarintzoff, N., *Russia The Country of Extremes*, London, Sidgwick & Jackson, 1914.

Judge, E. H., *Plehve, Repression and Reform in Imperial Russia, 1902–4*, Syracuse University Press, 1983.

Karavia, M., *Odissos*, Athens, Nea Eilora, 1995.

Kennan, George, *Siberia and the Exile System*, 2 Vols, London, James R. Osgood, McIlvaine & Co., 1891.

Kent, W. (ed.), *An Encyclopaedia of London*, London, J. M. Dent, 1937.

Knesel, F. (trans.), *Leon Trotsky, Autobiography, 1879–1917*, Cambridge, Mass., Iskra Research Publishing House, 1999.

Kropotkin, Peter, *In Russian and French Prisons*, London, Ward & Downey, 1887.

Krupskaya, N., *Reminiscences of Lenin*, English edition, International Publishers, n.p., 1970.

Kynaston, D., *The City of London*, Vol. 2, 'Golden Years', London, Chatto & Windus, 1995.

Lancaster, O., *All Done from Memory*, London, John Murray, 1963.

Lucas, E. V., *'EV Lucas' London'*, London, Methuen, 1926.

McAuley, M., *Russia's Politics of Uncertainty*, Cambridge, CUP, 1997.

McKibbin, R., *Class and Culture in England 1918–51*, Oxford, OUP, 1998.

Marchand, Leslie A., *Byron – A Portrait*, London, John Murray, 1973.

Marsden, K., *On Sledge and Horseback to Outcast Siberian Lepers*, London, Record Press, 1892.

Maynard, J., *The Russian Peasant*, London, Gollancz, 1942.

Merridale, Catherine, *Nights of Stone, Death and Memory in Russia*, London, Granta, 2000.

Mico, T. et al, *Past Imperfect – History According to the Movies*, NY, Henry Holt, 1995.

Middelton, N., *The Bloody Baron*, London, Short Books, 2001.

Mortimer, J., *Clinging to the Wreckage*, London, Penguin, 1983.

Nash, G., *The Tarasov Saga*, Kenthurst (Australia), Rosenberg Publishing, 2002.

Norman, H., *All The Russias*, New York, Scribner, 1902.

Obraztsev, V., *Les Chemins de Fer de la URSS*, Paris, n.d.

Orwell, G., 'Books v. Cigarettes', in *George Orwell: Essays*, London, Penguin Classics, 2000.

Petrie, Sir C., *Scenes of Edwardian Life*, London, Eyre and Spottiswoode, 1965.

Plotke, A. J., *Imperial Spies Invade Russia, The British Intelligence Intervention 1918*, Westport, Conn., Greenwood Press, 1993.

Pipes, Richard, *The Russian Revolution 1899–1919*, London, Harvill, 1990.

Pipes, Richard, *Russia under the Bolshevik Regime*, New York, Alfred A. Knopf, 1994.

Pipes, Richard, *The Degaev Affair*, London and New Haven, Yale University Press, 2003.

Priestley, J. B., *Angel Pavement*, London, William Heinemann, 1930.

Pyman, A., *A History of Russian Symbolism*, Cambridge, CUP, 1994.

Rappaport, E. D., *Shopping for Pleasure*, New Jersey, Princeton University Press, 2000.

Rappoport, A. S., *Home Life in Russia*, New York, The Macmillan Co., 1913.

Rappoport, A. S., *Pioneers of the Russian Revolution*, London, Stanley Paul, 1918.

Rasmussen, S. E., *London, The Unique City*, revised English edition, London, Jonathan Cape, 1937.

Read, D., *The Power of News – The History of Reuters*, 2nd Edition, Oxford, OUP, 1999.

Reid, Anna, *Borderland*, London, Weidenfeld & Nicolson, 1997.

Reid, Anna, *The Shaman's Coat: A Native History of Russia*, London, Weidenfeld and Nicolson, 2002.

Reynders-Ristiano, M., *Port of Last Resort, The Diaspora Communities of Shanghai*, California, Stanford University Press, 2001.

Roth, Joseph (trans. Michael Hofmann), *The Wandering Jews*, New York, W.W. Norton, 2001.

Rothstein, A., *Lenin in Britain*, London, The Communist Party, 1970.

Royle, E., *Modern Britain – A Social History 1750–1985*, London, Edward Arnold, n.d.

Sebag Montefiore, S., *Stalin – At the Court of the Red Tsar*, London, Weidenfeld, 2003.

Seton Watson, H., *The Russian Empire 1801–1917*, Oxford, Clarendon Press, 1967.

Seymour, H. D., *Russia on the Black Sea and the Sea of Azof*, London, John Murray, 1855.

Shentalinsky, V., *The KGB's Literary Archive*, London, Harvill, 1997.

Shukman, Harold (ed.), *The Blackwell Encyclopaedia of the Russian Revolution*, Oxford, Basil Blackwell, 1988.

Shukman, Harold, *The Russian Revolution*, Stroud, Sutton Publishing, 1998.

Shukman, Harold, *Stalin*, Stroud, Sutton Publishing, 1999.

Singer, I. B., *The Slave*, New York, Farrar Straus Giroux, 1962.

Smith, Gordon E. (ed.), and Beskrovny, L.G. (trans.), *The Russian Army and Fleet in the 19th Century*, Florida, Academic International Press, 1996.

Sobranie (Holdings) Ltd, Stock Exchange Prospectus, London, 1948, and later Annual Reports.

Solzhenitsyn, Alexander (trans. H. T. Willetts), *Lenin in Zurich*, London, The Bodley Head, 1976.

Strachan, Hew, *The First World War*, Vol. 1, Oxford, OUP, 2001.

Swain, Geoffrey, *Russia's Civil War*, Stroud, Tempus, 2000.

Szryma, Col. Lacch (ed.), *Eva, Felinska, Revelations of Siberia*, London, Colbourn & Co., 1853.

Taylor, A. J. P., *English History 1914–45*, Oxford, Clarendon Press, 1945.

Thubron, C., *In Siberia*, London, Chatto & Windus, 1999.

Tolz, V., *Inventing the Nation*, London, Hodder Headline, 2002.

Trotsky, L., *My Life*, at www.marxist. org./archive/Trotsky.

Trotsky, L., *My Life*, 1905; London, Penguin, 1971.

Tupper, H., *To The Great Ocean*, London, Secker & Warburg, 1965.

Ullman, R. H., *Britain and the Russian Civil War*, Vol. 2, New Jersey, Princeton University Press, 1962.

Vitebsky, Piers, *The Shaman*, London, Duncan Baird Publishers, 2001.

Volkogonov, Dmitry (trans. Harold Shukman), *Stalin – Triumph and Tragedy*, London, Weidenfeld and Nicolson, 1991.

Volkogonov, Dmitry (trans. Harold Shukman), *Trotsky – The Eternal Revolutionary*, New York, The Free Press, 1996.

Walsh, J., *Are You Talking to Me?*, London, HarperCollins, 2003.

Weinreb, B., and Hibbert, C. (eds), *The London Encyclopaedia*, London, Book Club Associates, 1983.

Wheatley, D., *Officer and Temporary Gentleman*, London, Hutchinson, 1978.

Wheatley, D., *Drink and Ink*, London, Hutchinson, 1979.

White, J., *London in the Twentieth Century*, London, Penguin, 2002.

Wilson, A., *The Ukrainians – Unexpected Nation*, London and New Haven, Yale University Press, 2000.

Wolff, David, *To the Harbin Station, The Liberal Alternative in Russian Manchuria*, California, Stanford University Press, 1999.

Wood, A. (ed.), *The History of Siberia*, London, Routledge, 1991.

Wynn, A., *Persia in the Great Game*, London, John Murray, 2003.

Yates, A., and Zvegintzov, N., *Siberian BAM Guide*, Hindhead, Surrey, Trailblazer Publications, 2nd edition, 2001.

Zeman, Z. A. B., and Scharlau, W. B., *The Merchant of Revolution, The Life of Alexander Israel Helphand (Parvus)*, Oxford, OUP, 1965.

Journals and Periodicals

Anon., 'Smoke Signals', *London*, Nos 218 and 219, May and June 1980; 'Tobacco', *London*, December 1949.

Ibid., David Redstone Obituary by Gordon West, March 1967.

Ibid., No. 1192, May 1980.

Barber, L., 'An Education', in *Granta*, No. 82, London 2003.

Benecke, W., 'The Soldiers' Library', *Jahrbucher Fur Geschichte Osteuropas*, 50(2) pp. 246–75, 2002.

Brett, C. E. B., 'Alupka Palace, Crimea', in *Country Life,* London, July 2002.

Gentes, A. [Reviews], *'Yakutiya v Sisteme Politicheskoi Ssylki Rossii 1826-1917 gg'* and *'Politicheskaya Ssylka v Sibiri: Nerchinskaya Katorga'* in Kritika, *Explorations in Russian and Eurasian History*, Slavica, 3.1 2002.

Giffin. F. C., 'The Russian Railway Service Corps', *The Historian*, n.p. June 1998.

Heydel-Mankoo, R., 'The Role of Public Transport in the Development of Suburban London 1900-1939', *London*, n.p. 2001.

Kapner, D. A., and Levine, S., 'The Jews of Japan', in *The Jerusalem Letter*, No. 425, March 2000.

Knight, Amy, 'Female Terrorists in the Russian Socialist Revolutionary Party', in *Russian Review*, No. 38, 1979.

Melancon, M., 'The Sixth Circle, The Lena Goldfield Workers and The Massacre of 4th April 1912', in *Slavic Review*, 53, No. 3, 1994.

Pron'ko, V. A., and Zemskov, V. N., *'Vklad Zaklyuchennykh Gulaga v Pobedu v Velikoi Otechenstvennoi Voine'*, in *Novaya I Noveishaya Istoriya*, No. 5, 1996.

Sabin, Burrit, 'The Pianos Fall Silent, The Tragic End of the Yokohama Colony of the Russian Diaspora', in *The East*, Vol. 37, No. 4, Tokyo, November–December 2001.

Spain, Nancy, 'Fortunes in Smoke', in *She*, August 1958.

Imperial Tobacco Company PLC, *The Tobacco Story*, at www.imperial-tobacco.com

The translation of Pushkin's 'Ovid' quotation is by Robin Edmonds and the rendering of the verse on Odessa is the author's own.

Index